Bal Gangadhar Tilak

Bal Gangadhar Tilak

Dr. C.P. Raj
Dr. Ved Prakash

AMIGA PRESS. INC
Delhi -110051

AMIGA PRESS. INC
H.O :- 28-A, Indra Park, Chander Nagar
Delhi :- 110051 (India)
Tel :- 011-22504028, +91-98736-57000
Email :- amigapress@gmail.com
amigaeditorial@gmail.com
Website :- www.amigapress@co.in

This edition is published by Amiga Press.Inc

ISBN : 978-93-84533-31-1

First Published 2018

PRINTED : THOMSON PRESS INDIA

Preface

Bal Gangadhar Tilak (July 23, 1856-August 1, 1920), was an Indian nationalist, social reformer and freedom fighter who was the first popular leader of the Indian Independence Movement and is known as "Father of the Indian unrest." Tilak was one of the first and strongest proponents for Swaraj (complete independence) in Indian consciousness, and is considered the father of Hindu nationalism as well. His famous quote, "Swaraj is my birthright, and I shall have it!" is well-remembered in India even today. Reverently addressed as Lokmanya (meaning "Beloved of the people" or "Revered by the world"), Tilak was a scholar of Indian history, Sanskrit, Hinduism, mathematics, law and astronomy.

Gangadhar Tilak joined the Indian National Congress in 1890. He soon started vocalizing his strong opposition to the moderate views of the party on self-rule. He maintained that simple constitutional agitation in itself was futile against the British. This subsequently made him stand against the prominent Congress leader, Gopal Krishna Gokhale. He wanted an armed revolt to broom-away the British. Following the partition of Bengal by Lord Curzon, Tilak wholeheartedly supported the Swadeshi (Indigenous) movement and Boycott of British goods. But his methods also raised bitter controversies within the Indian National Congress (INC) and the movement itself.

Bal Gangadhar Tilak's contribution to modern India stands on par with that of Mahatma Gandhi's. Tilak was a great Sanskrit scholar and astronomer. He fixed the origin and date of Rigvedic Aryans, which was highly acclaimed and universally accepted by orientalists of his time. His role in Congress and advocating Home Rule for India were enormous. His newspaper (Kesari) founded in 1881 is going strong even today. Hundreds of schools in India were result of his vision. We owe the mass celebration of the Ganesh festival (see: Ganesh Chaturthi) only to Tilak. He was Guru to Savarkar (biography) and hundreds of nationalists and thousands of Indians. Actually he set up the platform for Gandhiji's leadership. Although Gandhi accepted Gokhale as his mentor, in practice, he adopted all of Tilak's ideas of *Swadeshi* and of social reform.

After Tilak's death on August 1, 1920, on the first day of Gandhi's first non-cooperation campaign, Gandhi paid his respects at his cremation in Mumbai, along with 20,000,000 people. Gandhi called Tilak "The Maker of Modern India". The court which convicted Tilak bears a plaque that says, "The actions of Tilak has been justified as the right of every individual to fight for his country. Those two convictions have gone into oblivion — oblivion reserved by history for all unworthy deeds". All the matter is just compiled and edited in nature. Taken from the various sources which are in public domain.

The book will prove an informative and most useful asset for students, scholars and teachers in this field. The book is of great importance for the scholars, researchers, students, teachers and historians as well pertaining to this sphere.

—*Editor*

Contents

Preface (*v*)

1. **Introduction** 1
Early Life; Political Career; Tilak and Comparative Mythology; British Colonial Period—Colonial Rule (1858–August 1918) ; Formation of Indian National Congress; First Partition of Bengal ; Formation of Muslim League (1906) ; Early Revolutionary Movement ; Alipore Bomb Case ; Hardinge Bomb Case ; Later Years and Legacy

2. **Tilak's Philosophy and Freedom Struggle** 40
Tilak's Philosophy for the Nation ; Pressures of Loyalism during British Rule ; Tilak and Home Rule Movement; Founding

3. **Tilak : Culture and Religion** 50
Tilak Claim of the Superiority of Hinduism; Claims that Hinduism is the most tolerant religion ; Promotion of Hindu Nationalism; A critical evaluation of Tilak's philosophy; Ethical Relativism and Intrinsic Goodness of Violence; Tilak and Ganesh Festivals

4. **Tilak View on Vedas** 94
Long Day and Long Night; Months and Seasons; The Cows' Walk

5. **Educational Views of Tilak** 185
Nature and Objectives of Education ; Education through National Festivals ; Tilak and Management of Educational Institutions ; Tilak's Views on Women's Education ; Tilak the Pioneer of National Education; Education-an Instrument of National Awakening ; Elphinstone's Educational Policy

Bibliography 221

Index 223

1

Introduction

Bal Gangadhar Tilak (July 23, 1856-August 1, 1920), was an Indian patriot, social reformer and opportunity warrior who was the principal mainstream pioneer of the Indian Independence Movement and is known as "Father of the Indian turmoil." Tilak was one of the first and most grounded advocates for Swaraj (finish autonomy) in Indian cognizance, and is viewed as the father of Hindu patriotism too. His popular quote, "Swaraj is my inheritance, and I should have it!" is very much recollected in India even today. Respectfully tended to as Lokmanya (signifying "Cherished of the general population" or "Loved by the world"), Tilak was a researcher of Indian history, Sanskrit, Hinduism, science, law and space science.

EARLY LIFE

Tilak was born in *Madhali Alee* (Middle Lane) in Ratnagiri, Maharashtra, into a middle class family. He graduated from Deccan College, Pune in 1877. After graduation, Tilak began teaching mathematics in a private school in Pune and later became a journalist. He became a strong critic of the Western education system, feeling it demeaned the Indian students and disrespected India's heritage. He organized the Deccan Education Society to improve the quality of education for India's youth. He taught Mathematics at Fergusson College.

POLITICAL CAREER

Tilak founded the Marathi daily *Kesari* (Lion) in 1880. In just two years 'Kesari' attracted more readers than any language news papers in India. The editorials gave a vivid picture of the people's sufferings and of actual happenings. They called upon every Indian to fight for his right.

The language was so sharp as to create in the most cowardly reader the thirst for freedom. Tilak used to say to his colleagues: "You are not writing for the university students. Imagine you are talking to a villager. Be sure of your facts. Let your words be clear as day light." Tilak strongly criticized the government for its brutality in suppressing free expression, especially in face of protests against the division of Bengal in 1905, and for denigrating India's culture, its people and heritage. He demanded that the British immediately give Indians the right to self-government.

Tilak joined the Indian National Congress in the 1890s, but soon fell into opposition of its liberal-moderate attitude towards the fight for self-government. In 1891 Tilak opposed the Age of Consent bill introduced after the death of a child bride from sexual injuries. The act raised the marriageable age of a child bride from 10 to 12 which was already 16 in Britain since 1885. This was one of the first significant reforms introduced by the British since Indian rebellion of 1857. The Congress and other liberals wholeheartedly supported it but Tilak raised a battle-cry terming it as 'Interference in Hindu Religion'. Since then he was seen as a hard-core Hindu nationalist.

When in 1897, bubonic plague spread from Bombay to Pune the Government became jittery. The Assistant Collector of Pune, Mr. Rand, and his associates employed extremely severe and brutal methods to stop the spread of the disease by destroying even "clean homes." Even people who were not infected were carried away and in some cases, the carriers even looted property of the affected people.

When the authorities turned a blind eye to all these excesses, furious Tilak took up the people's cause by publishing inflammatory articles in his paper *Kesari,* quoting the Hindu scripture, the Bhagavad Gita, to say that no blame could be attached to anyone who killed an oppressor without any thought of reward. Following this, on 27 June, Rand and his assistant were killed. Tilak was charged with incitement to murder and sentenced to 18 months' imprisonment. When he emerged from prison, he had become a national hero and adopted a new slogan, "Swaraj (Self-Rule) is my birth right and I will have it."

Tilak opposed the moderate views of Gopal Krishna Gokhale, and was supported by fellow Indian nationalists Bipin Chandra Pal in Bengal and Lala Lajpat Rai in Punjab. They were referred to as the Lal-Bal-Pal triumvirate. In 1907, the annual session of the Congress Party was held at Surat (Gujarat). Trouble broke out between the moderate and the extremist factions of the party over the selection of the new president of the Congress and the party split into the *Garam Dal* ("Hot Faction," or extremists), led by Tilak, Pal and Lajpat Rai, and the *Naram Dal* ("Soft Faction," or moderates).

On 30 April 1908 two Bengali youths, Prafulla Chaki and Kudiram Bose, threw a bomb on a carriage at Muzzafurpur in order to kill a District Judge

Douglass Kenford but erroneously killed some women travelling in it. While Chaki committed suicide when caught, Bose was tried and hanged. British papers screamed for vengeance and their shrill cries became even more insistent when Police raided and found a cache of arms at Calcutta. But Tilak in his paper Kesari defended the revolutionaries and called for immediate Swaraj or Self-rule. The Government swiftly arrested him for sedition. He asked a young Muhammad Ali Jinnah to represent him. But the British judge convicted him and he was imprisoned from 1908 to 1914 in Mandalay, Burma.

Much has been said of his trial of 1908, it being the most historic trial. His last words on the verdict of the Jury were such: *"In spite of the verdict of the Jury, I maintain that I am innocent. There are higher powers that rule the destiny of men and nations and it may be the will of providence that the cause which I represent may prosper more by my suffering than my remaining free"*. These words now can be seen imprinted on the wall of Room. No. 46 at Bombay High Court.

Upon his release from Mandalay, Tilak re-united with his fellow nationalists and re-joined the Indian National Congress in 1916. He also helped found the All India Home Rule League in 1916-18 with Annie Besant and Muhammad Ali Jinnah. Tilak was impressed by the Russian Revolution, and expressed his admiration for Lenin. Tilak, who started his political life as a Maratha Protagonist, during his later part of life progressed into a prominent nationalist after his close association with Bengal nationalists following the partition of Bengal. When asked in Calcutta whether he envisioned a Maratha type of government for Free India, Tilak replied that the Maratha dominated Governments of 16th and 17th centuries were outmoded in 20th century and he wanted a genuine federal system for Free India where every religion and race were equal partners. Only such a form of Government would be able to safeguard India's freedom he added.

TILAK AND COMPARATIVE MYTHOLOGY

We propose in this section to look at whether and how far the conclusions we have concluded from the Vedic and the Avestic confirmation are supported by the myths and conventions of the European branches of the Aryan race. Without a doubt the proof, gathered in the prior sections, is so broad in character that it will must be considered, regardless of the possibility that the customs of different races are found to strife with it in any capacity.

At the end of the day, it has nothing extraordinarily Asiatic in it and without further support we can, accordingly, securely say that the first home of the Indo-Iranians, before the last Glacial age, should likewise be the home of the other Aryan individuals in those remote times.

Yet we may conveniently look at the conventions of other Aryan races, and check whether the last have protected any memories of the first home, either in their old timetable or in their other old myths or legends. Obviously the confirmation can't be required to be as dependable as that found in the Veda or the Avesta, yet it has its own esteem for substantiating purposes. The History of near mythology and philology demonstrates that when Vedic writing and dialect got to be available to European researchers, a significant new light was tossed along these lines on the Greek and the Roman mythology; and it is not impossible that the disclosure of the Vedic and the Avestic prove, for the Arctic home may also serve to clarify a few focuses in the fanciful writing of the Aryan races in Europe. In any case, the subject is vast to the point that it can't be dealt with in a solitary part of this book, nor do I have the essential intends to attempt the errand.

I should, accordingly, placate myself with an announcement of such certainties as evidently demonstrate the memory of an antiquated Arctic home in the conventional writing of the Greek, Roman, Celtic, Teutonic and Slavonic branches of the Aryan race; and I may here express that I am enormously obligated for this reason to that scholarly and excellent work, The Hibbert addresses, by Prof. Rhys. On the birthplace and development of religion as outlined by Celtic Heathendom. Taking after the request received in the talk of the Vedic confirmation, we should first take up the subject of the antiquated date-book, and check whether the conventions saved by the western Aryan races about the old year bring up to any Arctic attributes, for example, the long day break; the difficult day, the taxing night, or a yearly time of daylight of under twelve months' term. We have seen that the Dawn is all the time discussed in the plural in the Rig-Veda and that a gathering of thirty Dawn-Sisters is really depicted as moving all around with one personality and in similar nook without being isolated from each other, a marvel which is unconventional just to the Arctic areas.

This Vedic record of the Dawn does not remain independent from anyone else. In this way in the Lettish mythology, the Dawn is called diewo dukte, or the sky-little girl or the god-girl, much in an indistinguishable route from the Ushas is called divo duhita in the Rig-Veda; "and the artists of the Lets talk similarly of numerous delightful sky-little girls, or goddaughters diewo dukruzeles." Prof. Max Muller; facilitate illuminates us that in the Greek mythology we can "without much of a stretch find among the spouses of Herakles, huge names, for example, Auge (daylight), Xanthis (yellow), Chryseis (brilliant), Iole (violet), Aglaia (radiant), and Eone, which can't be isolated from Eos, day break." similar story shows up again in the Celtic mythology where Cuchulainn, the Sunhero, is depicted as having a wife, who is differently named as Emer, Ethne Ingubai. Upon this Prof. Rhys watches that "it might be that the myth imagined the sunrise not as one but rather the same number of to every one of whom the Sun-god had intercourse throughout the three hundred and more days of the year." It has been demonstrated already that the depiction of the Vedic first lights, as a firmly joined band, blocks us from seeing them as three hundred and more day breaks of the year; and that the main surmising we can draw from a firmly joined gathering of day breaks is that it speaks to the long and ceaseless Arctic day break separated into various parts of twenty-four hours each for accommodation.

The description of the dawn in the Lettish mythology does not seem to be so full as that in the Vedas and by itself it may not be sufficient to indicate the Polar dawn; but considering the fact that the dawn is described as sky-daughter and spoken of in the plural by the poets of the Lets and the poets of the Rig-Veda alike, we may safely extend to the Lettish mythology the conclusion we have drawn from the more detailed description of the Dawn in the Rig-Veda, and the same may be said of the Celtic and the Greek stories of the dawn given above.

In treating of the *Gavam-ayanam* and the corresponding legend of the Dashagvas, a reference has already been made to the Greek legend of Helios, who is described as having 350 oxen and as many sheep, obviously representing a year of 350 days and nights, and to the Roman tradition about *December* being the tenth and the last month of the year as denoted by its etymology. Prof. Lignana in his essay on *The Navagvas and the Dashagvas of the Rig-Veda,* published in the proceedings of the seventh International Congress of the Orientalists, 1886, however, remarks that the passage of Plutarch in the life of Numa, where this tradition is mentioned, does not support the view that the Romans originally counted not more than ten months. It is true that Plutarch mentions an alternative story of Numa's altering the order of months "making March the third which was the first, January first which was the eleventh of Romulus, and February the second which was the twelfth and last."

But immediately afterwards Plutarch says, "Many, however, assert that two months of January and February were added by Numa, whereas before they had reckoned ten months in the year"; and in the next paragraph gives his own opinion, "That the Roman year contained at first ten months only and not twelve, we have a proof in the name of the last; for they still call it *December,* or the tenth month; and that March was first is also evident, because the fifth from it was called *Quintilis,* the sixth *Sextilis,* and so the rest in their order."

I have referred to this passage previously and shown that Plutarch's reasoning about the order of the months as indicated by their numerical names cannot be lightly set aside. If January and February were the last two months in the ancient calendar of the Romans, we should have to assume that the numerical order from *Quintilis* to *December* was abruptly given up after December which does not seem probable.

It is, therefore, more reasonable to hold that: Numa actually added two months to the old year, and that the story of the transposition of the two months of January and February from the end to the beginning of the year was a later suggestion put forward by those who knew not how to account for a year of ten months, or 304 days only. But besides Plutarch, we have also the testimony of Macrobius, who, as stated before, tells us that Romulus had a year of ten months only. There can, therefore, be little doubt about the existence of a tradition of the ancient Roman year of ten months and we now see that it is thoroughly intelligible by comparison with the annual sacrificial *sattras* of ten months mentioned in the Vedic literature. The names of the Roman months from *Quintilis* to *December* further show that the months of the year had no special names in ancient times, but were named simply in their numerical order, a fact which accounts for the absence of common names for the months of the year in different Aryan languages.

The evidence regarding the ancient year of Celts, Teutons and Greeks is not however so definite, though it may be clearly shown that in each case the year was marked by a certain period of cold and darkness, indicating the Arctic, origin of the ancient calendar. Speaking of the ancient Celtic year Prof. Rhys observes, "Now as the Celts were in the habit formerly of counting winters, and of giving precedence in their reckoning to night and winter over day and summer, I should argue that the last day of the year in the Irish story of Diarmait's death meant the eve of November of All-Halloween, the night before the Irish *Samhain*, and known in Welsh as *Nos Galangaeaf*, or the Night of the winter Calends.

But there is no occasion to rest on this alone, for we have the evidence of Cormac's Glossary that the month before the be ginning of winter was the last month, so that the first day of the first month of winter was also the first day of the year." Various superstitious customs are then alluded to, showing that the eve of November was considered to be the proper time for prophecy or the appearance of goblins; and the Professor then closes the discussion regarding the above-mentioned last day of the Celtic year with the remark that "It had been fixed upon as the time of all others, when the Sun-god whose power had been gradually falling off since the great feast associated with him on the first of August, succumbed to his enemies, the powers of darkness and winter. It was their first hour of triumph after an interval of subjection, and the popular imagination pictured them stalking aboard with more than ordinary insolence and aggressiveness; and if it comes to giving individuality and form to the deformity of darkness, to describe it as a sow, black or grisly, with neither ears nor tail, is not perhaps very readily surpassed as an instance of imaginative aptitude." The shows that the ancient Celtic year closed with the season of autumn and the beginning of winter which corresponded with the last day of October, or the eve of November, and was marked by festivals which indicated the victory of darkness over light.

As regards the middle of the year or summer in the Celtic traditions, the same authority further informs us that "The Lammas fairs and meetings forming the Lugnassad in ancient Ireland marked the victorious close of the sun's contest with the powers of darkness and death, when the warmth and light of that luminary's rays, after routing the colds and blights, were fast bringing the crops to maturity. This, more mythologically expressed, was represented as the final crushing of Fomori and Fir Bolg, the death of their king and the nullifying of their malignant spells, and as the triumphant return of Lug with peace and plenty to marry the maiden Erinn and to enjoy a well-earned banquet, at which the fairy host of dead ancestors was probably not forgotten. Marriages were solemnized on the auspicious occasion; and no prince, who failed to be present on the last day of the fair, durst look forward to prosperity during the coming year.

The Lugnassad was the great event of the summer half of the year, which extended form the calends of May to the calends of winter. The Celtic year was more thermometric than astronomical, and the Lugnassad was so to say its summer solstice, whereas the longest day was, so far as I have been able to discover, of no special account." The great feast of the Lugnassad thus marked the middle of the year or summer, and it was held at the beginning of August.

Therefore, "the First of May must, according to Celtic ideas, have been the right season for the birth of the summer sun-god"; and this is confirmed by the story of Gwin and Gwythur, who fought for the same damsel, and between whom peace was made on the condition that they were to fight for the damsel "on the Calends of May every year thenceforth till the Day of Doom, and he who should prove victorious on the Day of Doom was to take the Damsel to wife." This is interpreted by Prof. Rhys to mean that "the Sun-god would recover his bride at the beginning of summer after his antagonist had gained possession of her at the beginning of winter;"§ and he compares the legend to the story of Persephone, daughter of Zeus carried away by Pluto, who was, however, able to retain her at his side only for six months in the year. We might also cite in this connection the legend of Demeter or Mother Earth, who is said to rejoice for six months in the presence of Proserpine, the green herb, her daughter, and for six months regret her absence in dark abodes beneath the earth. The ancient Celtic year thus seems to nave been divided into two halves, one representing the six summer months and the other, which commenced on the eve of November, the six months of winter darkness.

But what is still more remarkable is that just as the Rig-Veda gives us the exact date of the commencement of the battle between Indra and Shambara, so Celtic myths record the exact date of the first battle of Moytura and also of the fight between Labraid of the Swift Hand on the Sword, king of an, Irish Hades, whom Cuchulainn goes to assist, and his enemies called the Men of F˙dga. They were fought on the eve of November, "when the Celtic year began with the ascendancy of the powers of darkness." Prof. Rhys further points out that the ancient Norse year was similar in character. The great feast of the Norsemen occupied three days called the Winter Nights and began on the Saturday falling on or between the 11th and the 18th of October; and according to Dr. Vigfusson this feast marked the beginning of the ancient year of the Norsemen.

The old Norse year thus appears to have been shorter by a few days than the Celtic one; but Prof. Rhys accounts for this difference on the ground "that winter, and therefore the year commences earlier in Scandinavia than in the continental centre from which the Celts dispersed themselves." As regards the ancient Greek calendar, Prof. Rhys has shown that the old year ended with the festival of Apaturia and the new one began with the Chalceia, an ancient feast in honour of Hephaestus and Athene, the exact date being the *enu kai nea* of the month of Pyanepsion, that is, approximately the last day of October.

Prof. Rhys then compares the Celtic feast of the Lugnassad with the Greek festival named Panathenæa, and the feast on the Calends of May with the Athenian Thargelia, and concludes his comparison of the Celtic and the Greek calendar by observing that "a year which was common to Celts with Greeks is not unlikely to have once been common to them with some or all other branches of the Aryan family."

This shows that the ancient Aryan races of Europe knew of six months' day and six months' night, and their calendars were the modifications of this Arctic division of the year. Comparative philology, according to Dr. Schrader, leads us to the same conclusion. Speaking of the ancient division of the year he says: "Nearly everywhere in the chronology of the individual peoples a division of the year into two parts can be traced. This finds linguistic expression in the circumstance that the terms for summer, spring, and winter have parallel suffix formations. As in the primeval period *jhi-m* and *sem* existed side by side, so in Zend *zima* and *hama* correspond to each other, in Armenian *amarn* and *jmern*, in Teutonic *sum-ar* and *wint-ar*, in Celtic *gam* and *sam*, in Indian *vasanta* and *hemanta*. There is absolutely no instance, in which one and the same language shows identity of suffixes in the names of the *three* seasons of the year. In Slavonic, also, the year is divided into two principal divisions, summer (*leto*) and winter (*zima*); and finally evident traces of old state of things are not wanting in Greek and Latin."

Dr. Schrader further remarks that the separate conceptions of winter and summer were combined in one whole even in primitive times; but there is no word for a year common to all or most of the Aryan languages, and it is not unlikely that the names of summer or winter were used to denote the return of the seasons more frequently than the conception of winter and summer combined into one whole.

As the length of summer, or the period of sunshine, as contrasted with the period of darkness, varied from six to twelve months in the Arctic regions the conception of a year of twelve months was perhaps less suited for practical reckoning in the primeval home than the conception of so many months' summer or so many months' winter taken singly, and this explains why in the Rig-Veda we have the expression "*manus ha yuga* and *kshapah*" to denote the whole year. In discussing the legend of the Navagvas and the Dashagvas we have shown that the numerals incorporated in their names must be interpreted as referring to the number of months during which they completed their annual sacrifices, and that Prof. Lignana's view that they refer to the months of pregnancy is not only improbable but opposed to the express Vedic texts which tell us that the Navagvas and the Dashagvas completed their sacrifices in ten months.

Let us now see if there are corresponding personages in other Aryan mythologies. Prof. Lignana has pointed out the resemblance between the Navagvas and the Novemsides of the Romans. The comparison is no doubt happy, but there is nothing in the cult of the Novemsides which gives us a clue to the original meaning of the word. We know nothing beyond the fact that Novemsides (also spelt Novemsiles) were, certain Latin gods, who according to the double etymology (*novam*, nine or *novus*, new) were taken for nine Muses, or for gods newly introduced, as after the conquest of a place in contrast with the old gods of the country. But the Celtic tradition of the Maid of Nine Forms is much more explicit, inasmuch as it is distinctly connected with the sun-hero Cuchulainn.

The story is thus narrated by Rhys: Conchobar had a passing fair daughter called Fedelm of the nine forms, for she had so many fair aspects, each of which was more beautiful, as we are told, than the others; and when "Cuchulainn had, at the news of the approach of the enemy from the west, advanced with his father to the frontier of the realm, he suddenly hastened away in the evening to a place of secret meeting, where he knew Fedelm to have a bath got ready for him, in order to prepare him for the morrow and his first encounter with the invading army."

This reminds us of the assistance rendered by the Navagvas and the Dashagvas to Indra by means of Sonia sacrifices performed by them and which sacrifices are said to have invigorated Indra and prepared him for his fight with the powers of darkness, repre ented by Vritra, Vala, Shambara and other demons. The Maid of Nine Forms is therefore a Celtic paraphrase of the Nine-going sacrifices in the Rig-Veda.

Prof. Rhys considers Fedelm to be a sort of Athene with nine forms of beauty, and refers to the story of Athene weaving a peplos for her favourite Herakles, or causing springs of warm water to gush forth from the ground, to supply him at the end of the day with a refreshing bath. But this comparison does not explain why there should be nine forms of beauty in either case.

The mystery is, however, cleared up, if we suppose these legends to refer to the nine months of sunshine at the end of which the setting sun-god is refreshed or invigorated for his struggle with the demons of darkness by the acts of or services of the Nine-going sacrificers or the Maid of Nine Forms. In the Norse literature we are told that Thor, the son of Earth, slays the World-dragon, walks nine paces and dies of the venom of the Serpent." If the slaying of the dragon be understood, as remarked by Prof. Rhys, to mean the conquest of the Sun-hero over the powers of darkness and the death of Thor be taken to represent the sinking of the summer-sun below the horizon, we have here a clear statement that Thor, the Sun-hero, walked nine paces during the time that intervened between the end of winter and the end of summer.

These nine paces could not be nine days or nine years; and there is therefore no alternative but to hold that the legend refers to the nine months' life of the Sun-god before he succumbed to the powers of darkness. The Avestic story of Vafra, or, according to Spiegel, Vifra Navaza (Yt. V, 61) belongs, I think, to the same class.

He is said to have been flung up in the air, in the shape of a bird by Thraetaona and was flying for three days and three nights towards his own house, but could not turn down. At the end of the third night when the beneficent dawn came dawning up, lie prayed unto Ardvi Sura Anahita to help him, promising to offer Haomas and meat by the drink of the river Rangha. Ardvi Sura Anahita listening to his prayer is then said to have brought him to his house safe and unhurt. Vifra Navaza in this legend is very likely Vipra

Navagva of the Rig-Veda. We have seen that the Navagvas and seven *vipras* are mentioned together in the Rig-Veda (VI, 22, 2) and that the Ashvins, who are called *vipra-vahasa* in (V, 74, 7), are said to have resided for three nights in the distant region. It is not unlikely, therefore, that the story of the Navagvas, who go to help Indra in the world of darkness after completing their sacrificial session of nine months, may have been combined with the story of the Ashvins in the Avestic legend of Vifra Navaza, Sanskrit *Vipra* being changed into Avestic *Vifra* and Navagva into Navaza. The above legends from the Greek, Celtic and Norse literatures show that a long winter-darkness was not unknown to the ancestors of the Aryan races in Europe, who have preserved distinct reminiscences of a year of ten or six months' sun-shine, and that the Navagvas and the Dashagvas of the Rig-Veda have again their parallels in the mythology of other Aryan races, though the resemblance may not be as obvious in the one as in the other case.

A year of six months' or ten months' sunshine necessarily implies a long continuous day and a long continuous night, and distinct references to these Arctic characteristics of day and night are found in Norse and Slavonic legends. Thus the Norse Sun-god Balder is said to have dwelt in a place in heaven called Breidablik or Broadgleam, the most blessed of all lands, where nought unclean or accursed could abide. Upon this Prof. Rhys observes, "It is remarkable that Balder had a dwelling place in the heavens, and this seems to refer to the Arctic summer when the sun prolongs his stay above the horizon. The pendant to the picture would naturally be his staying as long in the nether world." This corresponds exactly with the Vedic description of the sun's unyoking his carriage and making a halt in the mid of the heaven, discussed in the sixth chapter.

The story of three brothers in the Slavonic literature also points out to the same conclusion. We are told that "Once there was an old couple who had three sons. Two of them had their wits about them, but the third, Ivan, was a simpleton. Now in the land in which Ivan lived, there was never any day but *always* night. This was a snake's doing. Well, Ivan undertook to kill that snake. Then came a third snake with twelve heads, Ivan killed it and destroyed the heads and immediately there was light throughout the whole land." This reminds one of the story of Trita in the Rig-Veda previously described.

Trita's abode is said to be in the distant region, and we have interpreted it to mean the nether world of darkness, an interpretation which amongst others is fully borne out by the story of Ivan and his two brothers. But the dark power takes a distinctive Russian appearance in the awful figure of Koshchei, the deathless, — a fleshless skeleton who squeezes heroes to death in his bony arms. He carries off a princess; after seven years the hero reaches his underground palace and is hidden; but is discovered by Koshchei who typifies winter in this case.

All these legends clearly indicate a dark winter of some months' duration, or the long winter-night of the Arctic regions. There are other stories in which the Sun-hero is said to have been detained in a place of darkness; but it is not necessary to refer to them in this place. For comparison I shall only refer briefly to a legend in the Finnish mythology, which, though not Aryan in origin, may yet serve to throw some light on the subject under consideration. In the mythology of the Finns, the Dawn is called Koi and "Koi, the Dawn (masc.), and Ammarik, the Gloaming (fem.), are said to have been entrusted by Vanna-issa, the Old Father, with lighting and extinguishing every morning and evening the torch of the day. As a reward for their faithful services Vanna-issa would allow them to get married.

But they preferred to remain bride and bride-groom, and Vanna-issa had nothing more to say. He allowed them, however, to meet at midnight during four weeks in summer. At that time Ammarik hands the dying torch to Koi, who revives it with his breath." If this legend has any meaning it signifies the cessation of extinguishing the torch of the day during four weeks in summer. Koi and Ammarik both leave their places and arrange to meet at midnight but without extinguishing the torch. This means a long day of four weeks, and as it must have a long night of four weeks to match it the story points out to a period of eleven months' sun-shine, and an Arctic night of four weeks.

From the legends mentioned, or referred to, or described above, it may be easily seen that many traces of the Arctic calendar are still discernible in the mythology of the western Aryan races like Celts, Teutons, Lets, Slavs, Greeks and Romans. Long dawns or a number of dawns, long days, long nights, dark winters, are all alluded to more or less explicitly in these myths, though none of these legends refers directly to the position of the primeval home and the cause of its destruction. But this omission or defect is removed by the evidence contained in the Veda and the Avesta; and when the European legends are viewed in the light of the Indo-Iranian traditions they clearly point to the existence of a primeval home near the North Pole. There are a number of other legends in the Celtic and Teutonic literatures which describe the victory of sun-hero over the demons of darkness every year, similar in character to the victory of Indra over Vritra, or to the achievements of the Ashvins, the physicians of the gods.

Thus in the Norse mythology, Hodur, the blind god of winter, is represented as killing Balder or Baldur, or the god of summer, and Vali the son of Odin and Rind is said to have avenged his brother's death afterwards. The encounters of Cuchulainn, the Celtic Sun-god, with his enemies, the Fomori or the Fir Bolg, the Irish representatives of the powers of darkness, are of the same character. It may also be remarked that according to Prof. Rhys the world of waters and the world of darkness and the dead are identical in Celtic myths, in the same way as the world of water, the abode of Vritra and the world of darkness are shown to be in the Vedic mythology.

The strange custom of *couvade*, by which the whole population of Ireland is described as being laid up in confinement or indisposed so as to be unable to defend their country against the invasion of Ailill and Medle with their Fig Bolg, excepting Cuchulainn and his father, again indicates, according to Prof. Rhys, a sort of decline in the power of gods like that witnessed in the case of the winter-sun; in other words, it was an indisposition or inactivity of the same sort which amounts in the Norse Edda to nothing less than actual death of the Anses at the hands of the powers of evil. This temporary affliction or the indisposition of the gods forms the subject of many other legends.

But we have no space to narrate all of them, and shall, therefore, only quote here the conclusion, which Prof. Rhys has been forced to adopt, regarding the meaning of these myths after a critical examination of the different Celtic and Teutonic legends. Speaking of Gods, Demons and Heroes, in the last lecture of his learned work, he thus sums up his views regarding the myths describing the encounters between Gods or Sun-heroes and the powers of darkness: "All that we have thus far found with regard to the contest of the gods and their allies against the powers of evil and theirs, would seem to indicate that they were originally regarded as yearly struggles.

This appears to be the meaning of the fore-knowledge as to the final battle of Moytura, and as to the exact date of the engagement on the Plain of Fidga in which Cuchulainn assists Labraid of the Swift Hand on the sword, a kind of Celtic Zeus, or Mars-Jupiter, as the ruler of an Elysium in the other world. It was for a similar reason that the northern Sibyl could predict that, after the Anses had been slain by Swart, aided by the evil brood, Balder would come to reign, when all would be healed, and the Anses would meet again in the Field of Ida. Nor can the case have been materially different with the Greek gods, as proved by the allusion to the prophecy about the issue of the war with the giants. And this was not all; for we are told that the Cretans represented Zeus as born and bred and also buried in their island, a view sometimes formally regarded as confirming the character ascribed to them for lying; but that deserves no serious consideration, and the Cretans in their mysteries are supposed to have represented the god going through the stages of his history every year. A little beyond the limits of the Greek world a similar idea assumed a still more remarkable form, namely, among the Phrygians, who are said by Plutarch to have believed their god (like the Puranic Vishnu) to sleep during the winter and resume his activity during summer.

The same author also states that the Paphlagonians were of opinion that the gods were shut up in a prison during winter and let loose in summer. Of these peoples, the Phrygians at least appear to have been Aryan, and related by no means distantly to the Greek; but nothing could resemble the Irish *couvade* of the Ultonion heroes more closely than the notion of the Phrygian god hibernating. This, in its turn, is not to be severed from the drastic account of the Zeus of the Greek Olympus reduced by Typho to a sinewless mass and thrown for a time into a cave in a state of utter helplessness.

Thus we seem to be directed to the north as the original home of the Aryan nations; and there are other indications to the same effect, such as Woden's gold ring Draupnir, which I have taken to be symbolic of the ancient eight-day week: he places it on Balder's pile, and with him it disappears for a while into the nether world, which would seem to mean the cessation for a time of the vicissitude of day and night, as happens in midwinter within the Arctic Circle. This might be claimed as exclusively Icelandic, but not if one can show traces, as I have attempted, of the same myth in Ireland. Further, a sort of complement to it is supplied by the fact that Cuchulainn, the Sun-hero, is made to fight several days and nights without having any sleep, which though fixed at the wrong season of the year in the epic tale in its present form, may probably be regarded as originally referring to the sun remaining above the horizon continuously for several days in summer.

Traces of the same idea betray themselves in Balder's son Forseti or the Judge, who according to a passage in old Norse literature, sits long hours at his court settling all causes in his palace of Glitnir in the skies. These points are mentioned as part of a hypothesis I have been forced to form for the interpretation of certain features of Aryan mythology; and that hypothesis, to say the least of it, will not now be considered so wild as it would have been a few years ago; for the recent researches of the students of language and ethnology have profoundly modified their views, and a few words must, at this point, be devoted to the change that has come over the scene."

Prof. Rhys then goes on to briefly describe how the views of mythologists and philologists regarding the primeval home of the Aryan race have been modified by the recent discoveries in Geology, Archeology and Craniology, and how the site of that home has been shifted from the plains of Central Asia to the northern parts of Germany or even to Scandinavia not only on ethnological but also on philological grounds. As we have discussed the subject previously, we omit this portion of Prof. Rhys' remarks and quote the concluding paragraph which runs as follows: "Thus the voice of recent research is raised very decidedly in favour of Europe, though there is no complete unanimity as to the exact portion of Europe, to regard as the early home of the Aryans; but the competition tends to lie between North Germany and Scandinavia, especially the south of Sweden.

This last would probably do well enough as the country in which the Aryans may have consolidated and organized themselves before beginning to send forth their excess of population to conquer the other lands now possessed by nations speaking Aryan languages. Nor can one forget that all the great states of modern Europe, except that of the sick man, trace their history back to the conquest of the Norsemen who set out from the Scandinavian land, which Jordanis proudly calls *officina gentium* and *vagina nationum.*

But I doubt whether the teachings of evolution may not force us to trace *them still further towards the North*: in any case, the mythological indications to which your attention has been called, point, if I am not mistaken, *to some spot within the Arctic Circle,* such, for example, as the region where Norse legend placed the Land of Immortality, somewhere in the north of Finland and the neighbourhood of the White Sea. There would, perhaps, be no difficulty in the way of supposing them to have thence in due time descended into Scandinavia, settling, among other places, at Upsala, which has all the appearance of being a most ancient site, lying as it does on a plain dotted with innumerable burial mounds of unknown antiquity. This, you will bear in mind, has to do only with the origin of the early Aryans, and not with that of the human race generally; but it would be no fatal objection to the view here suggested, if it should be urged that the mythology of nations beside the Aryans, such as that of the Paphlagonians, in case of their not being Aryan, point likewise to the north; for it is not contended that the Aryans may be the only people of northern origin. Indeed, I may add that a theory was, not long ago, propounded by a distinguished French savant, to the effect that the entire human race originated on the shores of the Polar Sea at a time when the rest of the northern hemisphere was too hot to be inhabited by man. M. de Saporta, for that is the learned writer's name, explains himself in clear and forcible terms; but how far his hypothesis may satisfy the other students of this fascinating subject I cannot say. It may, however, be observed in passing that it need not disconcert even the most orthodox of men, for it supposes all the races of mankind traceable to a single non-simian origin, and the Bible leaves it an open question where exactly and when the Garden of Eden flourished."

I have very little to add to the views expressed in the above passages; in fact Prof. Rhys has left us little to be done so far as Celtic and Teutonic myths are concerned. The way in which he proceeds to analyze the legends and show that they all point to a primeval home in the Arctic regions is at once interesting and instructive. He first clears the ground by ascribing the different prophecies occurring in the legends not to any fore-knowledge on the part of the poet, but to the simple fact that the events spoken of were of annual occurrence, and as they were known to recur regularly it was not difficult to adopt the language of prophecy and predict the happening of these events in future. He then collects a number of facts which go to prove that gods and heroes were afflicted with some disability of distress at certain intervals of time, which rendered them incapable to carry on the annual struggle with the powers of evil and darkness. The only physical phenomena corresponding to such distress of the solar hero, or the sun, are his daily setting, the decay of his powers in winter and his disappearing below the horizon for some months in the Polar regions. As the struggle between the Sungod and his enemies is, as stated above, determined to be annual, the daily setting of the sun does not come within the range of the possible explanations of the temporary distress of the sun-god. Out of the two remaining physical phenomena, the decay of sun's power in winter would have answered the purpose, had there been no legends or myths which indicated the cessation of the vicissitude of day and night for some time. I have pointed out before how Prof. Max Muller, who has followed the same method of interpretation in his discussion of the achievements of the Ashvins, has failed to grasp the real meaning of the Ashvins' legends by disregarding the statements which distinctly speak of the proteges of the Ashvins as dwelling or laboring in darkness. Prof. Rhys is more cautious in this respect, and is anxious to account for all the incidents in the legends if they could possibly be accounted for on any theory. The result is that he has been gradually led, or we might even say forced, to adopt the theory of the ancient Arctic home of the Aryan people inasmuch as all the different incidents in the legends under consideration can be accounted for only by this theory.

In short, Prof. Rhys has this book in regard to the Vedic and Avestic traditions. This has considerably lightened our labour in regard to the examination of Celtic and Teutonic myths from our point of view, and our thanks are due to Prof. Rhys for the same. But we feel sure that if the Vedic evidence and facts stated and discussed in the foregoing chapters had been known to the learned Professor before he wrote his work, he would have expressed himself still more confidently regarding the inference to be drawn from the traces of Arctic origin discernible in Teutonic myths; but even as it is, the value of his testimony stands very high in the decision of the question before us. It is the testimony of an expert given after a critical and careful examination of all Celtic and Teutonic Myths, and after comparing them with similar Greek traditions; and when this testimony falls in so completely with the conclusions we have drawn from an independent consideration of the Vedic and Avestic myths, our results may, so to say, be regarded as doubly proved. It has already been shown that the results of comparative philology also support, or, at any rate, are not inconsistent with our conclusions. The theory of the Asiatic home may be said to have been now abandoned on linguistic or etymological grounds, but it has not yet been proved that the Neolithic Aryan races of Europe were autochthonus in the countries where their remains are now found.

Therefore the question of the original home of the Aryan people is still an open question, and we are free to draw any conclusion regarding the ancient home from a legitimate consideration of the traditional evidence before us. Prof. Rhys has well described the situation by observing that the teachings of evolution may force us to look for the original home still farther north in the Arctic regions. In fact we have to go to a latitude which will give us seven months' sunshine, or a hundred nights' continuous darkness, or thirty days' continuous dawn. The question whether the home of other nations, beside the Aryan, can be traced to the North Pole, has been ably discussed by Dr. Warren in his *Paradise Found*, or the Cradle of the Human Race at the North Pole.

It is an important question from an anthropological point of view; but its very comprehensiveness precludes us from collecting evidence from the traditional literatures of the different human races living on the surface of this earth. It is true that we sometimes derive help from the discussion of the broader questions at first; but for all practical purposes it is always desirable to split up the inquiry into different sections, and when each section has been thoroughly investigated to combine the results of the different investigators and see what conclusions are common to all.

Our inquiry of the original Aryan home is, therefore, not only not inconsistent with the general theory about the, cradle of the human race at the North Pole, but a necessary complement to it; and it matters little whether it is undertaken as an independent inquiry as we have done, or as a part of the general investigation. Anyhow ours is a limited task, namely, to prove that the original home of the Aryan people was situated in the Arctic regions before the last Glacial epoch and that the oldest ancestors of the Aryan race had to abandon it owing to its destruction by ice and snow of the Glacial period.

The Vedic and the Avestic passages, quoted in the previous chapters, directly point to such a home in primeval times, and we now see that the testimony of scholars, like Prof. Rhys, who have independently examined the Celtic, Teutonic and other mythologies of the European branches of the Aryan race, fully bears out the conclusion we have deduced from the Indo-Iranian traditions.

We have also seen that our view is supported by the latest scientific researches, and is not inconsistent with the results of comparative philology. We may, therefore, take it as established that the original home of the Aryan people was in the far north, in regions round about the North Pole, and that we have correctly interpreted the Vedic and the Avestic traditions which had long remained misinterpreted or misunderstood.

BRITISH COLONIAL PERIOD – COLONIAL RULE (1858–AUGUST 1918)

After 1858, India turned out to be formally a British province as British crown took control of India from East India Company. The British crown put a Secretary of State for India in change of India. Indian Council who had just consultative forces helped him. India was isolated into three regulatory zones (Bengal, Madras and Bombay). Various managerial and legitimate changes were presented. In 1861 Indian Councils Act, High Courts Act and Penal code were passed. English kept on growing the railroads and transmitted system and in 1868 new Ambala – Delhi railroad line was begun. A blend of regulatory disappointments and characteristic elements brought about expansive number of starvations in India that murdered a large number of individuals:

1861 Famine in North West

1866 Famine in Bengal and Orissa – 1 million perished

1869 Intense famine in Rajasthan – 1.5 million perished

1874 Famine in Bihar

1876–78 Famine in Bombay, Madras and Mysore – 5 million perished.

During this time, India was forced to produce cash crop, which were to be sold by the British. India was also forced to accept British goods that destroyed cottage industries. Many peasants had to borrow money to pay the extremely high taxes imposed on them. 1st January 1877, Queen Victoria was proclaimed Empress of India at a *Durbar* (assembly of notables and princes), in Delhi. The Viceroy Lord Lytton represented the Sovereign, who incidentally never visited her Indian Empire. In 1878 Vernacular Press act was introduced in India that imposed severe limitations on the rights of the press. In the same year there was 'Rendition of Mysore' and Mysore was returned to its original Wodeyar rulers. In 1883 the Ilbert Bill Act was passed which allowed Indian magistrates to try Europeans. This angered the Europeans and the bill was withdrawn.

Indians suffered from growing unemployment while most well paying jobs were reserved for the British. Racial discrimination against Indian's forced the Indian nationalists into organizing themselves for getting their demands accepted.

Hindu renaissance movement – During this period several great saints and religious leaders were responsible for revival of Hinduism in different parts of India. Ramkrishna Paramhansa (1836-1886), Swami Vivekananda (1863-1902) and Ishwar Chandra Vidyasagar (1820-1891) led the Hinduism renaissance in Bengal that later spread to other parts of India. Swami Dayananda Saraswati (1824-1883) formed Arya Samaj, which became a major religious movement in north India.

FORMATION OF INDIAN NATIONAL CONGRESS

Allen Octavian Hume at last shaped the Indian National Congress. The First meeting was in December 1885 in Bombay. Womesh Chandra Banerjee turned into the primary president of Indian National Congress. It met each year in December in various parts of the nation. In the early years, the congress utilized just Petition, Prayer and Protest to attempt to get their requirements met. In 1891 Indian plant Act was passed and in 1892 Indian Councils Act was changed to incorporate new arrangements for administrating India. Bubonic Plague in Bombay, 1896-1914 and Indian Famine 1897-1901:

The epidemic spread from Bombay City, western and northern India, was hardest hit. Around 200,000 people died of plague in Bombay alone. Between October 1896 and February 1897, nearly half of Bombay's estimated 850,000 populations left the city resulting in great loss to commerce and industrial life and helped the disease to spread in countryside and other parts of India. Along with plague many parts of India were devastated by famine during 1897-1901 that killed around 2 million people.

FIRST PARTITION OF BENGAL

Following the 'divide and rule' policy Bengal was divided by the British, on October 16, 1905, into Hindu and Muslim areas. By doing this British had hoped to increase tensions between the Hindus and the Muslims. Lord Curzon was the British governor general at this time. The following excerpts from Curzon's letter of 2nd February 1905 to St. John Brodrick, Secretary of State for India, give an idea of his aims in partitioning Bengal.

"CALCUTTA is the center from which the Congress Party is manipulated throughout the whole of Bengal, and indeed the whole of India. Its best wire pullers and its most frothy orators all reside here. The perfection of their

machinery, and the tyranny which it enables them to exercise are truly remarkable. They dominate public opinion in Calcutta; they affect the High Court; they frighten the local Government, and they are sometimes not without serious influence on the Government of India. The whole of their activity is directed to creating an agency so powerful that they may one day be able to force a weak government to give them what they desire. Any measure in consequence that would divide the Bengali-speaking population; that would permit independent centres of activity and influence to grow up; that would dethrone Calcutta from its place as the centre of successful intrigue, or that would weaken the influence of the lawyer class, who have the entire organization in their hands, is intensely and hotly resented by them. The outcry will be loud and very fierce, but as a native gentleman said to me – 'my countrymen always howl until a thing is settled; then they accept it'."

Protest meetings against the partition were organized in all parts of the country on and after 16 October 1905. Partition of Bengal also saw a strong polarization in Indian National Congress between 'moderates' and 'hardliners'. Moderates such as Gopal Krishan Gokhale believed in making "loyal" representations to the government for small reforms, while hardliners like Lokmanya Bal Gangadhar Tilak complete freedom or 'purna swarajya'.

Tilak announced his slogan "Swaraj is my birthright and I shall have it" in his newspaper and became the speaker for the new group of nationalists. The primary leaders of the nationalist movement were Lala Lajpat Rai (1865-1928) from Punjab, Lokmanya Bal Gangadhar Tilak (1856-1920) from Maharashtra and Bipin Chandra Pal from Bengal. Together, they were called Lal-Bal-Pal. Ajit Singh in Punjab and Chidambaram Pillay in Tamil Nadu were other important leaders of the Nationalistic Movement.

In 1906, Tilak set forth a programme of passive resistance, known as the Tenets of the New Party, that he hoped would destroy the hypnotic influence of British rule and prepare the people for sacrifice in order to gain independence. Mahatma Gandhi later adopted these forms of political action initiated by Tilak-the boycotting of goods and passive resistance-in his programme of non-cooperation with the British.

The Nationalistic movement adopted the slogan of "Swadeshi and Swaraj". Swadeshi means our country and promoted the use of Indian products and the boycott of foreign goods. Swaraj means self-government.

Tilak aimed at Swarajya (Independence), not piecemeal reforms, and attempted to persuade the Congress to adopt his purna swarajya programme. On this issue, he clashed with the moderates at the Surat session of the Congress in 1907. Taking advantage of the split in the nationalist forces, the government again prosecuted Tilak on a charge of sedition and inciting terrorism and deported him to Mandalay, Burma (Myanmar), to serve a sentence of six years' imprisonment.

FORMATION OF MUSLIM LEAGUE (1906)

Huge numbers of the Indian Muslims were taken in by British divisive approach of 'partition and run the show'. Despite the fact that Muslims had a reasonable representation in Congress some of them needed a different stage for Indian Muslims. In 1906 Muslim League was shaped to speak to Indian Muslims.

By the segment of Bengal in 1905 British effectively sowed the seeds of division amongst Hindus and Muslims that lead at last to the segment of India in 1947. Apparitions of the British 'gap and run' approach, keep on haunting free India and Pakistan in present times with proceeding with strains and fringe question.

EARLY REVOLUTIONARY MOVEMENT

Partition of Bengal created a massive outburst of public anger against British rule. Intellectual people as well as common man took part in mass agitation. Poet Rabindranath Tagore actively supported the movement. Bankim Chandra Chatterjee's '*Bande Matram*' was taken up as the soul-stirring slogan. Several groups of revolutionaries started operating in Bengal. Aurobindo Ghosh (later known as Sri Aurobindo), Rasbihari Bose and Jatindranath Mukherjee (Bagha Jatin) were some of the important leaders of these revolutionary groups.

ALIPORE BOMB CASE

On 30th April, 1908 in Muzzafarpur Bihar, Khudiram Bose and Prafulla Chaki tried to kill the Chief Presidency Magistrate Kingsford who was notorious for passing out stiff sentences against the nationalist activists Kingsford escaped the bomb attack which unfortunately killed two innocent British ladies died in the bomb attack. Following a massive manhunt, Khudiram was arrested on 1st May 1908; Prafulla evaded arrest by shooting himself. On 11th August 1908, eighteen-year-old Khudiram Bose was hanged and became a martyr. Aurobindo Ghosh was arrested on charges of masterminding the attacks on Kingsford but a young lawyer Chittaranjan Das ably defended him. Aurobindo later left politics and became a Yogi and philosopher and became famous as Maharishi Aurobindo or Sri Aurobindo. A Durbar was held in Delhi on December 12, 1911, to celebrate the visit of King George V. King was welcomed with great pomp and show and given numerous priceless gifts. In 1911 British government under pressure from increasing agitations in Bengal and other parts of India modified the 'partition of Bengal' to make again a united Presidency of Bengal.

HARDINGE BOMB CASE

British shifted the imperial capital from Calcutta to Delhi in 1912. On December 23, 1912 to mark the entry of the Governor-general of India into the new Capital, an imperial procession was taken out in Delhi, with Lord Hardinge seated on a caparisoned elephant. As the procession was passed through Chandni Chowk, a bomb was thrown on the elephant, killing the *mahawat*. Lord Hardinge escaped with injuries. Many persons including Master Amir Chand, a school teacher of Delhi, Bhai Balmukand, Master Awadh Behari, Basant Kumar Biswas, Ganeshilal Khasta, Vishnu Ganesh Pingley, Charan Das, Balraj, Lachhmi Narain Sharma and Lala Hanwant Sahey, and many others were arrested. L.N Sharma and G. Khasta were taken to Varanasi and sentenced to life imprisonment. V.G Pingley was taken to Lahore and was hanged. Master Amir Chand, Bhai Balmukand and Master Awadh Behari were executed on May 8, 1915 in Delhi Jail and Basant Kumar Biswas was executed the next day on May 9, 1915 in Ambala Central Jail.

Ras Bihari Bose, who masterminded the Chandni Chowk incident, escaped to Japan and continued the struggle against British rule from abroad. He was the President of Indian Independence League and head of the first Indian National Army (INA) founded by General Mohan Singh.

In 1914 Britain became engaged in World War I. Shortly after declaration of war, two infantry divisions and a cavalry brigade of the Indian Army were sent to Europe. In all 140,000 men served on the Western Front, 90,000 in the Indian Corps and 50,000 in the Labour Companies. Indian troops also played important role in operations in Mesopotamia, Palestine, and Gallipoli. They also served in the West and East African campaigns and in China.

On 16 June 1914, Bal Gangadhar Tilak was released after serving a prison sentence of 6 years, most of which he had spent in Mandalay in Burma. In 1915-1916, under the leadership of Tilak, Annie Besant and Subramaniya Iyer, the Home Rule League was started. January 9, 1915, saw the beginning of a new phase in India's struggle for independence with arrival of Mohandas Karamchand Gandhi to Bombay from South Africa. Two major events took place at the Lucknow session of the Indian Nation Congress in 1916. First, the moderate and hardliner groups were united. Second, the Muslim League put aside old differences and joined hands with the Indian National Congress. Responding to Gandhi's call for helping British in World War I, a large number of Indians joined British Indian Army during 1916-1917. By the end of the World War I in 1918, the numerical strength of Indians in British Indian Army had increased to nearly 600,000.

First Stirrings of Nationalism

On Tuesday, June 22, 1897, the British in India were engaged in celebrating the Diamond Jubilee of the Queen-Empress Victoria. They did so with military parades, dances and champagne dinners. At Poona, the summer seat of the Governor of Bombay, the festivities were particularly glittering. That night there was a dinner-party at Government House. As the guests left in their carriages they were startled by the sound of firing. A woman's screams brought the guests and guards to two carriages in which one man, Walter Rand lay dying and another, Charles Ayrest, was dead. Political assassination had emerged as a weapon against the British Raj.

The authorities were caught off balance, but not for long. Surprise was replaced by angry panic. Was the murder of Englishmen an signal for a popular uprising? The Indians certainly had many reasons to revolt. A serious famine in Western India followed by the appearance for the first time in India of bubonic plague. Doctors knew neither the cause of, nor the cure for this terrifying scourge. In Bombay alone, 20,000 died, and by 1897 the disease had spread to the countryside. In Poona, the Chief Plague Officer, Mr. Rand, whose reputation as a stern disciplinarian had preceded him, had adopted brutal methods to prevent the spread of infection. British troops had been called in to destroy property believed contaminated. Men, women and children, from allegedly infected areas had been segregated in special plague camps. The troops were not gentle. While searching houses for suspected victims, they damaged religious shrines, looted, and often sent to camps people who were in fact free from the plague.

To the inhabitants of Poona, Mr. Rand's men appeared to be carry on a reign of terror. The native-language press demanded retaliation. Everyone has the right of self defence. According to certain Hindu sects, no blame was attached even to killing if it were disinterested and a group of young men had therefore established a "society for removing obstacles to the Hindu religion" and murdered Mr. Rand and his assistant.

The authorities moved a large force of police into Poona. Secret agents moved among the people, but they could not find the assassins or any clue t their identity. A collective fine on the city produced no more than money. But the failure of the police resulted in calls for strong action in the English-language newspapers. Indian nationalism seemed about to embrace violent revolution-a radical and frightening move away from the quiet nationalism that had been the pattern over the previous 30 years.

Indian nationalism was a child of the Raj-at first uncritical and only gradually becoming rebellious. The effects of English education in 19th Century India had been to produce a middle-class identifying itself in many ways with the alien rulers, speaking their language, cherishing their political philosophy, and hoping that the promises so frequently made to them that one day they would be accepted as partners would be fulfilled. As the second half of the 19th Century moved to its close, that fulfilment seemed as far away as ever. The reluctance of the government to share its powers with educated Indians and the unquestioning belief by the British in their racial superiority pushed the middle-classes into action.

At the turn of the century, members of Congress had no desire for independence for India, but only for active participation in the government of the country. They were not anti-British. On the contrary, they believed that the British had brought many blessings to India, and that being a part of the British Empire was not only a gift of Providence but good fortune as well.

The man who emerged during this time as leader of Congress, Gopal Krishna Gokhale, typified these middle-class Indians. He had many British friends and had visited England many times. He believed that the inequalities and inadequacies of Hindu society were the only reason for India's political subordination to their foreign rulers. A cautious rather sickly man, he wanted India to progress gradually in partnership with "the genius of the British people."

But there were others who did not share the faith and hope -and the innocence-of these fully Westernised Indians. Most of them were western educated also, but for them western education had brought unease-and unemployment. In British India there were only a limited number of outlets for the educated. The unemployed found themselves without a place in Westernised society, or in that from which their education cut them off. In fact they began to look upon those Indians who *had* found a place in the world of the British-as government servants, lawyers or businessmen -as just as much their enemies as the British themselves. Had they not become bastard Englishmen? To the educated unemployed, the appeal of religious nationalism offered a refuge, a chance of identity with something greater than themselves.

Given that the first stirrings of religious nationalism occurred in Bengal with the writings of Bankim Chandra Chatterji, there were others too, who claimed to find in the Hindu past a real hope for the future, for an India that was Indian rather than fake British. It was in the province of Bombay that his looking backwards in order to see the shape of the future first took the form of positive political action. The man who gave it that form was Bal Gangadhar Tilak. Western educated, at first cooperative with the moderate English-thinking liberals but soon realised that they represented only a minority, cut away from the people of India.

The British, Tilak was convinced, would never give India their freedom, and if they granted some political power it would only be to those who were most in sympathy with their rule. Tilak turned to the organisation of mass action in Bombay province whose inhabitants looked back in admiration to the 17th Century Maratha Empire, which had contained Bombay. There was a recent tradition of Maratha independence.

Tilak quickly assumed leadership of the Hindu masses in Western India. In doing so he was, paradoxically, taking a more orthodox western view of the tools of political change than the Liberal moderates of the Indian National Congress. The history of European democracy in the 19th Century, he said, was the history of revolution not reform. The British did not fear the men of Congress, but they had every reason to fear a popular uprising-and was not assassination a weapon of revolution? This fear turned the British against Tilak and the murders at Poona in 1897.

Yet try as they did, the police could find no connection between Tilak and the murders at Poona. He was therefore charged with sedition. The Governor was reluctant to press such vague charges, but gave in to the clamour of the English press. The trial was a travesty. Two articles by Tilak were subjected to the most perverse interpretation by the presiding judge who defined sedition as "the disaffection" or "want of affection" for British rule. The jury found Tilak guilty by a majority and he was sent to prison for 18 months.

The Politics of Disaster

When natural disasters-famine or plague-hit the sub-continent of India, its British rulers faced up to their responsibilities with varying degrees of vigour and success. The administration's battle against the particularly severe famines at the end of the 19th Century was both energetic and effective. Development projects were set up in affected areas to provide work and wages, the construction of new railways was launched, partly to carry grain to where it was most needed, rent was remitted and a certain amount of free relief was granted. Mercifully, the measures had some effect. The administration's fight against plague, however, was not successful and the Indians were left with an abiding memory of the peremptory and often brutal nature of British paternalism. Well-intentioned action thus intensified nationalism.

The Great Bombay Blunder

The British learned with a vengeance the inadequacies of their short-sighted philanthropy during the Bombay plague of 1896-7. After a disastrous famine in 1896, bubonic plague broke out in Bombay and spread to Poona. Within a year it had killed 34,000 people. The British adopted drastic measures in their attempt to combat it. Lieutenant Walter Rand a man with a reputation as a strict disciplinarian, was appointed Plague Officer and decided on a draconian policy of isolation. Anyone showing symptoms or suspected of being a contact was shut away in a plague camp. Houses were broken into, hosed down, fumigated and limewashed with no concern for the sensibilities of the inhabitants. The soldiers carried out Rand's orders with a toughness that, on occasion, became brutality. Complaints poured in about women being raped and money stolen.

All sections of the Indian community were outraged. The extremist Bal Gangadhar Tilak, who himself had asked the British for strong measures, headed a deputation to the Governor with suggestions about how the searches could be conducted more humanely. He was politely shown the door. As a direct result of British insensitivity, in 1897, Rand and his deputy were murdered by terrorists. Assassination had for the first time become a political weapon to be used against the British Raj.

Doctor Brighton

In the First World War, when India forgot her quarrel with Britain and helped close the Imperial ranks, 139,000 Indians fought in the mud of the Western front. The British responded generously to such loyalty and to care for the wounded, set up special hospitals along the south coast most notably in Brighton, long known as" Doctor Brighton" for bracing air. George IV's elaborate Indian style Pavilion was aptly fitted out as a hospital, as was the town's 'workhouse,' tactfully renamed the Kitchener Hospital. Every attempt was made to provide comfort for Britain's Eastern soldiers. Different kitchens were opened for different religions. Untouchables were banished to the lawns and the wounded were cared for by orderlies of the same caste. The dead were treated with respect. Muslims were taken for burial to the nearby mosque and Hindus were cremated on a specially built *ghat* near Brighton, and their ashes scattered in the sea.

India Claims Nationhood

The news of Tilak's sentence spread his fame-and his ideas. Young men began to think that their future lay in manipulation of the masses and the use of violence. The moderates had failed them, with their obsequious flattery of alien ideas and their feeble requests for a slice of the cake. Tilak's experience dramatised a conflict of generations. The leaders of Congress were men aware of the century of anarchy that had preceded British rule; but the young felt only the tensions of the time, and their own frustrations. The impatient young men of India, organising themselves into secret societies, reading about European revolutionary terrorism, waited another eight years for some great event that would make them the spearhead of mass protest. The British supplied it with their high-handed decision to divide up the province of Bengal. It had proved too large to be administered as a single unit; now it was to become two separate provinces -West Bengal with a Hindu, and East Bengal and Assam, with a Muslim majority. Here at last was the tinder to spark the flame of Hindu nationalism. Two weapons of protest emerged-the economic boycott of British goods and the terrorists bombs.

The Viceroy, Lord Curzon, who in March 1905 had dismissed the anti-partition agitators as "petty volcanoes" by October, was forced to admit ""the agitation is now being conducted by methods of open terrorism and violence." During 1906, violence spread throughout Bengal. Now secret societies were formed, bomb factories set up. The government assumed special security powers. Leaders were deported without trial, political organisations were declared illegal, many arrests were made and sentences of flogging imposed for many minor crimes. These methods appear to have worked to a certain extent. An attempt by young advocates of violent struggle to capture the leadership of Congress failed. The extremists suffered further setbacks. Their leader Tilak, was once more sentenced in 1908 to eight years in jail. As a sop to the nationalists, 'safe men' *i.e.* Indians with little leverage, were elected to Legislative Councils at vice regal level.

These reforms were the work of Lord Minto, and the cautious Secretary of state for India, John Morley. Both believed that small concessions would encourage those Indians who were loyal to Britain and that India's future would remain firmly in British hands. Morley told Parliament that universal suffrage in India was "a fantastic and ludicrous dream."

The reforms were also well received by Indian Muslims who in 1906-scared at the growing strength of Hindu nationalism and anti-Muslim sentiment, had founded their own political organisation, the Muslim League. They asked for, and were granted separate electorates for Muslims. A dangerous precedent. The commencement of hostilities in Europe in August 1914, produced an outburst of loyal enthusiasm in India, which in the light of subsequent events seems almost incomprehensible. Over a million men volunteered for the armed forces, messages of support came from every level of Indian life, and there were large cash contributions of war loans.

In November 1914, the Under Secretary of State for India emphasised the point in a statement in the House of Commons. "It is clear," he said, "that India claims to be not a mere dependent but a partner in the Empire, and her partnership with us in spirit and on battlefields cannot but alter the angle from which we shall henceforth look at the problems of government of India." By 1915, the extremists had again emerged to voice popular fears and aspirations, their task eased by the death of Gokhale and Sir Pherozshah Mehta, the two most implacable opponents of the extremists in that year.

Indian Muslims too, were no longer so pro-British. The revocation of the partition of Bengal announced at the magnificent Delhi Durbar of 1911, as a sop to Hindu nationalism, had shocked them deeply. They were further alienated from the British by the fact that their spiritual overlord, the Caliph of Turkey, found himself at war with their temporal master the King-Emperor of Britain. Under this pressure, many Muslims, among them the future creator of Pakistan, Muhammad Ali Jinnah urged the League to re-establish the link with the Congress party. In 1916, this occurred, and Britain was once again faced with a united Indian opposition. But the Congress was about to change from a body whose watchword was caution, into a mass rally and the vanguard of militant Hindu nationalism which in turn again split the Muslims from them.

The British managed to dissipate any remaining goodwill by one of the most unimaginative and ill-timed moves they had made during their rule of the Indian subcontinent. At the same time as the Secretary-of-State for India, Edwin Montagu, arrived in India to consult with Indian leaders and the Viceroy, Lord Chelmsford, about impending reforms, a committee under Mr. Justice Rowlatt was sitting to "investigate and report on the nature and extent of the criminal conspiracies connected with the revolutionary movement in India." The Rowlatt Bills effectively guaranteed that Indian nationalists would be suspicious of the proposed reforms.

These reforms-incorporated in the Montagu-Chelmsford Report-which the British hoped would both reward Indian loyalists and stifle unrest, were in fact quite radical, even by the changed standards of the time. The British government not only accepted the principle of self-government for India but was actually ready to prepare for it. But between the announcement of these reforms and their coming into force three years later events took place which were to produce a new national leader-Gandhi-who was to condemn any cooperation with "this satanic government." The Rowlatt Acts were the turning point for the growth of nationalistic fervour in India for, in the atmosphere of tension and indignation which united the political classes and the people as never before, a new leader, Mohandas Karamchand Gandhi, emerged, who was to become the symbol of India to the world. Gandhi, a lawyer of 49, had recently returned from South Africa where he had spent almost the whole of his adult life. There he had made his name as the leader of the Indian community in their fight against discrimination by the South African government, using his own method of protest which he called *Satyagraha* or "soul force" To draw suffering upon oneself and thus shame ones opponent into a change of heart, to die-but not to kill-for the truth. When Gandhi returned to India in 1915, he found his own country strange to him and spent a year or two travelling around, finding out what the people were thinking.

Gandhi

At that time, although his reputation had preceded him, his views had always been those of moderates, and no one had really considered him as either a spokesman or potential leader. He believed however that experiments in passive resistance in India had shown that there was a place for his kind of nonviolent approach to political action. Gandhi was right. His moral condemnation of the new security laws struck a chord in the hearts of all classes. By using religion he made the political movement acceptable to all the people of India. He proposed a traditional Hindu method of protest-the *hartal* a closing of all shops and places of business as a sign of mourning. All over India people responded to Gandhi's call. The Hartal in many places led to violent rioting. Horrified, Gandhi tried to call off the strike but it was like reasoning with a whirlwind, it merely grew more violent particularly in the Punjab. Thousands of demobilised soldiers had returned home with little hope of a future. The government of the Punjab, believing the 'hartal' to be merely a cloak for rebellion was determined to suppress any signs of revolt. The situation was ripe for an explosion. It took place on April 13, 1919 in the town of Amritsar.

Bal Gangadhar Tilak was a great Sanskrit scholar and astronomer. He fixed the origin and date of Rigvedic Aryans, which was highly acclaimed and universally accepted by orientalists of his time. His role in Congress and advocating Home Rule for India were enormous. His newspaper (Kesari) founded in 1881 is going strong even today. He was Guru to V.D. Savarkar and hundreds of nationalists and thousands of Indians. He led the Indian Freedom Movement, till 1920, his death. After him Gandhiji took over. Although Gandhi accepted Gokhale as his mentor, in practice, he adopted all of Tilak's ideas of Swadeshi and of social reform.

His words, "Swaraj is my birthright and I shall have it!" roused a sleeping nation to action, making Indian people aware of their political plight under a foreign rule. Tilak did not question the British Sovereignty nor his demands were rebellious or revolutionary. All he was asking was favourable conditions in India, to enable people to learn to govern themselves. May be all over the world, the separatist forces should follow his vision and define freedom as ability to govern one's land. But the handful rulers who ruled India's millions thought otherwise. They thought that Tilak was whipping a rebellion and he was imprisoned twice; two years for the first and six during the second. They said, he had committed treason.. Tilak rightly calculated the attitude of the British towards the economic exploitation of the Indians. The British used the raw material from the Indian soil and produced finished products in their country, which in turn were sold in India. This made the Indians totally dependent on the British. In the process, all the self-employing industries of India like spinning, weaving, glass making, sugar, dyeing, paper making were destroyed. People became destitute for no fault of theirs to help an empire become richer and stronger. To fight this situation, he gave four mantras called Chatuhsutri: (1). Boycott of foreign goods (2) National Education (3) Self Government (4) Swadeshi or self reliance. He realized that mere protest against British rule was not going to help and insisted on native production and reliance. He founded Deccan Education Society to give better education as per the country's needs. He wrote articles over inhuman punishment meted out to the nationalist youth who protested the division of Bengal (Vanga Bhanga). Indian newspapers were not to criticize the British policy in those days and two articles titled "Has the Government lost its head ?".and "To Rule is not to wreak vengeance" appearing in Kesari landed him in jail, after a namesake trial. For the first time in British history, intellectuals in England (including the great orientalist, Max Muller) were able to convince the Government that the trial was unfair. But the second time (1908) was no different. Tilak advocated his own case and when the judgment of six years of black-waters (kala pani) imprisonment was pronounced, he gave the famous statement :

> *"All I wish to say is that in spite of the verdict of the jury, I maintain my innocence. There are higher powers that rule the destiny of men and nations. It may be the will of Providence that the cause I represent may prosper by suffering than by remaining free".*

His trial and punishment led to national upheaval. But the British were careful enough to arrange everything in secret and the judgment was delivered at midnight and Tilak was taken under military vigil to be deported to Burma (present Myanmar, which was also under British control).

At 52, Tilak wrote his famous commentary on Bhagavad-Gita, the sacred book of Hindus; Gita-Rahasya in the jail. By the time Tilak completed his six year prison term, he was the unquestioned leader of the Indians-the uncrowned king. He was known as the Tilak Maharaj. There was unprecedented jubilation after Tilak was free and back in India.

Civil resistance, the concept of Swaraj, and nationalism had taken deep roots. Tilak's suffering did not go in vain. A band of leaders, full of zeal for nationalism and self-sacrifice was coming up. National schools were coming up in all corners of India. He paved the way for Khadi (hand woven cloth), picketing against foreign goods and alcoholism. His death in 1920 brought Mahatma Gandhi on the scene and Gandhiji gave a concrete shape to Tilak's ideas of Swadeshi.

LATER YEARS AND LEGACY

Tilak was a critic of Mahatma Gandhi's strategy of non-violence, civil disobedience. Although once considered an extremist revolutionary, in his later years Tilak had considerably mellowed. He favoured political dialogue and discussions as a more effective way to obtain political freedom for India.

When Tilak died in 1920, Gandhi paid his respects at his cremation in Bombay, along with 200,000 people. Gandhi called Tilak *"The Maker of Modern India"*. Tilak is also today considered the father of Hindu Nationalism. He was the idol of Indian revolutionary Vinayak Damodar Savarkar, who penned the political doctrine of Hindutva. He realized that the constitutional agitation in itself was futile against the British and that, moreover, India was ill prepared for an armed revolt.

As a result, although he was helpful to revolutionaries such as Savarkar, Aurobindo Ghosh and Chaphekar, he did not venture into it himself. Instead, he martialled the extremist wing of Indian National Congress. His movement was based on the principles of Swadeshi (Indigenous), Boycott and Education. It was he who, through his own example, gave prestige to imprisonment in freedom struggle. It is a tragedy that his work is not given the recognition due to it.

Tilak is often misinterpreted. Perhaps it is so because of his style of operation which raised bitter controversies and still more bitter opponenents even outside the beurocracy. Violent arguements characterized his relationship with social reformists such as Agarkar, Ranade and moderates like Ferozshah Mehta. Many blame him for opposing the Age of Consent Bill which raised the age limit for marriage of girls to 12 (from 10). But is fact that at the same time he had signed a counter-proposal where in one of the clauses was that the girls (boys) should not be married until they are 16 (20). He educated all of his daughters and did not marry them till they were over 16. There are instances when he privately paid for the education of women. Still it remains true that he was a reactionary and did not use his considerable influence to give a much-needed support to the social reformists. Probably, he did not want to offend the prevalent rigid system-he, himself, having been brought up in the culturally narrow surroundings of Pune. It seems as if his canvas presented him no room for active social reforms.

He had several discussions with Shankaracharya of Sankeshwar and asserted that like Swami Vivekananda, the modern Shankaracharya must be educated on modern lines. Tilak received Bachelor of Arts degree from The Deccan College, Pune in 1879 and L.L.B. from the Elphinston College, Mumbai in 1882.

He was among the founders of the New English School, Pune (1881) of which Prof Chiplunkar became the Principal. He had a genius for organisation and with Agarkar, the then foremost social reformist, started the newspapers 'Kesari' and 'The Maratha' in 1881 and in 1890's started the annual celebration of 'Shivaji Festival' and 'Ganapati Festival' which served a platform for people to join in the nationalist movement against the British. Soon he came to be regarded as the undisputed leader of Maharashtra and was honoured with the title 'Lokamanya' in 1893 which became synonymous with him in the 1900.

As the nation fumed over the partition of Bengal (1905), Tilak assumed the national leadership with his extremist attitude and stated his position unequivocally as "Swarajya (self rule) is my birth right and I shall have it."

Ganesh Festival and Shiv Jayanti

In order to inspire the common man he started these two festivals which were celebrated across cast and creed. There are many festive days and different festivals in the Hindu religion, but they are celebrated individually and privately. For national awakening Tilak initiated Ganeshotsav and Shivaji Utsav in 1894. Shivaji Utsav started on Fort Raigad in 1894 and reached as far as Japan by 1905. In 1896 Ganeshotsav attained national importance. The next three years saw meteoric rise in his stature and the British power which had long since considered him their chief concern and had sent him to prison twice already, decided on a firmer measure.

Much has been said of his trial of 1908. He utilized his time in prison in scholarly pursuits and wrote "Gita Rahasya", a commentary on the Gita. He returned to Indian political scene in 1915. The political situation was fast changing under the shadow of World War I. Mahatma Gandhi's star was on rise with Satyagraha at Sabarmati in 1914. The British charged Tilak in 1918.

He fought those charges both in India and England, and was judged guilty. Amidst rumours of yet another sentence, he headed the Home-Rule commission in England to debate India's constitutional demands. By that time, Gandhi had made preparations of the first nation wide non-cooperation movement and, perhaps, it was to make way for Gandhi that Tilak left for England. Tilak was, probably, the only leader who could have put brakes on Gandhi. Both had conflicting approaches. Gandhi had the courage to address and solve the issue of untouchability once and forever. He, unlike Tilak, was a fluent speaker in Hindi and could thus reach the masses more easily. It is no secret that he had little respect for Tilak's real politick and Tilak hated adopting means which killed self pride of the masses. Whereas Gandhi preached, "Overcome hatred with love", Tilak pooh poohed moderates saying, "There is no empire lost by a free grant of concession by the rulers to tne ruled." In both world wars, Gandhi encouraged Indians to fight for the British Empire unconditionally whereas Tilak held that if Indians were to remain slaves then it mattered little whether they joined army or not. The Mahatma was modern with novel methods. His was a welcome arrival both for the Moderates who needed an answer to the Extremists and Tilak, in particular, and the British who would rather acknowledge and have a saint as the foremost adversary.

In the 20's many of Tilak's followers, Dadasaheb Khaparde and N.C. Kelkar being the most prominent among them, supported Gandhi but none could have his say in the new order. Aurobindo Ghosh had retired to an ascetic life and Savarkar was serving two life sentences in Andaman. The Lokamanya had no worthy successor. Tilak's health continued to deteriorate rapidly at end of July 1920 and he went delirious and was unconscious for 3 days. His last words in the final momentary recovery were, "This happened in 1818 (End of Peshwai) and this in 1918. A hundred years' history-what a life of servitude...Unless Swaraj is obtained, India shall not prosper. It is necessary for our very own existence."

Tilak's father, Gangadhar Shastri, was a good Sanskrit scholar and a friend of Ramakrishna Bhandarkar. Tilak's mother's name was Paravti Bai Gangadhar. Tilak's father, Gangadharpanth, started his career as a school teacher at Ratnagiri. In 1886 he was transferred to Poona as an Assistant Deputy Education Inspector for Primary Schools. In spite of the ancient aristocratic heritage, the family belonged to the lower-middle class when Bal Gangadhar Tilak was born. In 1871 Tilak married Tapibai. After marriage her name was changed to Satyabhamabai. She belonged to the Ballal Val Chitpavan family of Ladghar village near Dapoli in Ratnagiri district.

Tilak received most of his education at Poona. A brilliant student, Tilak was known even in his childhood for his fierce self-respect, regard for truth and his intense reaction to injustice. He passed his B.A. in the first class with Mathematics and Sanskrit (1876) and completed his education with a Law degree in 1879. While he was a student at the Deccan College, Poona, he was much influenced by the teaching of Professor Wordsworth and Professor Shoot. The former taught him English Literature and the latter taught him History and Political Economy which helped him to appreciate English ideas. Tilak, in spite of his Hindu conservatism, was much influenced by Western thought on Politics and Metaphysics. He was particularly fond of Hegel, Kant, Spencer, Mill, Bentham, Voltaire and Rousseau. As he himself expressed it in the 'Gita Rahasya' : "To a certain extent my line of argument runs parallel to the line of thinking followed by Green in his book on Ethics."

After completing his education, Tilak spurned the lucrative offers of Government service and decided to devote himself to the larger cause of national awakening. He firmly believed that modern education had to be taken to the masses by the Indians themselves if they were to grow in stature to overcome the pathetic acceptance of the concept of the rulers and the ruled which the Britishers wanted to preserve so assiduously.

He joined Agarkar, Chiplunkar and Namjoshi in starting the New English School and later in founding the Deccan Education Society and the Fergusson College in 1885. He, however, parted company with them in 1890, following serious differences about the fundamental commitments of the members of the Society.

In a way it could be said that Tilak's true public life started only after his dissociation from the Deccan Education Society in 1890, by which time he had acquired complete control over the Kesari and the Mahratta, the two newspapers unfold before the reader the many facets of Tilak's complex but captivating personality, many of them inexplicably contradictory. A radical so far as his political views were concerned, Tilak was a conservative so far as the question of social reforms was concerned.

Social reforms did not receive a high priority in his programme of opposition to the Age of Consent Bill. Once he took tea in a Christian Missionary School and underwent a penance for it. On 24 March 1918 an All India Depressed Classes Conference was held under the Presidentship of Sayajirao Gaikwad, the a Maharaja of Baroda. Although Tilak spoke for the removal of untouchability, he refused to sign a manifesto declaring that the signatories would not observe untouchability in their day-to-day life.

Through his writings and speeches, he led the radicals in rousing public indignation against the ways of the British administration, their callous indifference to the sufferings and indignities which the Indian people were made to suffer at the hands of the British officers. The famine of 1896 and the subsequent plague epidemic in the Bombay Province brought Tilak into conflict with the Government. Through the columns of the Kesari and the Mahratta he roused the people to demand from the Government what was due to them and demand it not as a favour but as a right. Tilak built up a new spirit of popular resistance against foreign rule and made the masses aware of their strength.

On the national plane also, Tilak's impact was equally forceful and revolutionary. He came on the national scene as a symbol of radical youth. During the 1896-97 plague in Maharashtra, Tilak bitterly criticised the Government for the plague measures taken and for the harassment to the public. The dissatisfaction among the Maharastrians led to the murder of Mr. Rand on 22 June 1897 at Poona. Tilak was accused of sedition and tried. On 14 September 1897 he was sentenced to eighteen months' imprisonment. But for a long time he was nowhere near the 'inner circle' which evolved the policies of the Congress. His concept of a political party was radically different from that of the other leaders. He wanted the Indian National Congress to be a rallying point for all classes and communities in India. He primarily strove to create a social sanction for the political ideals of the generation which was oppressed by an alien rule.

Tilak essentially aimed at building up a militant mass movement is support of the political objectives which he had in mind. These extreme political views of Tilak alarmed the moderates in the Congress Party. Tilak expressed his views on Swaraj strongly at the Calcutta session of the Congress in 1906.

But it was not long before Tilak's ideology appealed to a people who were completely disillusioned by the indifference of the Government to their sufferings. His thesis of national education, Swadeshi and Boycott leading to Swarajya was revolutionary in concept and it fired the imagination of the people.

While addressing an audience at Calcutta in January 1907, Tilak said : "Your future rests entirely in your hands. If you mean to be free you can be free. If you have not the power of active resistance, have you not the power of self-denial and self-abstinence in such a way as not to assist this boycott. We shall not give the Government assistance to collect revenue and keep peace. We shall not assist them in fighting beyond our frontiers; we shall not assist them in carrying on the administration of justice and when time comes we shall not pay taxes. If you can do that by your united efforts, you are free tomorrow. The point is to have the entire control in out hands. I want to have the key of my house and not merely one stranger turned out. Self-government is our goal" (Bal Gangadhar Tilak-'Writings and Speeches'). This was unusual language which exuded self-confidence which was contagious. It infused a new spirit of defiance into the people. Tilak's uniqueness lies in the fact that at a time when British imperialism was at its zenith, he aroused a desperate people to demand 'Swarajya' as a matter of right. The partition of Bengal gave a sharper edge to the struggle for freedom.

Tilak, as a gifted general with a clear political vision, used this tension to created unrest all over India through his speeches and writings. He was also in close touch with the revolutionaries of his time and was not unreceptive to their plan to open another front for the freedom struggle. In 1907, when the Indian National Congress was held at Surat, there was an open split between the Moderates and the Extremists. The Extremists were supposed to be followers of Tilak and were mostly members of the Revolutionary Partyin Bengal led by Aurobindo Ghose.

Tilak wrote two articles in the Kesari. "The Country's Misfortune" and "These Remedies Are Not Lasting". He pleaded with the Government to try to appreciate the changed psychology of the people. On 22 July 1908 Tilak was charged for bringing into people hatred and contempt and exciting disloyalty and feelings of enmity towards His Majesty and the Government established by Law in British India and was sentenced to transportation. Tilak spent six years in the Mandalay Jail, Burma, and was released on 17 June 1914.

After his released from Jail, Tilak soon returned to the arena of battle. Along with Annie Besant, he launched the Home Rule agitation for obtaining autonomy within the Empire in 1916. In the whirlwind campaign (1917), Tilak carried the message of Home Rule to the farthest corners of the country. It was because of the untiring efforts of Tilak and his band of dedicated colleagues that the Home Rule Movement spread like wildfire and forced the Government to come out with the declaration that the goal of British Policy was the realisation of responsible government in India.

This was not enough to meet the aspirations of Tilak. But while he declared the Indian Reforms Act of 1919 as inadequate, unsatisfactory and disappointing, he was too much of a pragmatist to let go whatever little gains it represented. He wanted to use the Act to gather more strength to demand more. He wanted to use the Act so as to organise the people to fight elections and to demonstrate effectively the intensity of the popular support for the freedom movement. He was confident of reaching in his lifetime. In April 1920 he started the Congress Democratic Party to carry on an agitation for Swarajya. Death, unfortunately, overtook him and he died in Bombay on 1 August 1920.

Tilak filed a law suit against Sit Valentine Chirol in 1918 for defaming him in his book 'Indian Unrest'. Tilak left Bombay on 19 September 1918 and reached London on 30 October 1918. He lost the Chirol Libel Case. But he started the activities of the Home Rule League in England. He returned to Bombay on 27 November 1919. During his stay in England Tilak established good relations with George Lansbury, the Socialist leader, Edgar Wallace, the well known journalist and author, and Ramsay Macdonald of the Labour Party. Tilak established such a friendly relationship with the Labour Party that from then on India became one of the major planks in the Labour Party's Programme.

Tilak had a remarkable personality. He was dark of complexion, of medium height and medium build. The forehead was broad, the eyes large and piercing, and the face was stern and had a grave look. The dress-toga-like upper garment, uttariya or loose cloth round the shoulder, dhoti, red shoes and red pugree-which was common when his public life began in 1880, he wore throughout his life, except when he visited England. His diet was simple; the only luxuries he allowed himself were tea and betelnut.

He bought the Gaikwad Wada in 1904, lived in a part of it and accommodated the printing press for his journals and his office in the rest. His office boasted of only a few pieces of furniture, a Victorian type of table, full of drawers and pigeonholes, a low chair from which he dictated his articles and cupboards and shelves stacked with books and journals. All his time was taken up in reading, writing, and discussions with his colleagues and public speeches. Not a week passed when he did not address a public meeting in one or another part of the country. His speeches and writings are marked by a vigorous and aggressive style which reflected his rugged personality.

Tilak's entire life was a "Karma Yajna'. He worked, ceaselessly and selflessly, to rouse a nation out of its slumber. With a dominant will power and tenacity, unique organising ability, and above all else an implicit faith in himself and his ideal of 'Sampoorna Swarajya', he refused to accepted defeat. With a remarkable degree of resilience Tilak always took setbacks to his activities philosophically and began to build up the edifice anew. Undaunted by the public hostility that he roused in England, he carried his message of freedom right up to Whitehall.

The composition of a treatise like 'Gita Rahasya', while undergoing a prison sentence at Mandalay, is another index of Tilak's ceaselessly working mind. As was only to be expected, his interpretation of the Gita is based on an activist philosophy. He was in the true sense of the word a 'Karma Yogi'.

When we come to assess the contribution of Tilak, we are faced with a difficult problem. His was a complex personality. Radical in political outlook and demands, Tilak was a conservative so far as social and religious reforms were concerned. He had his own views about social change. He has said :"a true nationalist desires to build on old foundations...but without detriment to progress and reform needed for our national conflict." For him, there was no question that was not dependent on Swaraj.

As Gandhiji had said, Tilak knew no other religion but love of the country. With his fearlessness and burning love for the country, he challenged both the westernised social reformer as well as the spirit of orthodoxy. Tilak, being a political realist, was aware that spirtualisation of politics could as well bring his dream of Swaraj nearer. Although an ardent Hindu, he believed in the fundamentals of secularism and tried to divorce the public life of the society from religious precepts.

He believed in Hindu-Muslim unity and was keenly aware that the yoke of foreign domination could not be thrown off unless the country stood united as one man. These contradictions make Tilak possibly the most controversial personality in recent Indian history. From his friends and followers he received the highest adulation; they called him 'Lokmanya'. To his opponents he was a social reactionary, a rabble-rouser. But nothing can detract from the monumental contribution that he made towards the Indian freedom struggle by rousing the political consciousness of the common people and by drawing them into the freedom struggle. He was perhaps the first leader who realised the strength of the masses-even unarmed, uneducated masses-in the fight against foreign domination. He had a rare insight into the working of society.

He evolved programmes, such as Shivaji Jayanti and Ganesh Pooja with the sole motive of bringing people together to ensure their awakening and involvement in the freedom struggle. He has been aptly described as the 'Father of Indian Unrest', because it was he who made people the moral courage to exert themselves to secure them.

His demand for 'Sampoorna Swarajya' as his birthright was radically and refreshingly different from what the moderate leaders of the Congress had been seeking. His speeches and writings had a new, vigorous and aggressive quality which electrified the country. It would not be wrong to say that Tilak laid the foundations on which, after him, Ganhiji built the edifice of the independence movement. The emergence of Tilak on the political horizon of the country was thus truly watershed in the life of the country. In a period of Indian history when the intellectual aristocracy was perhaps at its best, he brought to the political arena a new kind of leadership which was highly intellectual, had a clear vision and an intense patriotism but at the same time had its roots and strength in the vast illiterate and poor masses. The Tilak era, is therefore, of special significance. The transformation of the Congress Party from a political platform of the sophisticated, westernised and educated few to a mass movement drawing strength from the millions of the poor and downtrodden was possible because of the new orientation given to the freedom struggle by Tilak. The 'Tilak Era' constitutes a significant landmark in our struggle for independence. It was essentially in this period that a moral strength was imparted to this movement and a new political strategy for the struggle came to be accepted.

Bal Gangadhar Tilak's contribution to modern India stands on par with that of Mahatma Gandhi's. Tilak was a great Sanskrit scholar and astronomer. He fixed the origin and date of Rigvedic Aryans, which was highly acclaimed and universally accepted by orientalists of his time. His role in Congress and advocating Home Rule for India were enormous. His newspaper (Kesari) founded in 1881 is going strong even today. Hundreds of schools in India were result of his vision. We owe the mass celebration of the Ganesh festival (see: Ganesh Chaturthi) only to Tilak. He was Guru to Savarkar (biography) and hundreds of nationalists and thousands of Indians. Actually he set up the platform for Gandhiji's leadership. Although Gandhi accepted Gokhale as his mentor, in practice, he adopted all of Tilak's ideas of *Swadeshi* and of social reform. In 1920, when Tilak passed away, 200,000 mourners assembled on Chowpati beach of Bombay, without a single untoward incident. It is very hard to condense the great man's contribution to our country, but I have made an attempt below.

2

Tilak's Philosophy and Freedom Struggle

TILAK'S PHILOSOPHY FOR THE NATION

Lord Macaulay's Indian intellectuals, the leaders of Westernisation in social and political reform, based their programme of social and political action almost entirely on the philosophy of life and action of nineteenth century Europe. They were truly more the products of Western civilization than Indian. Tilak was not satisfied with the Western values and was not ready to reject India's own philosophy of life in order to imitate the philosophy of the British.

For Tilak, there was no reason for India to feel ashamed of her civilization when compared to the west. Just the contrary, India should feel great pride. Indian values were different from but not inferior to western values. Dharma, according to Tilak was the integrative principal, and Swadharma the spiritual and social duty of each individual. Here was the guide to social and political action. The Westernized intellectuals (mainly social reformers) wanted to change and remake India in an alien faith. But they were wrong. Tilak reminded them, "How can a man be proud of the greatness of his own nation if he feels no pride of his own religion?" It was the Bharadharma that provided an understanding of the moral purposefulness of the universe, which is the necessary basis of a philosophy of life. It provided Tilak and the nationalists like Ghose, Pal, and Lal with a guide to concrete action in personal, social and political matters.

From an Indian philosophy of life Tilak and the nationalist leaders began to construct an Indian philosophy of politics that was to become the political theory of the Indian Independence Movement. He became the chief architect of the political philosophy of the Indian independence movement as he was one of the most important leaders of India at that time.

Two Festivals

Perhaps the most effective way in which he reached the people was through the employment of national festivals. He was instrumental in popularizing two great festivals, one to Ganapati, the Hindu deity of learning and propitiousness, and a festival to revive the memory of glory of Shivaji, the liberator of Maharashtra, and the restorer of Swaraj through his battle with the Mughal Empire. He especially emphasised the dynamic spirit of Shivaji. He believed it was the spirit which actuated Shivaji in his doings that is held forth as the proper idea to be kept constantly in view of the rising generation. To keep this spirit constant, Tilak worked ceaselessly to reach the people and to educate them through the festivals. He carried his doctrine throughout Maharashtra and waged his battle. Education through religion and history, through the association in the popular mind with gods and heroes, through recreating an appreciation of the heritage of the past as a guide to the future. This was the way he educated the people.

First Sedition Case (1897)

Tilak was aggressive and writing very strongly through the editorials of Kesari against the British bureaucracy.

The British bureaucracy and the Anglo-Indian press realised that Tilak was an emerging leader of the people and of a new spirit in India. Those who lacked foresight began to fear him.

In the tense atmosphere of famine and a plague—racked Pune, a young man, Damodar Chaphekar assassinated Rand. Rand was the British official in charge of the plague. Those who feared Rand, were quick to blame Tilak for the death, and hinted at his complicity in a conspiracy for political assassination. Tilak was, of course, innocent of any knowledge of or collaboration in this crime. He had publically disagreed with Rand for his unsympathetic behaviour towards the plague stricken people. Tilak had condemned the inhuman aspects of the British anti-plague campaign, but he had never contemplated or encouraged the assassination of the British official in charge. Tilak, nevertheless, was brought to trial in 1897, not as an accessory to assassination, not as being involved in the plot to commit murder, but rather on the charge of 'sedition'. The court allowed the prosecution to argue hat he had written seditious matter and his criminal sedition constituted, in effect, 'dissatisfaction' with the British Raj. It was brought to the notice of the court that Tilak was not positively "affectionate for" British officialdom. This was one of the most unusual interpretations of 'sedition and disaffection' in the annals of British justice. Nevertheless Tilak was convicted and sentenced to two years' imprisonment.

The British had miscalculated both the effect of this sentence on Tilak and on public opinion.

N. C. Kelkar observes, "His arrest and prosecution in 1897 was a sensation that nearly pulled the mind of the country by its roots, as political prosecutions were then extremely rare, and Tilak was, in himself a man big enough to mark an epoch by his personal misfortune."

But this was not Tilak's last imprisonment. The British Indian Government endeavoured to convict him of perjury in connection with the well-known Tai Maharaj case in 1904. They did not succeed as he was acquitted by the High Court. In 1908, he was sentenced to six years' imprisonment, again for sedition; but in 1916, he was acquitted of a similar charge. For two decades he was persecuted by the British Indian Government because they saw in him the greatest challenge to their rule over the Indian empire.

The seditation case in 1897 roused sympathy not only in Maharashtra but also in Bengal. In Bengal, Shishir Kumar Motilal Ghosh and Surendranath Bannerjee started raising funds for the defense of Tilak. The court found Tilak guilty but Tilak's prestige rose very high in the minds of the people. Max Mueller and Indian leaders submitted a memorial to the government for the early release of Tilak. The government also soon realised the mistake and released Tilak.

Tilak emerged from prison in 1899 (first sedition) after serving eighteen months of his sentence. Now he became a national hero. He got following outside Maharashtra. He became the first all-India national leader. He had been persecuted for his political opinions. He was now the acknowledged political leader of the nation and the nation was prepared to heed his opinions. He had begun as an awakener of the people and as a critic of bureaucratic abuses. He emerged from prison with the responsibility of leading the Nationalist cause to political self-determination (Swatantrya). He was acclaimed the Lokmanya, the honoured and respected of the people.

Tilak's knowledge and love of the great classical Indian values had prepared him with a personal philosophy and a frame of reference for his battles with social reformism and with the spirit of orthodoxy. It also provided him with the foundation of his emerging political philosophy. He had fought against injustice, he had argued against the placating policies of the moderates. Now he began to put forward a positive political programme centred around the concept of Swaraj, self-rule for India. He realised that the self-rule must precede the meaningful social reform.

National self-rule, he believed, was the only enduring basis for national unity and national self-respect. He reminded people that Shivaji had recreated Swaraj as a necessary foundation of social and political freedom, progress and morality. He, therefore, declared, which in course of time became a famous slogan, that "swaraj is my birth right and I shall have it".

PRESSURES OF LOYALISM DURING BRITISH RULE

Even as loyalist pressures cast a long shadow on political currents that were to influence the Indian elite of the late nineteenth century, rapidly deteriorating economic conditions also led to a heightened degree of radicalization amongst the most advanced sections of the new Indian intelligentsia. Ajit Singh in Punjab, Bal Gangadhar Tilak in Maharashtra, Chidambaram Pillay in Tamil Nadu and Bipin Chandra Pal in Bengal formed the nucleus of a new nationalist movement that tried valiantly, but mostly unsuccessfully to move the conservative leadership of the Indian National Congress in a more radical direction. Most charismatic amongst the new national leaders was Bal Gangadhar Tilak (b. 1856, d. 1920).

Portrayed as anti-Muslim by the Muslim-League, maligned by India's colonial rulers and British loyalists as an "extremist", and misrepresented as a sectarian Hindu revivalist by some historians, Tilak was in fact, one of the leading lights of the Indian freedom movement. Best remembered for his slogan *"Swaraj is my birth-right "*, he was one of the first to call for complete freedom from British rule, and fought a long and sometimes lonely political struggle against the forces of "moderation" that held sway over the Indian National Congress in the early part of the last century.

After the defeat of 1858, one of the most significant challenges to British imperial authority in India had appeared in the form of Vasudeo Balvant Phadke's revolt of 1879, and amongst his many youthful followers and trainees in Pune was the young Tilak. Along with Chiplunkar, Agarkar and Namjoshi, Tilak initially concentrated on launching a nationalist weekly-the *Kesari* (1881), the publishing house-*Kitabkhana*, and developing Indian educational institutions such as the Deccan Education Society (1884). Tilak and his friends saw the right kind of education as being a crucial element in the task of national regeneration, and in this respect appeared to be continuing in the tradition of Jyotirao Phule (1827-1890) and Gopalrao Deshmukh (1823-1892) who was more known by his pen-name 'Lokahitwadi'. Foremost amongst the social revolutionaries of nineteenth century Maharashtra, Phule and his wife Savitribai, had advocated a radical restructuring of Hindu society on the basis of equality of caste, gender and creed. Phule, (who belonged to the *Mali* caste) was unsparing in his criticism of Brahminical society that looked down upon the *shudra jatis,* prevented the *atishudra* (untouchable) *jatis* from attending school, and treated young widows (particularly Brahmin widows) as outcastes.

One of the first to start a school for girls (1848), Phule went on to found the first school for the *atishudras* (1851), a home for young widows (1863), and also the first to open the family well to *atishudra* women (1868). Social reformers in Maharashtra also emerged from the upper castes, such as Gopalrao Deshmukh, who although a Chitpawan Brahmin was a sharp critic of Brahminical society, and worked primarily through reformist middle-class organizations such as the Prasthana Samaj and the Arya Samaj to fight against caste inequities.

But amongst Tilak's colleagues, not all were well-disposed towards Phule and Deshmukh (Lokahitwadi). Chiplunkar was particularly vitriolic in his criticism of Phule. Tilak, on the other hand, was not unsympathetic to the need for social reforms, and was opposed to evils like child-marriage, casteism and untouchability. Many years later, (at a conference in Bombay in 1918), he was to declare: *"If God were to tolerate untouchability, I would not recognize him as God at all"*. However, he was reluctant to give precedence to social reforms over political struggle, believing that social change ought to come gradually, through the growth of enlightened public opinion, rather than through the legislative authority of an alien government. He was convinced that no significant social progress was possible in a country that wasn't politically free. He was particularly critical of loyalist or moderate "reformers" who were unwilling to practice what they preached, yet frequently baited him as being against social reforms.

Neither a sectarian religious revivalist in the mold of Chiplunkar, nor willing to confine himself exclusively to the cause of radical social reforms like Agarkar, Tilak eventually parted ways with his colleagues in 1888. Working through the *Kesari,* (and later also the *Maratha*) he gradually developed a more advanced nationalist perspective based on the pillars of nationalist education, *Swaraj* (self-rule) *and Swadeshi* (self-reliance). One of the first to take the nationalist message to the Indian masses, he played a particularly important role in organizing western Maharashtra's peasant and artisan communities during the 1897 famine under the auspices of the Sarvajanik Sabha. By 1905, popular resistance movements had developed in both Bengal and Maharashtra, calling for the boycott of British goods and non-payment of land revenues and other taxes. Between 1905 and 1908 the national movement intensified, workers participated in strikes and work-stoppages, women and students joined the boycott movements-picketing at shops that sold imported goods, and an ever-growing mass of people began joining mass meetings and street processions.

Only too aware of the economic devastation that British rule had brought on the country, India's broad masses were responding eagerly to the nationalist message. But the nationalist movement was also becoming exceedingly divided between two poles representing radically different currents and tendencies. Whereas one side (even as it recognized the many negative aspects of alien rule) clung to the British umbilical chord, and attempted to restrict the national movement to a struggle for political reforms, the other side correctly saw British rule as an unmitigated disaster for the Indian people and called for the complete liberation from colonial rule.

Tilak eloquently and succinctly summarized the sentiments of the new and increasingly militant national movement. He spoke of British rule as having ruined trade, caused the collapse of industry, and destroyed the people's courage and abilities. Under the colonial regimen, Tilak asserted that the country was offered neither education, nor rights, nor respect for public opinion. Without prosperity and contentment, the Indian people suffered constantly from the three 'd's'-*i.e. daridra* (poverty), *dushkal* (famine) and *dravyashosha* (drain). And he saw only one remedy: for the Indian people to take political power without which Indian industry could not develop, without which the nation's youth couldn't be educated, and without which the country could win neither social reforms nor material welfare for it's people. Tilak saw colonial rule as being inimical to India's progress, and the contradictions between the British oppressors and the Indian people as being irreconcilable.

But "moderates" such as Gokhale (President of the Congress in 1905) while cognizant of how *"deplorable"* Britain's industrial domination of India was, and how the economic drain from India to Britain was *"bleeding India"*, were nevertheless all praise for the British educational system in India, ascribing to the British the virtues of introducing liberal "social reforms", governmental "peace and order" and such modern conveniences as the railways, post and telegraphs, and new industrial appliances. (That all these things benefited a miniscule Indian elite did not appear to bother such admirers of the empire, nor did it occur to them that this and much more could have just as easily been achieved under self-rule.)

Tilak and Gokhale were clearly seeing Indian reality from very different vantage points. From the point of view of the ordinary masses, British rule had already bankrupted the nation, left intolerable misery in it's wake, and offered no hope for the future. Tilak's assessment of the situation reflected bleak reality-as experienced not only by the oppressed and downtrodden Indian masses, but by an overwhelming majority of all Indians. But Gokhale's ambivalence and his more cautiously expressed (though clearly articulated) concerns reflected the position of those who had at least partially shared in the spoils of the empire, but saw with some trepidation how the growing poverty of the nation might unravel the British empire. Reluctant to make common cause with the masses, "moderates" such as Gokhale did everything in their power to restrain the growing national movement-even branding Tilak and his allies as "extremists".

The British took full advantage of this schism, and proceeded to bring the full weight of their administrative and military might in crushing the new national movement. Communal forces such as the Muslim League were also employed in the battle to extinguish radical tendencies. (See note below) The years 1905-1908 were thus extremely critical in shaping the direction of the Indian national movement. Increasingly, the Indian masses were looking to Tilak and his compatriots for direction. But, in direct opposition to the energizing of the Indian peasantry, and mass of workers and students across the country, the elite was reasserting it's loyalty to British rule.

In Punjab, the polarization was especially sharp. The boycott movement had struck deep roots within the peasantry, and made it difficult for British troops to find porters and other logistical help from the poor peasants. Roused by calls to protest the British land revenue policy, Sikh and Jat agricultural workers were becoming strongly politicized. In a rousing speech, Tilak's close associate in Punjab, Ajit Singh made a secular appeal to the masses of Punjab to rise against the British: *"Hindu brothers, Mohammedan brothers, Sepahi brothers-we are all one. The government is not even dust before us....What have you got to fear?....Our numbers are much greater. True they have guns, but we have fists...You are dying from the plague and other diseases, so better sacrifice yourselves to your motherland. Our strength lies in unity..."* (Excerpts from an April 21, 1907 speech in Rawalpindi)

On May 1, 1907, a spontaneous outburst of popular discontent shook the British administration in Rawalpindi when seething crowds, reinforced by striking workers marched through the streets-throwing mud and stones at passing Britishers, attacking government offices, cottages of Christian missionaries, British enterprises and commercial establishments. Although the uprising was effectively quelled by a large contingent of British troops who were close at hand, it shook the colonial administration enough to hastily evacuate families of colonial officials and military officers from Punjab, and extend term of the Commander-in-Chief of the British Army, Lord Kitchener. The colonial police and troops were also ruthless in crushing such uprisings in Lahore and Amritsar. Ajit Singh and Lala Lajpat Rai were summarily deported to Burma, without trial or right of appeal. Arrests and persecution of other patriots followed, and a state of emergency was declared in a number of Punjab districts. In 1908, uprisings on a similiar scale broke out in the South, in Trivandrum, Tirunelveli, and Tuticorin. In Trivandrum, police stations were attacked, prisoners liberated, and offices of the repressive colonial state were set on fire. When Chidambaram Pillay, another important Tilak ally was put on trial, he refused to disown his national goals, and was sentenced to life imprisonment.

Russian consular official Chirkin had been quite prophetic in his May 28, 1907 report when he wrote:*"The outburst in Punjab is by it's character more dangerous than the Bengal unrest.....This outburst has roused all India."* But equally powerful forces were working to stem and reverse the radical tide that had the potential of upturning colonial rule.

Bengal zamindars who had agitated against the partition of Bengal declared their loyalty to the Raj. The Maharajas not only offered armed personnel to help the British but some (such as the Maharaja of Jammu and Kashmir) themselves initiated repressive measures against those deemed "extremist".

The Congress who under the leadership of Dadabhai Naoroji had accepted the demands put forth by the Tilak group or Swaraj, Swadeshi and National Education in 1906, reneged on it's previous position, and at it's Surat session in 1907 decided to limit the struggle to a *"constitutional manner"*. *"Swaraj"* was reinterpreted to mean *"self-rule"* as a colony, and rather than fighting the colonial power, the Congress decided to cooperate with it in effecting *"reforms"*.

A motion to elect Tilak (who was unquestionably the most popular leader of the national-liberation movement) was turned down, as was a compromise motion to elect Lala Lajpat Rai. The triumph of the "moderate" wing was total and complete. Gokhale's "moderate nationalism" which was simply another face of loyalism succeeded to the utter exclusion of all the popular forces aligned with Tilak, and returned the Congress to a broadly loyalist track.

Tilak and his supporters were thus compelled to regroup outside the stifling confines of the Congress and continued a vigorous struggle against the British. But in July 1908, after having removed most of Tilak's serious compatriots from the national scene, Tilak himself was brought to trial. The English majority outvoted the Indian jurors to issue a guilty verdict, and Tilak was sentenced to six years of transportation. This evoked a mass protest wave which swept a number of Indian cities culminating in a massive strike of 100,000 workers and a city-wide 'hartal' (shutdown) in Bombay. Tilak's sentence had to be commuted to simple imprisonment, but it was sufficient to deal a severe blow to the Indian freedom movement.

By 1914, the Congress had so deteriorated that a majority of it's members failed to admonish the young Mohandas Karamchand Gandhi when he embarked on a campaign to seek volunteers for the British war efforts in World

War I. The man who was to repeatedly chastise the Indian masses for being insufficiently "nonviolent", had in 1914, no compunctions in seeking sacrificial lambs for a war in which India's only interest should have been for the defeat of it's colonial master.

But Gandhi, who had been born the son of the Prime Minister of the princely state of Rajkot in Kathiawar, was simply following the lead of the Indian Maharajas, such as that of Bikaner-who needed little prodding in offering his troops for a war that essentially pitted Europe's older and stronger imperial powers against their emerging rivals.

Unsurprisingly, it was to Gokhale that the young Gandhi looked for inspiration, not Tilak. But others recognized his pre-eminent role in giving new direction and leadership to the Indian freedom movement.

Nehru pointed out that the *"real symbol of the new age was Bal Gangadhar Tilak"*, and recognized that *"the vast majority of politically-minded people in India favoured Tilak and his group"*. This was acknowledge as much by Sir Valentine Chirol, foreign editor of the *The Times,* who noted how Tilak's imprisonment deprived India of it's most able and determined leader, perhaps the only one capable of providing the Indian national movement (with it's different and often contradictory trends), the organization and unity that had been lacking thus far. N.C. Kelkar, a biographer and follower of Tilak echoed such sentiments.

TILAK AND HOME RULE MOVEMENT

Home Rule Flag

The All India Home Rule League was a national political organization founded in 1916 to lead the national demand for self-government, termed *Home Rule,* and to obtain the status of a Dominion within the British Empire as enjoyed by Australia, Canada, South Africa, New Zealand and Newfoundland at the time.

In Context of World War I

Most Indians and Indian political leaders had been divided in their response to World War I and the Indian soldiers fighting on behalf of the British Empire against Germany, the Austro-Hungarian Empire and the Ottoman Empire. The latter's involvement irked India's Muslims, who saw the Sultan as the Caliph of Islam. Many Indian revolutionaries opposed the war, while moderates and liberals backed the war. The issue divided India's political classes and left the increasing demand for self-government going nowhere.

FOUNDING

Between 1916 and 1918, when the war was closing, prominent Indians like Muhammad Ali Jinnah, Bal Gangadhar Tilak and the leader of the Theosophical Society, Annie Besant decided to organize a national alliance of leagues across India, specifically to demand *Home Rule,* or self-government within the British Empire for all of India. Tilak founded the first League in the city of Pune, Maharashtra. Muhammad Ali Jinnah headed up the League's Bombay Branch. With its national headquarters in Delhi, the main cities of activity were Bombay, Calcutta and Madras.

The move created considerable excitement at the time, and attracted many members of the Indian National Congress and the All India Muslim League, who had been allied since the 1916 Lucknow Pact. The leaders of the League gave fiery speeches, and petitions with hundreds of thousands of Indians as signatories were submitted to British authorities.

Unification of moderates and radicals as well as unity between Muslim League and Indian National Congress was a remarkable achievement of Mrs Annie Besant. Later when government arrested Annie Besant the movement actually spread out and made its impact in interior villages of India. League spread the political awareness in new areas like Sindh, Punjab, Gujarat, United Provinces, Bihar, Orissa as well as Madras and all stood up for an active political movement, qasdas sdl, las, md asda.

3

Tilak : Culture and Religion

There is, consequently, nothing abnormal if a portion of the sections in the Rig-Veda and the Avesta reveal to us thoughts which the antiquated pundits couldn't and did not see in them; and I would ask for the peruser to tolerate this as a top priority in looking at the elucidations and clarifications proposed by me in the previous parts with the present translations of these entries by eastern or western Vedic researchers. In any case, our decisions don't lay just on the elucidation of entries which, if appropriately interpreted, uncover climatic attributes impossible to miss to the Arctic districts; however this proof is, independent from anyone else, adequate to demonstrate our speculation. We have seen that in the conciliatory writing of the Vedic individuals and in addition in their mythology there are numerous signs which indicate similar conclusion; and these are completely substantiated by the old conventions and legends in the Avesta furthermore by the mythologies of the European branches of the Aryan race.

A conciliatory session of ten months held by the Dashagvas, or a yearly sattra of similar span, contrasted and the most seasoned Roman year finishing in December or the tenth month, are the key cases on the point; and they have been completely examined in the prior sections. I have additionally demonstrated that the information of the half-year-taxing day or night is not bound to the customs of the eastern Aryas, yet is basic likewise to the European branches of the Aryan race.

The custom saved in the Vendidad about the antiquated Iranian Paradise in the far north, so that a year was equivalent to a day to the tenants thereof, and its devastation by snow and ice covering the land under a thick icecap, again bears the most striking and relevant verification of the hypothesis we have attempted to demonstrate in these pages. Thus if the traditions of the western Aryas point out, according to Prof. Rhys, to Finland or the White Sea as the original home of the Aryan people, the Vedic and the Avestic traditions carry us still farther to the north; for a continuous dawn of thirty days is possible only within a few degrees of the North Pole. But though the latitude of the original home can be thus ascertained more or less definitely, yet there is unfortunately nothing in these traditions which will enable us to determine the longitude of the place, or, in other words, whether the original home of the Aryan race was to the north of Europe or Asia.

But considering the fact that the traditions of the original Polar home are better preserved in the sacred books of the Brahmins and the Parsis, it is not unlikely that the primeval home was located to the north of Siberia rather than to the north of Russia or Scandinavia. It is, however, useless to speculate on the point without further proof. The Vedic and the Avestic evidence clearly establish the existence of a primeval Polar home, the climate of which was mild and temperate in ancient times, before it was invaded by the Glacial epoch; and with this result we must rest content, until we get sufficient new materials to ascertain the exact position of the Aryan home within the Arctic regions.

We commenced the book with a summary of the results of the latest geological and archeological researches regarding the history of primitive humanity and the invasion of northern Europe and Asia by a series of glacial epochs in the Quarternary era. This discussion was prefixed to the book with the object of clearing up certain misapprehensions regarding the early history of our planet based on knowledge derived from older geological works, when man was believed to be postglacial; and it will now be seen that our theory of the primeval Arctic home of the Aryan races is in perfect accord with the latest and most approved geological facts and opinions.

A primeval Arctic home would have been regarded an impossibility, had not science cleared the ground by establishing that the antiquity of man goes back to the Tertiary era, that the climate of the Polar regions was mild and temperate in interglacial times, and that it was rendered cold and inclement by the advent of the Glacial epoch. We can now also understand why attempts to prove the existence of an Arctic home by discovering references to severe winter and cold in the Vedas did not succeed in the past.

The winter in the primeval home was originally, that is, in interglacial times, neither severe nor inclement, and if such expressions as "a hundred winters" (*shatam himah*) are found in the Vedic literature, they cannot be taken for reminiscences of severe cold winters in the original home; for the expression came into use probably because the year in the original home closed with a winter characterized by the long Arctic night. It was the advent of the Ice Age that destroyed the mild climate of the original home and converted it into an ice-bound land unfit for the habitation of man. This is well expressed in the

Avesta which describes the Airyana Vaejo as a happy land subsequently converted by the invasion of Angra Mainyu into a land of severe winter and snow. This correspondence between the Avestic description of the original home and the result of the latest geological researches, at once enables us to, fix the age of the Arctic home, for it is now a well-settled scientific fact that a mild climate in the Polar regions was possible only in the inter-Glacial and not in the post-Glacial times.

But according to some geologists 20,000 or even 80,000 years have passed since the close of the last Glacial epoch; and as the oldest date assigned to the Vedic hymns does not go beyond 4500 B.C., it may be contended that the traditions of the Ice Age, or of the inter-Glacial home, cannot be supposed to have been accurately preserved by oral transmission for thousands of years that elapsed between the commencement of the post-Glacial era and the oldest date of the Vedic hymns. It is, therefore, necessary to examine the point a little more closely in this place. In my *Orion or Researches into the antiquity of the Vedas*, I have shown that while the Taittiriya Samhita and the Brahmans begin the Nakshatras with the Krittikas or the Pleiades, showing that the vernal equinox then coincided with the aforesaid asterism (2500 B.C.), the Vedic literature contains traces of Mriga or Orion being once the first of the Nakshatras and the hymns of the Rig-Veda, or at least many of them, which are undoubtedly older than the Taittiriya Samhita, contain reference to this period, that is, about 4500 B.C. approximately It is also pointed out that there are faint traces of the same equinox being once in the constellation of Punarvasu, presided over by Aditi, which was possible in about 6,000 B.C. I have in my later researches tried to push back this limit by searching for the older zodiacal positions of the vernal equinox in the Vedic literature, but I have not found any evidence of the same.

My attention was, however, directed more and more to passages containing traces of an Arctic calendar and an Arctic home, and I have been gradually led to infer therefrom that at about 5000 or 6000 B.C., the Vedic Aryas had settled on the plains of Central Asia, and that at the time the raditions about the existence of the Arctic hone and its destruction by snow and ice, as well as about the Arctic origin of the Vedic deities, were definitely known to the bards of these races.

In short, researches in Vedic chronology and calendar do not warrant us in placing the advent of the last Glacial epoch, which destroyed the ancient Aryan home, at a time several thousands of years previous to the Orion period; and from what has been stated in the first two chapters of the book, it will be seen that this estimate well agrees with the conclusions of American geologists, who, from an examination of the erosion of valleys and similar other well-ascertained facts, assign to the close of the last Glacial epoch a date not older than about 8000 B.C.

We might even go further and say that ancient Vedic chronology and calendar furnish an independent corroboration of the moderate view of the American geologists; and when two independent lines of research unexpectedly lead us to the same result, we may very well reject, at least in the present state of our knowledge, the extravagant speculations of Croll and his followers, and, for all practical purposes, adopt the view that the last Glacial epoch closed and the post-Glacial period commenced at about 8000 B.C. From this to the Orion period is an interval of about 3000 years, and it is not at all improbable that the traditions of the ancient home should have been remembered and incorporated into hymns whose origin can be clearly traced to that period.

In short, the Vedic traditions, far from being contradictory to the scientific evidence, only serve to check the extravagant estimates regarding the age of the last Glacial epoch; and if the sober view of American geologists be adopted, both geology and the traditions recorded in the ancient books of the Aryan race will be found alike to point out to a period not much older than 8000 B.C. for the commencement of the post-Glacial era and the compulsory migration of the Aryan races from their Arctic home.

And not only Vedic but also Puranic chronology, properly understood, leads us to the same conclusion. According to the Puranas the earth and the whole universe are occasionally subjected to destruction at long intervals of time, the earth by a small and the universe by a grand deluge.

Thus we are told that when the god Brahma is awake during *his* day the creation exists; but when at the end of the day he goes to sleep, the world is destroyed by a deluge, and is re-created when he awakes from his sleep and resumes his activity the next morning. Brahma's evening and morning are thus synonymous with the destruction and the re-creation of the earth. A day and a night of Brahma are each equal to a period of time called a *Kalpa*, and a *Kalpa* is taken for a unit in measuring higher periods of time. Two *Kalpas* constitute a nycthemeron (day and night) of Brahma, and 360 × 2 = 720 *Kalpas* make his year, while a hundred such years constitute his life-time, at the end of which a grand deluge overtakes the whole universe including Brahma.

Now according to the Code of Manu and the Mahabharata the four yugas of Krita, Treta, Dvapara and Kali form a yuga of gods, and a thousand such yugas make a Kalpa or a day of Brahma of 12,000,000 years, at the end of which a deluge destroys the world. The Puranas, however, have adopted a different method of computation. The four yugas of Krita, Treta, Dvapara and

Kali are there said to constitute a Mahayuga; 71 such Maha-yugas constitute a Manvantara, and 14 Manvantaras make a *Kalpa*, which, according to this method of counting, contains 4,320,000,000 years. The difference between the durations of a *Kalpa* according to these two methods is due to the fact that the years making up the four yugas of Krita, Treta, Dvapara and Kali are considered to be *divine* in the latter, while they are obviously human in Manu and the Mahabharata.

For further details the reader is referred to the late Mr. S. B. Dixit's *History of Indian Astronomy* in Marathi, Prof. Rangacharya's essay on *Yugas*, and Mr. Aiyer's *Chronology of Ancient India*, a book, in which the question of yugas and especially that of the beginning of the Kali yuga, is subjected to a searching and exhaustive examination. The Hindu writers on astronomy seem to have adopted the same system, except Aryabhatta, who holds that 72, and not 71, Mahayugas make a Manvantara, and that a Mahayuga is divided into four equal parts which are termed Krita, Treta, Dvapara and Kali.

According to this chronological system, we are, at present, in the 5003rd year (elapsed) of the Kali yuga of the 28th Maha-yuga of the 7th (Vaivasvata) Manvantara of the current Kalpa; or, 1,972,949,003 years have, in other words, elapsed since the deluge which occurred at the beginning of the present or the Shveta-varaha Kalpa. This estimate is, as observed by Prof. Rangacharya, quite beyond the limit admitted by modern geology; and it is not unlikely that Hindu astronomers, who held the view that the sun, the moon, and all the planets were in a line at the beginning of the Kalpa, arrived at this figure by mathematically calculating the period during which the sun, the moon and all the planets made an integral number of complete revolutions round the earth.

We need not, however, go into these details, which howsoever interesting are not relevant to the subject in hand. A cycle of the four yugas, *viz.*, Krita, Treta, Dvapara and Kali, is, it will be seen, the basis of this chronological system, and we have therefore to examine more critically what this collection of four yugas, otherwise termed a Maha-yuga, really signifies and whether the period of time originally denoted by it was the same as it is said to be at present. Prof. Rangacharya and especially Mr. Aiyer have ably treated this subject in their essays, and I agree in the main with them in their conclusions. I use the words "in the main" deliberately, for though my researches have independently led me to reject the hypothesis of "*divine* years," yet there are certain points which cannot, in my opinion, be definitely settled without further research. I have shown previously that the word *yuga* is used in the Rig-Veda to denote "a period of time," and that in the phrase *manusha yuga* it cannot but be taken to denote "a month."

Yuga is, however, evidently used to denote a longer period of time in such expressions as *Devanam prathame yuge* in the Rig-Veda, X, 72, 3; while in the Atharva Veda VIII, 2, 21, which says "We allot to thee a hundred, ten thousand years, two, three, (or) four *yugas*," a *yuga* evidently means a period of not less than 10,000 years; and Mr. Aiyer is right in pointing out that the omission of the word "one" in the above verse is not accidental.

According to this view a *yuga* may be taken to have, at the longest, denoted a period of 10,000 years in the days of the Atharva Veda Samhita. Now it is found that Manu and the Mahabharata both assign 1000, 2000, 3000 and 4000 years to the four yugas of Kali, Dvapara, Treta and Krita respectively. In other words, the durations of Dvapara, Treta and Krita are obtained by doubling, trebling and quadrupling the duration of Kali; and taking into consideration that Krita (which Mr. Aiyer compares with Latin *quatuor*) means "four" in Sanskrit literature, the names of the yugas may perhaps be derived from this fact. We are, however, concerned with the duration of the four yugas, and adding up the numbers given above, we obtain 10,000 years for a cycle of four yugas, or a *Maha-yuga* according to the terminology explained above. Manu and Vyasa, however, add to this 10,000 another period of 2,000 years, said to represent the Sandhya or the Sandhyamsha periods intervening between the different *yugas*. Thus the Krita age does not pass suddenly into Treta, but has a period of 400 years interposed at each of its ends, while the Treta is protected from the contact of the preceding and the succeeding yuga by two periods of 300 years each, the Dvapara of 200 and the Kali of 100 years.

The word *Sandhya* denotes the time of the dawn in ordinary literature; and Mr. Aiyer points out that as the period of the dawn and the gloaming, or the morning and the evening twilight, is each found to extend over three out of thirty *ghatis* of a day, so one-tenth of the period of each yuga is assigned to its *Sandhya* or the period of transition into another yuga: and that these supplementary periods were subsequent amendments. The period of 10,000 years for a cycle of the four yugas is thus increased to 12,000, if the *Sandhya* periods are included in it, making Krita comprise 4800, Treta 3600, Dvapara 2400 and Kali 1200 years. Now at the time of the Mahabharata or the Code of Manu, the Kali yuga had already set in; and if the yuga contained no more than 1000, or, including the Sandhyas, 1200 *ordinary* years, it would have terminated about the beginning of the Christian era.

The writers of the Puranas, many of which appear to have been written during the first few centuries of the Christian, era, were naturally unwilling to believe that the Kali yuga had passed away, and that they lived in the Krita yuga of a new Maha-yuga; for the Krita yuga meant according to them a golden age, while the times in which they lived showed signs of degeneration on all sides. An attempt was, therefore, made to extend the duration of the Kali yuga by converting 1000 (or 1200) ordinary human years thereof into as many *divine* years, a single *divine* year, or a year of the gods, being equal to 360 human years. A Vedic authority for such an interpretation was found in the text from the Taittiriya Brahmana, which, we have quoted and discussed previously, *viz.*, "That which is a year is a day of the gods." Manu and Vyasa simply assign 1000 years to the Kali yuga.

But as Manu, immediately after recording the duration of the *yugas* and their *Sandhyas*, observes "that this period of 12,000 years is called the yuga of the gods," the device of converting the ordinary years of the different yugas into as many divine years was, thereby, at once rendered plausible; and as people were unwilling to believe that they could be in a yuga other than the Kali, this solution of the difficulty was universally adopted, and a Kali of 1200 ordinary years was at once changed, by this ingenious artifice, into a magnificent cycle of as many divine, or 360 × 1200 = 432,000 ordinary years. The same device converted, at one stroke, the 12,000 ordinary years of a Maha-yuga, into as many divine, or 360 × 12,000 = 4,320,000 ordinary years, affecting in a similar way the higher cycles of time like Manvantaras and Kalpas.

How the beginning of the Kali yuga was thrown back, by astronomical calculations, to 3102 B.C., when this hypothesis of "divine years" was adopted is a separate question by itself; but not being pertinent to the subject in hand we need not go into it in this place. Suffice it to say that where chronology is invested with semi-religious character, artifices or devices, like the one noticed above, are not unlikely to be used to suit the exigencies of the time; and those who have to investigate the subject from a historical and antiquarian point of view must be prepared to undertake the task of carefully sifting the data furnished by such chronology, as Prof. Rangacharya and Mr. Aiyer have done in their essays referred to above.

From a consideration of the facts stated above it will be seen that so far as the Code of Manu and the Mahabharata are concerned, they preserve for us a reminiscence of a cycle of 10,000 years comprising the four yugas, the Krita, the Treta, the Dvapara and the Kali; and that the Kali yuga of one thousand years had been already set in. In other words, Manu and Vyasa obviously speak only of a period of 10,000, or, including the Sandhyas, of 12,000 ordinary or human (not divine) years, from the beginning of the Krita to the end of the Kali yuga; and it is remarkable that in the Atharva Veda we should find a period of 10,000 years apparently assigned to one yuga. It is not, therefore, unlikely that the Atharva Veda takes the Krita, the Treta, the Dvapara and the Kali together, and uses the word *yuga* to denote the combined duration of all these in the passage referred to above. Now considering the fact that the Krita age is said to commence after a *pralaya* or the deluge, Manu and Vyasa must be understood to have preserved herein an old tradition that about 10,000 years before their time (supposing them to have lived at the beginning of the Kali age of 1200 years), the new order of things commenced with the Krita age; or, in other words, the deluge which destroyed the old order of things occurred about 10,000 years before their time.

The tradition has been very much distorted owing to devices adopted in later times to make the traditional chronology suit the circumstances of the day. But still it is not difficult to ascertain the original character of the tradition; and when we do so, we are led to conclude that the beginning of the new order of things, or, to put it more scientifically, the commencement of the current post-Glacial era was, according to this tradition, not assigned to a period older than 10,000 years before the Christian era. We have shown that researches in Vedic chronology do not allow us to carry back the date of the post-Glacial era beyond this estimate, for traditions of the Arctic home appear to have been well understood by the bards of the Rig-Veda in the Orion period.

It is, therefore, almost certain that the invasion of the Arctic Aryan home by the last Glacial epoch did not take place at a time older than 10,000 B.C. The American geologists, we have seen, have arrived at the same conclusion on independent scientific grounds; and when the Vedic and the Puranic chronology indicate nearly the same time,— a difference of one or two thousand years, in such cases, does not matter much,— we may safely reject the extravagant estimates of 20,000 or 80,000 years and adopt, for all practical purposes, the view that the last Glacial epoch closed and the post-Glacial period commenced at about 8,000, or, at best, about 10,000 B.C.

We have now to consider how the tradition about the existence of the original home at the North Pole and its destruction by snow and ice of the Glacial epoch, and other cognate reminiscences were preserved until they were incorporated into the law-book of the Mazdayasnians and the hymns of the Rig-Veda. That a real tradition is preserved in these books is undoubted, for we have seen that an examination of the traditions preserved by the European branches of the Aryan rage have led Prof. Rhys to the same conclusion; and those who know the history of the preservation of our sacred books will see nothing improbable herein.

In these days of writing and printing, we have no need to depend upon memory, and consequently we fail to realize what memory, kept under the strictest discipline, is capable of achieving. The whole of the Rig-Veda, nay, the

Veda and its nine supplementary books, have been preserved by the Brahmins of India, letter for letter and accent for accent, for the last 3000 or 4000 years at least; and priests who have done so in recent times may well be credited with having faithfully preserved the traditions of the ancient home, until they were incorporated into the sacred books. These achievements of disciplined memory may appear marvellous to us at present; but, as stated above, they were looked upon as ordinary feats when memory was trusted better than books, and trained and cultivated with such special care as to be a faithful instrument for transmitting along many generations whatever men were most anxious to have remembered.

It has been a fashion to cry down the class of priests who make it their sole profession to cultivate their memory by keeping it under strict discipline and transmit by its means our sacred writings without the loss of a single accent from generation to generation. They have been described, even by scholars like Yaska, as the carriers of burden, and compared by others to parrots who repeat words without understanding their meaning. But the service, which this class has rendered to the cause of ancient history and religion by preserving the oldest traditions of the race, is invaluable; and looking to the fact that a specially disciplined memory was needed for such preservation, we cannot but gratefully remember the services of those whose hereditary devotion to the task, we might say, the sacred religious task, rendered it possible for so many traditions to be preserved for thousands of years. Pandits might analyze and explain the Vedic hymns more or less elaborately or correctly; but for that reason, we cannot forget that the very basis of their labours would have been lost long ago, had the institution of priests who made disciplined memory their exclusive business in life not been in existence. If the institution has outlived its necessity,—which is doubtful, for the art of writing or printing can hardly be trusted to the same extent as disciplined memory in such matters,—we must remember that religious institutions are the hardest to die in any country in the world.

We may, therefore, safely assert that Vedic and Avestic traditions, which have been faithfully preserved by disciplined memory, and whose trustworthiness is proved by Comparative Mythology, as well as by the latest researches in Geology and Archaeology, fully establish the existence of an Arctic home of the Aryan people in interglacial times; and that after the destruction of this home by the last Glacial epoch the Aryan people had to migrate southwards and settle at first in the northern parts of Europe or on the plains of Central Asia at the beginning of the post-Glacial period, that is about 8000 B.C. The antiquity of the Aryan race is thus carried back to interglacial times, and its oldest home to regions round about the North Pole, where alone a long dawn of thirty days is possible.

Whether other human races, beside the Aryan, lived with them in the circumpolar country is a question which does not fall within the purview of this book. Dr. Warren, in his *Paradise Found,* has cited Egyptian, Akkadian, Assyrian, Babylonian, Chinese and even Japanese traditions indicating the existence of an Arctic home of these races in ancient times; and from a consideration of all these he arrives at the conclusion that the cradle of the *whole human race* must be placed in the circum-polar regions, a conclusion in which he is also supported by other scholars. But, as observed by Prof. Rhys, it is no fatal objection to the view we have endeavoured to prove in these pages, that the mythologies of nations, beside the Aryan, also point to the North Pole as their original home; for it is not contended that the Aryans may be the only people of northern origin. On the contrary, there are grounds to believe that the five races of men (*pancha janah*) often mentioned in the Rig-Veda may have been the races which lived with the Aryans in their original home, for we cannot suppose that the Vedic Aryas after their dispersion from the original home met only with five races in their migrations, or were divided only into five branches. But the question is one which can be finally decided only after a good deal of further research; and as it is not necessary to mix it up with the question of the original home of the Aryans, we may leave it out for the present.

If the North Pole is conclusively shown to be the cradle of the human race hereafter, it would not affect in the least the conclusion we have drawn in these pages from a number of definite Vedic and Avestic traditions, but if the existence of the Aryan home near the North Pole is proved, as we have endeavoured to do in the foregoing pages, by independent testimony, it is sure to strengthen the probability of the northern home of the whole human race; and as the traditions of the Aryan people are admittedly better preserved in the Veda and the Avesta than those of any other race, it is safer and even desirable to treat the question of the primeval Aryan home independently of the general problem taken up by Dr. Warren and other scholars. That the Veda and the Avesta are the oldest books of the Aryan race is now conceded by all, and we have seen that it is not difficult to ascertain, from traditions contained therein, the site of the Aryan Paradise, now that we begin to search for it in the light thrown upon the subject by modern scientific researches.

But if the fact of an early Aryan home in the far north is once established by indisputable traditional evidence, it is sure to revolutionize the existing views regarding the primitive history or religion of the Aryan races. Comparative philologists and Sanskritists, who looked for the primeval home "somewhere in Central Asia," have advanced the theory that the whole progress of the Aryan race, intellectual, social or moral from primeval savagery to such civilization as is disclosed by the Vedic hymns, was effected on the plains of Central Asia. It was on these plains, we are told, that our oldest ancestors gazed upon the wonders of dawn or the rising sun with awe and astonishment, or reverentially watched the storm-clouds hovering in the sky to be eventually broken up by the god of rain and thunder, thereby giving rise to the worship of natural elements and thus laying down the foundations of later Aryan mythology.

It was on these plains that they learnt the art of weaving, the products of which superseded the use of hides for clothing, or constructed their chariots, or trained their horses, or discovered the use of metals like gold and silver. In short, all the civilization and culture which Comparative Philology proves on linguistic grounds to have been common to the different Aryan races before their separation is regarded to have, first originated or developed on the plains of Central Asia in post-Glacial times. Dr. Schrader, in his *Prehistoric Antiquities of the Aryan Peoples*, gives us an exhaustive summary of facts and arguments regarding primitive Aryan culture and civilization which can be deduced from Linguistic Palaeology, or Comparative Philology, and as a repertory of such facts the book stands unrivalled.

But we must remember that the results of Comparative Philology, howsoever interesting and instructive they may be from the linguistic or the historical point of view, are apt to mislead us if we know not the site of the original home, or the time when it was inhabited or abandoned by the ancestors of our race. Comparative Philology may teach us that cow was an animal known and domesticated before the Aryan separation, or that the art of weaving was known in those old days, because the words "cow" and "weave" can be traced in all the Aryan languages. But it is now found that equations like these do not help us much in definitely ascertaining where the united Aryans lived and when they separated; while recent researches in Archaeology and Anthropology have exhibited the improbability of a Central Asian home of the Aryan races and successive migrations therefrom to European countries. The hypothesis of a Central Asian home is, therefore, now almost abandoned; but strange to say, that those, who maintain that Europe was inhabited at the beginning of the Neolithic age by the ancestors of the races who now inhabit the same regions, are prepared to leave undetermined the question whether these races originated in Europe or went there from some other land.

Thus Canon Taylor, in his *Origin of the Aryans*, confidently advises us that we need not concern ourselves with the arguments of those who assert that

Europe was inhabited by the ancestors of the existing races even in the Paleolithic period; for, says he, "philologists will probably admit that within the limits of the Neolithic age, it would be possible to find sufficient time for the evolution and the differentiation of the Aryan languages." In the last chapter of the same book we are further informed that the mythologies of the different branches of the Aryan race must have been developed after their separation, and that resemblances, like Dyaus-pitar and Jupiter, or Varuna and Uranus, must be taken to be merely verbal and not mythological in their origin. In short, the advocates of the Central Asian as well, as of the northern European home of the Aryans are both unwilling to carry back the beginning of the Aryan civilization beyond post-Glacial times, and we are told that Aryan mythology and religion cannot, therefore, claim any higher antiquity.

All such guesses and speculations about the origin of the Aryan race and its civilization will have now to be revised in the new light thrown upon the subject by the theory of the Arctic home in pre-Glacial times. We cannot now maintain that primitive Aryans were a post-Glacial race, or that they advanced from barbarism to civilization in the Neolithic period either in Central Asia or in the northern parts of Europe; nor it is possible to argue that because the mythologies of the different branches of the Aryan race do not disclose the existence of common deities, these mythologies must be taken to have developed after the separation of the Aryan races from their common home. Thus, for instance, we are told that though the word *Ushas* occurs in Zend as *Ushangh*, and may be compared to Greek *Eos*, Latin *Aurora*, Lithuanian *Auszra*, Teutonic *Asustro* and Anglo-Saxon *Eostra*, yet it is only in the Vedic mythology that we find Ushas raised to the dignity of the goddess of the morning; and from this we are asked to infer that the worship of the dawn was developed only on the Indian soil.

The theory of the Arctic home, however, makes it impossible to argue in this way. If Vedic deities are clothed with attributes which are unmistakably polar in their origin,—and in the case of Ushas, the polar character has been shown to be unquestionable,—we cannot hold that the legends pertaining to these deities were developed on the plains of Central Asia. It was impossible for the Indian priests to conceive or picture the splendours of the dawn in the way we meet with in the Rig-Veda; for it has been shown that the evanescent dawn, with which they were familiar, is quite dissimilar in character to the Arctic dawn, the subject of the Vedic hymns. And what applies to the dawn can be predicated as well of other deities and myths, *e.g.*, of Indra and Vritra or the captive Waters, of Vishnu hibernating for four months in a year, or of Trita or the Third going down in a well, or of the Ashvins rescuing or saving the gods from the temporary affliction to which they were again and again subjected.

These very names may not be found in the Celtic or the Teutonic mythology, but an examination of the latter has been found to disclose the same polar characteristics which are possessed by Vedic deities or myths; and so long as this fundamental coincidence exists between the two, it is unreasonable to contend that the mythologies of the different branches of the Aryan race had no common origin, or that the resemblances between the names of the deities are more linguistic than mythological.

The destruction of the ancient Aryan home by glaciation and deluge introduces a new factor in the history of the Aryan civilization; and any shortcomings or defects in the civilization of the Aryan races, that are found to have inhabited the northern parts of Europe in the beginning of the Neolithic age, as distinguished from the civilization of the Asiatic Aryan races, must now be accounted for as the result of a natural relapse into barbarism after the great catastrophe. It is true that ordinarily we cannot conceive a race that has once launched on a career of progress and civilization suddenly retrograding or relapsing into barbarism. But the same rule cannot be applied to the case of the continuation of the ante-diluvian civilization into post-diluvian times. In the first place very few people could have survived a cataclysm of such magnitude as the deluge of snow and ice; and those that survived could hardly be expected to have carried with them all the civilization of the original home, and introduced it intact in their new settlements, under adverse circumstances, amongst the non-Aryan tribes, in the north of Europe or on the plains of Central Asia.

We must also bear in mind the fact that the climate of northern Europe and Asia, though temperate at present, must have been very much colder after the great deluge, and the descendants of those who had to migrate to these countries from the Polar regions, born only to a savage or nomadic life, could have, at best, preserved only fragmentary reminiscences of the ante-diluvian culture and civilization of their forefathers living in the once happy Arctic home. Under these circumstances we need not be surprised if the European Aryas are found to be in an inferior state of civilization at the beginning of the Neolithic age. On the contrary the wonder is that so much of the antediluvian religion or culture should have been preserved from the general wreck, caused by the last Glacial epoch, by the religious zeal and industry of the bards or priests of the Iranian or the Indian Aryas.

It is true that they looked upon these relics of the ancient civilization, as a sacred treasure entrusted to them to be scrupulously guarded and transmitted to future generations. Yet considering the difficulties with which they had to contend, we cannot but wonder how so much of the ante-diluvian civilization, religion or worship was preserved in the Veda or the Avesta. If the other Aryan races have failed to preserve these ancient traditions so well, it would be unreasonable to argue therefrom that the civilization or the culture of these races was developed after their separation from the common stock.

It has been shown previously that the climate of the Arctic regions in the inter-Glacial period was so mild and temperate as to be almost an approach to a perpetual spring, and that there was then a continent of land round about the Pole, the same being submerged during the glacial epoch. The primitive Aryans residing in such regions must, therefore, have lived a happy life. The only inconvenience experienced by them was the long Arctic night; and we have seen how this phenomenon has served to give rise to various myths or legends describing the struggle between the powers of light and darkness. The occurrence of the Arctic night, its tiresome length, and the long expected morning light on the horizon after some months were, naturally enough, the most important facts which attracted the attention of our primeval forefathers, and it is no wonder if they believed it to be the greatest exploit of their gods when the beneficent dawn came dawning up, after several months of darkness, from the nether world of aerial waters, inaugurating a new yearly round of sacrifices, festivals, or other religious or social ceremonies.

It was the beginning of the Devayana, when the powers of light celebrated their victory over the demons of darkness, and the Child of the Morning, the Kumara, the leader of the army of gods, walked victoriously along the Devayana path commencing the cycle of human ages, or *manusha yuga,* as mentioned in the Rig-Veda. The Pitiyana, or the walk of the Manes, corresponded with the dark winter, the duration of which extended in the original home from two to six months. This was the period of rest or repose during which, as observed previously, people refrained even from disposing the bodies of the dead owing to the absence of sunshine. All social and religious ceremonies of feasts were also suspended during this period as the powers of darkness were believed to be in the ascendant.

In short, the oldest Aryan calendar was, as remarked by Dr. Schrader, divided into two parts, a summer of seven or ten months and a corresponding winter of five or two months. But it seems to have been an ancient practice to reckon the year by counting the recurrence of summers or winters rather than by combining the two seasons. It is thus that we can account for a year of seven or ten months in old times, or annual sacrificial *sattras* extending over the same period. This calendar is obviously unsuited to places to the south of the Arctic circle; and the Aryans had, therefore, to change or reform the same, as was done by Numa, in postglacial times, when, expatriated from their mother-land, they settled in the northern parts of Europe and Central Asia. But the reminiscence of the Devayana as a special period of sacrifices and ceremonies was tenaciously preserved, and even now it is looked upon as a season of special religious merit. We can, on this theory, easily explain why the Grihya-Sutras attach special importance to the *Uttarayana* from a ceremonial point of view, and why death during the *Dakshinayana* is regarded as inauspicious.

How the inter-Glacial year of seven or ten months was changed to a year of twelve months in post-Glacial times, and how the equinoctial division which obtained at first on the analogy of the Devayana and the Pitiyana, was subsequently altered to the solstitial one, the old meaning of the word*Uttarayana* undergoing (*Orion*, p. 25*f*.) a similar change, are questions, which, though important in the history of the Aryan calendar, are not relevant in this place; and we shall, therefore, proceed with the subject in hand. It is urged by some writers that though the worship of natural elements is found to obtain in several ancient Indo-European religions, yet its beginnings cannot be supposed to go back to the time of the common origin of the related peoples.

Dr. Schrader has ably refuted this view in the concluding pages of his book on the prehistoric antiquities of Aryan peoples; and the theory of the Arctic home powerfully supports Dr. Schrader in his conclusions. "If we put aside every thing unsafe and false," observes Dr. Schrader, "that Comparative Mythology and History of Religion has accumulated on this subject, we are solely, from the consideration of perfectly trustworthy material, more and more driven, on all sides, to assume that the common basis of ancient European religions was a worship of the powers of Nature practiced in the Indo-European period."

The fact that the Vedic deities like Ushas, the Adityas, the Ashvins or the Vritrahan are found invested with Polar characteristics, further goes to confirm the conclusion based on linguistic grounds, or common etymological equations for sky, morning, fire, light or other natural powers. In short, whatever be the stand-point from which we view the subject in question, we are led to the conclusion that the shining sky (*Dyaus pita*), the sun (*Surya*), the fire (*Agni*), the Dawn (*Ushas*), the storm or thunder (*Tanyatu*) had already attained to the dignity of divine beings or gods in the primeval period; and etymological equations like Sanskrit *yaj*, Zend *yaz* and Greek *azomai*, show that these gods were worshipped and sacrifices offered to them to secure their favour even in primeval times. Whether this worship originated, or, in other words, whether the powers of nature were invested with divine honours only in inter-Glacial times or in times anterior to it, cannot, as stated above, be ascertained from the materials in our hands at present.

But this much is beyond question that the worship of these elements, as manifestations of divine power, had already become established amongst the undivided Aryans in the Arctic home, and the post-diluvian Aryan religions were developed from this ancient system of worship and sacrifices. We have seen that the Rig-Veda mentions the ancient sacrificers of the race like Manu, Angirases, Bhigus and others, and the fact that they completed their sacrificial sessions in seven, nine or ten months proves that they were the sacrifices of the undivided Aryans in their Arctic home.

It was these sacrificers who performed the sacrifices of, the people during a summer of seven or ten months and worshipped the mutational deities with offerings in primeval times. But when the sun went down below the horizon, these sacrificers naturally closed their sessions and made their offerings *only* to Vritrahan, the chief hero in the struggle with the demons of darkness, in order that he may, invigorated by their offerings eventually bring back the light of the dawn to these worshippers. I do not mean to assert that an elaborate system of sacrifices existed in inter-Glacial times; but I do maintain that sacrifice was the main ritual of the primeval Aryan religion, and that it is a mistake to suppose that it originated or was invented only in post-Glacial times. I have dwelt at some length on the question of ancient religious worship and ritual in this place because the theory of the Arctic home very well exposes, in my opinion, the fallacious character of many of the existing views on this subject.

A people, who had come to worship the powers of Nature as manifestations of divine will and energy, who had a well-developed language of their own, and who had already evolved a legendary literature out of the Arctic conditions of the year in their congenial home near the North Pole, may well be expected to have made a good advance in civilization. But we have at present very few means by which we can ascertain the exact degree of civilization attained by the undivided Aryans in their primitive home. Comparative Philology tells us that primitive Aryans were familiar with the art of spinning and weaving, knew and worked in metals, constructed boats and chariots, founded and lived in cities, carried on buying and selling, and had made considerable progress in agriculture.

We also know that important social or political institutions or organizations, as, for instance marriage or the laws of property, prevailed amongst the forefathers of our race in those early days; and linguistic palaeontology furnishes us with a long list of the fauna and the flora known to the undivided Aryans. These are important linguistic discoveries, and taking them as they are, they evidently disclose a state of civilization higher than that of the savages of the Neolithic age. But in the light of the Arctic theory we are naturally led to inquire if the culture of the primitive Aryans was confined only to the level disclosed by Comparative Philology, or whether it was of a higher type than the one we can predicate of them simply on linguistic grounds. We have seen above that in the case of the mythological deities and their worship the Polar character of many of the deities at once enables us to assign them to the primitive period even when their names are not found in all the Aryan languages; and the results of Comparative Philology regarding primitive Aryan culture will have to be checked and revised in the same way.

The very fact that after compulsory dispersion from their mother-land the surviving Aryans, despite the fragmentary civilization they carried with them, were able to establish their supremacy over the races they came across in their migrations from the original home at the beginning of the post-Glacial period, and that they succeeded, by conquest or assimilation, in Aryanising the latter in language, thought and religion under circumstances which could not be expected to be favourable to them, is enough to prove that the original Aryan civilization must have been of a type far higher than that of the non-Aryan races, or than the one found among the Aryan races that migrated southward after the destruction of their home by the Ice Age. So long as the Aryan races inhabiting the northern parts of Europe in the beginning of the Neolithic age were believed to be autochthonous there was no necessity of going beyond the results of Comparative Philology to ascertain the degree of civilization attained by the undivided Aryans. But now we see that the culture of the Neolithic Aryans is obviously only a relic, an imperfect fragment, of the culture attained by the undivided Aryans in their Arctic home; and it would, therefore, be unreasonable to argue that such and such civilization, or culture cannot be predicated of the undivided Aryans simply because words indicating the same are found only in some and not in all the Aryan languages.

In other words, though we may accept the result of Comparative Philology so far as they go, we shall have to be more cautious hereafter in inferring that such and such a thing was not known to the primitive Aryans because common etymological equations for the same cannot be discovered in all the Aryan languages. We have, it is true, no means of ascertaining how much of the original civilization was lost in the deluge, but we cannot, on that account, deny that some portion of it must have been irrecoverably lost in the great cataclysm that destroyed the original home. Under these circumstances all that we can safely assert is that the degree of culture disclosed by Comparative. Philology is the *lowest* or the *minimum* that can be predicated of the undivided Aryans.

his important to bear this reservation in mind because undue importance is sometimes attached to the results of Comparative Philology by a kind of reasoning which appeared all right so long the question of the site of the original home was unsettled. But now that we know that Aryan race and religion are both inter-Glacial and their ultimate origin is lost in geological antiquity, it does not stand to reason to suppose that the inter-Glacial Aryans were a race of savages.

The archaeologists, it is true, have established the succession of the ages of Stone, Bronze and Iron; and according to this theory the Aryan race must have once been in the Stone age. But there is nothing in archeology which requires us to place the Stone age of the Aryan races in post-Glacial times; and when Comparative Philology has established the fact that undivided Aryans were acquainted with the use of metals, it becomes clear that the degree of civilization reached by the undivided Aryans in their Arctic home was higher than the culture of the Stone age or even that of the age of metals. I have referred in the first chapter of the book to the opinion of some eminent archaeologists that the mete] age was introduced into Europe from other countries either by commerce or by the Indo-European race going there from outside, and the theory of the Arctic home with its inter-Glacial civilization lends support to this view. I might in passing here refer to an instance which illustrates the danger of relying exclusively on Comparative Philology in this respect. Dr. Schrader has shown that copper, at any rate, was known to the primitive Aryans; and he admits the possibility that this metal may, in isolated cases, have been employed in the manufacture of weapons like fighting knives or lance-heads.

But we are told that there are linguistic difficulties which prevent us from assuming that gold and silver were known in the primitive period. On an examination of the subject it will, however, be seen that in cases like these the philologist relics too much on his own methods or follows them too rigidly. For instance *khalkos* (copper or bronze) is mentioned by Homer as a medium of exchange (II, vii, 472); and Comparative Philology discloses two etymological equations, one derived from the root *mei* (Sans. *me*) denoting "barter," and the other derived from the Sanskrit *kri* Greek *priamai,* meaning purchase. The Rig-Veda (VIII, 1, 5) also mentions a measure of the value called *shulka,* and, as, the word is used in later Sanskrit literature to denote a *small* payment made at a toll-house, it is not unlikely that *shulka,* originally meant a small coin of copper or bronze similar in character to the *khalkos* mentioned by Homer. Now it is true that ordinarily Greek *kh,* is represented by *h* in Sanskrit, and that if this rule be rigidly applied to the present case it would not be possible to phonetically identify *khalkos* with *shulka.* Philologists have, therefore, tried to compare *khalkos* with Sanskrit *hriku* or *hliku.*

But, as remarked by Dr. Schrader, the connection seems to be altogether improbable. *Hriku* is not a Vedic word, nor does it mean copper or bronze. Despite the phonetic difficulty, — and the difficulty is not so serious as it seems to be at the first sight, for Sanskrit *sh* is represented by *k* in Greek, and this *k* sometimes gives place to the aspirated *kh*, — I am, therefore, inclined to identify *khalkos* with *shulka*; and if this is correct, we must conclude that undivided Aryans were familiar with some metal, either copper or, bronze, as a medium of exchange. There are many other points similar in character. But it is impossible to go further into this subject in this place. I only want to point out the reservation with which we shall have now to accept the results of Comparative Philology in forming our estimate of the degree of culture reached by the primitive Aryans, and show that when the primitive Aryan culture is carried back to the inter-Glacial age, the hypothesis that primitive Aryans were hardly better than the savage races of the present day at once falls to the ground. If the civilization of some Aryan races in the Neolithic age appears to be inferior or imperfect it must, therefore, be, as observed above, ascribed to relapse or retrogression after the destruction of the ancient civilization by the Ice Age, and the necessarily hard and nomadic life led by the people who survived the cataclysm.

The Asiatic Aryans, it is true, where able to preserve a good deal more of the original religion and culture, but it seems to be mainly due to their having incorporated the old traditions into their religious hymns or songs; and made it the exclusive business of a few to preserve and hand down with religious scrupulosity these prayers and songs to future generations by means of memory specially trained and cultivated for the purpose. But even then how difficult the task was can be very well seen from the fact that a greater portion of the hymns and songs originally comprised in the Avesta has been lost; and though the Veda is better preserved, still what we have at present is only a portion of the literature which is believed on good grounds to have once been in existence.

It may seem passing-strange that these books should disclose to us the existence of an original Arctic home so many centuries after the traditions were incorporated into them. But the evidence in the foregoing pages shows that it is a fact; and if so, we must hold that the Neolithic Aryan people in Europe were not, as Prof. Max Muller thinks, progressive, but, for the time at least, necessarily retrogressive savages working only with such residua of the antediluvian civilization as were saved from its general wreck.

But though the Vedic or Aryan people and their religion and culture can thus be traced to the last inter-Glacial period, and though we know that the degree of culture attained by the primitive Aryans was of a higher type than some scholars seem to be willing to assign to them, yet there are many points in the primitive Aryan history which still remain unsolved. For instance, when and where the Aryan race was differentiated from other human races, or how and where the Aryan speech was developed, are important questions from the anthropological point of view, but we have, at present, no, means to answer the same satisfactorily.

It is quite possible that other human races might have lived with the Aryans in their home at this time; but the Vedic evidence is silent on this point. The existence of the human race is traced by geologists to the Tertiary era; and it is now geologically certain that the gigantic changes wrought on this globe by glacial epochs were witnessed by man. But anthropology does not supply us with any data from which we can ascertain when, where, or how the human race came to be differentiated according to colour or language. On the contrary, it is now proved that at the earliest date at which human remains have been found, the race was already divided into several, sharply distinguished types; and this, as observed by Laing, leaves the question of man's ultimate origin completely open to speculation, and enables both monogenists and polygenists, to contend for their respective views with plausible arguments and without fear of being refuted by facts. The evidence, set forth in the foregoing pages, does not enable us to solve any of these questions regarding the ultimate origin of the human race or even of the Aryan people or their language and religion. We have nothing in this evidence for ascertaining how far the existence of the Aryan race can be traced back to pre-Glacial, as distinguished from inter-Glacial times; or whether the race was descended from a single pair (monogeny) or plurality of pairs (polygeny) in the remotest ages.

The traditional evidence collected by us only warrants us in taking back the Aryan people and their civilization from the Temperate zone in post-Glacial to the Arctic regions in inter-Glacial times. It is true that: Aryans and their culture or religion cannot be supposed to have developed all of a sudden at the close of the last inter-Glacial period, and the ultimate origin of both must, therefore, be placed in remote geological times. But it is useless to speculate on this question without further evidence, and in the present state of our knowledge we must rest content with the result that though Aryan race or religion can be traced to the last inter-Glacial-period yet the ultimate origin of both is still lost in geological antiquity.

I cannot conclude this chapter without briefly examining the bearing of our results on the views entertained by Hindu theological scholars regarding the origin, character and authority of the Vedas. It is a question which has been discussed with more or less acuteness, subtlety, or learning ever since the days of the Brahmans; and frond a purely theological point of view I do not think there remains anything to be now said upon it. Again, for the purposes of scientific investigation, it is necessary to keep the theological and the antiquarian aspect of the question quite distinct from each other. Yet when our investigation, conducted on strict scientific lines, is completed, we may usefully compare our conclusions with the theological views and see how far they harmonize or clash with each other. In fact no Hindu who reads a book like the present, can avoid making such a comparison; and we shall be lightening his task by inserting in this place a few remarks on this subject. According to the view held by Hindu theologians, the Vedas are eternal (*nitya*), without a beginning (*anadi*), and also not created by a human author (*apaurusheya*); and we are told that these attributes have been predicated of our sacred books from the most ancient times known to our divines or philosophers.

The whole of the third Volume of Dr. Muir's *Original Sanskrit Texts* is devoted to the discussion of this subject, a number of original passages and arguments bearing on which are there collected, including Sayana's lucid summary in the introduction to his commentary on the Rig-Veda; and more recently the late Mahamahopadhyaya Rajarama Shastri Bodas, the editor of the Bombay edition of the Rig-Veda, has done the same in a Sanskrit pamphlet, the second edition of which is now published by his son, Mr. M. R. Bodas, of the Bombay High Court Bar. I shall, therefore, give in this place only a summary of the different views of Hindu theologians, without entering into the details of the controversy which can be studied from the above books. The question before us is whether the Vedic hymns, that is, not only the words of the hymns but also the religious system found or referred to therein, are the compositions of the Rishis to whom they are assigned in the Anukramanikas, or the ancient Indexes of the Veda, in the sense in which the Shakuntala is a composition of Kalidasa; or whether these hymns existed from times immemorial, in other words, whether they are eternal and without a beginning. The hymns themselves are naturally the best evidence on the point. But, as shown by Dr. Muir in the second chapter (pp. 218-86) of the Volume above mentioned, the utterances of the Vedic Rishis on this point are not unanimous.

Thus side by side with passages in which the Vedic bards have expressed their emotions, hopes or fears, or prayed for worldly comforts and victory over their enemies, condemning evil practices like gambling with dice (X, 34), or have described events, which on their face seem to be the events of the day; side by side with passages where the poet says that how has made (*kri*) generated (*jan*), or fabricated (*taksh*) a new (*navyasi* or *apurvya*) hymn, much in the same way as a carpenter fashions a chariot (I, 47, 2; 62, 13; II, 19, 8; IV, 16,

20; VIII, 95, 5; X, 23, 6; 39, 14; 54, 6; 160, 5; &c.); or with hymns in which we are plainly told that they are composed by so and so, the son of so and so, (I, 60, 5; X, 63, 17; 67, 1; &c.), there are to be found in the Rig-Veda itself an equally large number of hymns where the Rishis state in unmistakable terms that the hymns sung by them were the results of inspiration from Indra, Varuna, Soma, Aditi, or some other deity; or that the Vedic verses (*richah*) directly emanated from the Supreme Purusha, or some other divine source; or that they were given by gods (*devatta*), or generated by them and only seen or perceived (*pashyat*) by the poets in later times, (I, 37, 4; II, 23, 2; VII, 66, 11; VIII, 59, 6; X, 72, 1; 88, 8; 93, 9; &c.). We are told that Vach (Speech) is *nitya* or eternal (VIII, 75, 6, also cf. X, 125); or that the gods generated the divine Vach and also the hymns (VIII, 100, 11; 101, 16; X, 88, 8). The evidence of the Vedic hymns does not, therefore, enable us to decide the question one way or the other; but if the composition of the hymns is once ascribed to human effort, and one to divine inspiration or to the gods directly, it is clear that at least some of these old Rishis believed the hymns to have been sung under inspiration or generated directly by the goddess of speech or other deities.

We may reconcile the former of these views with the passages where the hymns are said to be made by human effort, on the supposition that the poets who sang the hymns believed themselves to be acting under divine inspiration. But the explanation fails to account for the statement that the Jik, the Yajus, and the Saman, all emanated from the Supreme Purusha or the gods; and we must, therefore, conclude that the tradition about the eternity of the Vedas, or their divine origin is as old as the Veda itself. Accordingly, when we come to the Brahmans and the Upanishads, we naturally find the same view prevailing.

They tell us that the Rig-Veda proceeded from Agni (fire), the Yajur-Veda from Vayu (wind), and the Sama-Veda from Surya (the sun), and that these three deities got their warmth from Prajapati who practiced lapas for the purpose (Shat. Brah, XI, 5, 8, 1 *f'*; Ait. Brah. V, 32-34; Chhan. Up. IV, 17, 1); or that the Vedas are the breathings of the Supreme Being (Brih. Up. II, 4, 10); or that Prajapati by means of the eternal Vach created the Vedas and everything else in this world; and the same view is met with in the Smritis like those of Manu (I, 21-23) and others, or in the Puranas, several extracts from which are given by Dr. Muir in the volume above referred to.

It is admitted that the Vedas, with other things, are destroyed, at the end of a Kalpa, by the deluge (*pralaya*) which overtakes: the world at the time. But we are told that this does not affect the question of the eternity of the new Kalpa by Brahma himself after the grand deluge, and by the Rishis, who survive, after minor deluges. The authority generally quoted in support of this view is a verse from the Mahabharata (Shanti-Parvan, Chap. 210, v. 19) which says, "The great Rishis, empowered by Svayambhu (the self-born), formerly obtained, through *tapas* (religious austerity), the Vedas and the Itihasas, which had disappeared at the end of the (preceding) *Yuga*." The Rishis are, therefore, called the *seers* and not the *makers* of the Vedic hymns; and the personal designation of some Shakhas, branches or recessions of Vedas, as Taittiriya, Kathaka, &c., as well as the statements in the Vedic hymns, which say that so and so has *made* or *generated* such and such a hymn, are understood to mean that the particular Shakha or hymn was perceived, and *only perceived*, by the particular Rishi or poet.

It is not, however, till we come to the works of the authors and expositors of the different schools of Hindu philosophy (*darshanas*) that we find the doctrine of the eternity of the Vedas subjected to a searching examination; and, as remarked by Dr. Muir, one who reads the discussions of these writers cannot fail to be struck "with the acuteness of their reasoning, the logical precision with which their arguments are presented, and the occasional liveliness and ingenuity of their illustrations."

They all bear witness to the fact that so far as tradition went, — an unbroken tradition of great antiquity, — there was no remembrance of the Vedas having been ever composed by or ascribed to any human author; and taking into consideration the, learning and the piety of these scholars, their testimony must be regarded as an unimpeachable proof of the existence of such a tradition, which was considered ancient several centuries before the Christian era. But though a tradition whose high antiquity can be so well established deserves to be seriously considered in our investigations regarding the character of the Vedas, yet it is, after all, a negative proof, showing, it may be urged, nothing more than no human author of the Veda has been known from times beyond the memory of all these ancient scholars.

Jaimini, the author of Mimamsa Sutras, therefore, further deduces (I, 1, 5) the eternity of the Vedas from the relation or connection between words and their meanings, which he holds to be eternal (*autpattika*) and not conventional. A word is defined to be an aggregate of letters in a particular order, and its sense is said to be conveyed by these letters following each other in a definite succession. But Grammarians are not satisfied with this view, and maintain that the sense of a word is not expressed by the aggregate of its constituent letters which are transient, but by a certain super-sensuous entity, called *sphota* (*i.e.*, manifester, from *sphut*), which supervenes the aggregate of the letters as soon as they are pronounced, and reveals their meaning. Jaimini denies that there are words in the Vedas which denote any transient objects, and as the

Vedic words and their sense are eternal, it follows, according to him, that the Vedas are self-demonstrative, or that they shine, like the sun, by their own light, and are, therefore, perfect and infallible.

If particular parts of the Vedas are designated after some Rishis, it does not, we are told, prove those sages to have been their authors, but merely the teachers who studied and handed them down. Badarayana, as interpreted by Shankaracharya (I, 31, 26-33), the great leader of the Vedanta School, accepts the doctrine of the eternity of sound or words, but adds that it is the species to which the word belongs, and not the word itself, that is eternal or indestructible, and, there fore, though the names of deities, like Indra and others, which are all created and hence liable to destruction, are mentioned in the Veda, it does not affect the question of its eternity as the species to which Indra and others are said to belong is still eternal. In short, Vedic names and forms of species are eternal, and it is by remembering these that the world is created by Brahma at the beginning of each Kalpa (Maitr. Up., VI, 22).

TILAK CLAIM OF THE SUPERIORITY OF HINDUISM

Tilak advocated the superiority of Hinduism over all other religions. During an address in Benaras in 1906 he said: "There is no other religion on the face of the earth except the Hindu religion wherein we find such a hopeful promise, a promise that God comes to us as many times as necessary. After Mahomed, no Prophet is promised, and Jesus Christ came once for ever. No religion holds such promise full of hope [....] A time will come when our religious thoughts and our rights will be vindicated"

According to Tilak, all the different sects of Hinduism are many branches of the Vedic religion. He claims that the term *sanatana dharma* ('eternal religion') shows that Hinduism is very old – as old as history of the human race itself. Vedic religion was the religion of the Aryans from a very early time.

Hindu religion as a whole is made up of different parts co-related to each other as many sons and daughters of one great religion. Tilak claims that all religions, except Hinduism, are partial truths. He says: "they [non-Hindu religions] are partial truth while our Hindu religion is based on the whole, the Sanatana truth". He adds: "Hindu religion is very comprehensive – as comprehensive as its literature itself; we have a wonderful literature. Wisdom, as is concentrated in the Gita and epitomised in about 700 verses, that wisdom, I am confident, cannot be defeated or overcome by any philosophy be it Western or any other".

In many of his speeches Tilak asked for greater co-ordination of all the sections of Hinduism under the banner of *Bharata Dharma Mahamandala* ('All

India Religious Association'). He also emphasised the value of numbers. He said: "Numerical strength also is a great strength. Can the religion which counts its followers by crores die? Never, unless the crores of our fellow-followers are suddenly swept away our religion will not die. All that is required for our glorious triumph and success is that we should unite all the different sects on a common platform and let the stream of Hindu religion flow through one channel".

CLAIMS THAT HINDUISM IS THE MOST TOLERANT RELIGION

Tilak proudly maintained that Hinduism is the most tolerant religion in the world. According to him it tolerates all religions. He asks: "If there be any religion in the world which advocates toleration of other religious beliefs and instruct [sic] one to stick to one's own religion, it is the religion of the Hindus alone". He adds: "Shri Krishna does not say that the followers of other religions would be doomed to eternal hell. I challenge anybody to point out to me a similar text from the scriptures of other religions. It cannot be found in any other religion".

PROMOTION OF HINDU NATIONALISM

Koenraad Elst watches that Tilak was the first to associate Hindu imagery with the opportunity battle and he translated the Gita as far as political activism. It was amid the British decide that Hindu patriotism took birth. 'The father of Indian agitation' was in numerous regards one of the figures who sustained it. Tilak was a Hindu patriot to the center who made – as Walport says – no qualification amongst religion and legislative issues. He was against Muslim and hostile to Gandhi. As indicated by Tilak, religion is a component of nationality. He buttressed the cases of Hindu closed-mindedness through his grant. He said: "The normal figure Indian Society is the sentiment Hindutva (Hinduness)". The Hindu religion gives to the Indian culture a good and in addition social tie. Amid the Vedic times India was an independent nation and an incredible country joined by a typical culture. That solidarity vanished and it brought upon the country incredible debasement. In any case, it is the obligation of the pioneers of India to restore that union.

Tilak remained for the foundation of a Hindu rashtra in India. It is contended that Tilak had a section in the purported 'Nepal plot'. The thought probably was to persuade the King of Nepal to attack India, starting thus an uprising inside the nation in his support, since if the free King of the main autonomous Hindu Kingdom vanquished India there would be one sovereign Hindu country. Imitating of an incredible past is proverbial to any social renaissance. Tilak contended that truths that are being found by the West were known to the rishis of India. Present day science is bit by bit advocating and vindicating the old insight of India. He says: "Are not these basic devotions to the Vedas, the Gita and the Ramayana our basic legacy? In the event that we lay weight on it overlooking all the minor contrasts that exist between various organizations, then by the beauty of provision we should [...] have the capacity to combine all the diverse groups into a relentless Hindu country. This should be the aspiration of each Hindu".

The Gitarahasya is basically a work of patriot writing than of logic. Through it he made a mixing call to his comrades to activity so as to claim their bequest which is swaraj (self run the show). He contended that in that procedure it is honest to goodness to enjoy savagery, in impersonation of Arjuna and Shivaji. It is the rationale as opposed to the activity in-itself that matters. As it were, end legitimizes the methods.

A CRITICAL EVALUATION OF TILAK'S PHILOSOPHY

Tilak created a revolution in the world of ethics with his *Gitarahasya*. It had far reaching consequences in the field of religion, politics, relationship with religious minorities and national struggle for independence. Below we take a critical look at his ethical views and its impact on the Hindutva ideology which is in vogue.

K.M.Panikkar observes that it is Tilak's *Gitarahasya* which marked the change in Indian political scenario. He showed for the first time that the message of the *Gita* was not renunciation as others had thought before, but it was essentially a scripture preaching a doctrine of social activism where action for human good without personal attachment is preached as the first imperative.

Subjective Interpretation of the *Gita*

Richard Charles Zaehner says that in interpreting the *Gita,* as in interpreting any sacred text, the danger is that the interpreter will quote all that is grist to his mill while failing to draw attention to what embarrasses him in other parts of the text.

Tilak introduced a new trend in the reading of scriptures with his *Gitarahasya*, namely, that of giving a subjective interpretation to the Hindu scriptures in order to give foundation for his concept of violence as higher duty. It is said that 'what one ought to do' is the problem of morality. The *Gita* says that what ought to be done is one's caste duty. If we follow Tilak's *Gitarahasya* the caste duty consists in action which may involve also violence, and it is fully justified. This is of course abuse of caste power.

The traditional Hindu texts like the *Gita* took on unprecedented importance with Tilak's *Gitarahasya*. The *Gita* became for the Hindu reformers a kind of counter Bible. Consequently many translations of the *Gita* were sponsored throughout the subcontinent in various languages. Until the advent of Tilak, the interpretations given to the *Gita* never really advocated violence. Many of the great Hindu reformers felt compelled to compose their own 'reading' or commentary of it. Thus not only do we hear from the more spiritual reformers such as, Swami Vivekananda (1863-1902), Sarveppalli Radhakrishnan (1888-1975) or Vinoba Bhave (1895-1994) but also men of action like Gandhi. But their concept of *karma yoga* differed from Tilak's.

The great commentators of the *Gita* preferred non-violence than violence. Some saw in the *Gita* action for social reform, others action for political independence, and some others saw in it a call to take up arms.

For the most part, the overwhelming majority of commentators read the *Gita* non-violently, as a spiritual or moral allegory and the desire to avoid violence was ever present. Many made allegorical readings of the battle between the Pandavas and the Kauravas. Gandhi saw the *Mahabharata* itself as a 'great anti-war epic' and Krishna's conversation with Arjuna as imaginary. This interpretation became the dominant reading of the *Gita* during the twentieth century. But with Tilak it was different.

In his own time Gandhi had rejected the views of Tilak. He said: "I do not find myself in agreement with everything he [Tilak] says"; "What we need to consider is whether Indians should accept the views of Mr.Tilak and his party. We submit, after great deliberation, that Mr.Tilak's views should be rejected".

K.M.Panikkar tells us that the British government was not unaware of the dynamite that the *Gita* contained, for long before Tilak's *Gitarahasya* had been published, he had been preaching its message. The authorities even considered seriously the question of proscribing the *Gita*; but a holy book which the Hindu masses use as daily prayer and which has been translated into every Indian language could not be proscribed as a seditious volume.

Divine Sanction to Violence

Tilak's interpretation of the *Gita* was an attempt to find justification for violence and militancy in the Hindu scriptures. An action may involve violence. But when that action is seen as a duty, violence becomes unavoidable and necessary. Tilak goes a step further and gives it a divine sanction. He presents Krishna as the new law-giver. This makes his ethics even more dangerous and diabolic. Thus violence becomes a religious activity, an obligation (*dharma*) for all Hindus and salvation is to be achieved through it. This makes us raise two pertinent questions: can a subjective interpretation of sacred scripture to rationalise violence be justified? Can such an interpretation be declared as divinely sanctioned? As we have seen above, according to Tilak, both are possible.

Tilak's ethics has been a great attraction for many Hindutva ideologues and organisations of modern and contemporary India. Hindu sacred scriptures like the *Bhagavadgita, Ramayana* and *Mahabharata* and even some *Puranas* are liberally interpreted in order to justify militancy, violence and extremism aganist both real and imaginary enemies in many parts of India. Ashis Nandy is correct to some extent when he says that South Asian gods and goddesses, like their Hellenistic counterparts, can sometimes be found on the wrong side of morality and law.

Many modern and contemporary Hindutva ideologues were inspired by Tilak's interpretation of the *Gita*. For example, M.S.Golwalkar, who was the leader of the RSS from 1940 to 1973 said: "Our Philosophy teaches us to fight with all our strength, [...] Sri Krishna commands Arjuna to fight, [...] and in a spirit of doing one's duty unwaveringly". Aurobindo said: "It is an error to think that the heights of religion are above the struggles of this world. The recurrent cry of Sri Krishna to Arjuna insists on the struggle: 'Fight and overthrow thy opponents'".

Pravin Togadia, a prominent leader of the VHP says: "during the Mahabharata, did God ask Arjuna not to fight, did God talk to Arjun about *Ahimsa*? What had Krishna Bhagawan said? Fight. [....] He told Arjuna to kill Karna. This is what Kyshtriya [sic] blood is made up of. Karna was killed. Did anyone tell Krishna that he had followed a path of *adharma*?".

There is nothing as dangerous as giving divine sanction to violence. It easily convinces the naive and the ignorant to indulge in violence as there is merit attached to it. It makes the criminals to commit violence with religious fervour.

Many instances of communal violence in India are violence justified by religion. In 1992 those who died during the *kar seva* in order to demolish the Babri mosque are considered as martyrs. On 6 December 1992 at Ayodhya in the midst of the hysterical cries of the *karsevaks, Jai siya Ram* the Babri mosque was razed to the ground. The attack on a century-old Christian Girl's school at Rajkot on 20 June 1998 was carried out amidst shouting slogans of *Jai Shri Ram*. The same slogan was heard when the Australian missionary Graham Staines and his two sons were burned alive in Orissa in 1999. When the Muslims women were being gang raped at Godhra in Gujarat in early 2002 the rapists shouted *har har Mahadev*.

Religious sanction to violence helps militants and extremists to plan to the finest details the execution of their misdeeds. Thus acts of violence become a sort of sacred ritual, the criminals assume the role of high priests and what is promised to the accomplices in the crime is merit.

Justification of Hindu Militancy

Tilak represented a militant version of Hinduism. He argues that Hinduism is a warrior religion with a warrior-morality. Lord Krishna did not send Arjuna to the woods as a mendicant or make a *sanyasin* out of him, filling his mind with apathy. He did not place in his hands cymbals or drum or harp but bow and arrows. His advice to Arjuna was to fight: "therefore, O Arjuna, fight"; "therefore, determine to fight and rise"; 'therefore, think of me [Krishna] and fight"; "the doer and the causer of everything is I myself [Krishna], and you [Arjuna] are only the tool; and therefore, fight and conquer your enemies". Tilak reminds us that Arjuna did really fight, and in the course of the fight he actually killed Bhisma, Karna, Jayadratha, and others as occasion arose. In other words, according to Tilak, in modern terms, a true patriot is one who holds the *Gita* on the one hand and pistol on the other.

Gandhi once remarked that Tilak seems to have said that in our language we have no word corresponding to conscience. Therefore, he rejected the idea of conscience. Gandhi was of the opinion that Tilak missed the inner meaning of the *Gita* when he used it to justify violence. He says: "But I have often felt that he [Tilak] has not understood the age-old spirit of India, has not understood her soul", which according to Gandhi, is non-violence (*ahimsa*).

During the trial of Tilak the judge said the following about him in the sentence he delivered: "It seems to me that it must be a diseased mind, a most perverted mind, that could say that the articles which you have written are legitimate weapons in political agitation. They are seething with sedition; they breathe violence; they speak of murder with approval, and the cowardly and atrocious act of committing murder with bombs not only seems to meet with your approval, but you hail that advent of the bomb in India as if something had come to India for good".

Violence is energy and talents wasted. The Judge added: "you [Tilak] are a man of undoubted talents and great power and influence. Those talents and influence if used for the good of your country would have been instrumental in brining about a great deal of happiness for those very people whose cause you expose".

Thus, as K.M.Panikkar observes, the terrorists and other political groups which worked for revolution believed frankly in violence and elevated it to a creed, and with the beginning of the twentieth century a new type of nationalism which believed in revolutionary methods emerged. The leaders of this new movement were Tilak in Western India and Aurobindo Ghose in Bengal.

ETHICAL RELATIVISM AND INTRINSIC GOODNESS OF VIOLENCE

The *Gitarahasya* advocates ethical relativism. Tilak believed in the principle of 'end justifies the means' which implies only that one's *motives* should be untainted by selfish interest and passion. The method does not matter. In other words, it is the motivation rather than the action in-itself which is important in determining culpability. He says: "'The Reason (*buddhi*) is of greater importance than the Action' [....] If one considers only the external Action, it is often misleading". Thus an action may be sinful. But from the fact that the external action is bad, one cannot draw the conclusion that the reason must also be bad.

Similarly with regard to truth. Under certain circumstances one has a higher obligation to lie. Tilak says: "telling a lie has been found, after mature deliberation, to be much better than speaking the truth"; "There is no sin in speaking the untruth on the following five occasions, namely, if in jock [sic] or while speaking with women or at the time of marriage, or if your life is in danger, or for protecting your own property". It is stated in the Vedas that even gods themselves broke the pledges made by them. There is then, in the strict sense, nothing called truth, justice, honesty, fairplay, charity, and the like. What exists is ethics of expediency. Everything is, therefore, relative. D.D.Pattanaik a pro-Hindutva writer admits: "Tilak was ready to condone occasional acts of terrorist violence on grounds of expediency". But the paradox is that, according to Tilak, even though one indulges in terrorist violence it may not be considered as sin so that one can still attain final liberation (*moksa*). He says: "the Gita has propounded the device of performing Action in such a way that one ultimately attains Release without committing sin".

Concerning the ethical problem involved in the killing Afzal Khan by Shivaji through treachery, Tilak said that great men are above the common principles of morality. Krishna preached in the *Gita* that we have the right even to kill our own *guru* and our kinsmen. Tilak openly approved the use of bomb as a legitimate weapon in political agitation. He wrote articles in defence and justification of political assassinations. He was accused of the offence of forgery by fraudulently altering documents. He came to be considered as the chief conspirator against the British government.

Here, it may be argued that the ethics of Tilak has a counterpart in Chanakya (Kautilya, 4th century B.C) who wrote a treatise on statecraft entitled

Arthasastra which contained a code of conduct for rulers that justified force, cunning and ruthlessness and endorsed real politic and dismissed considerations of morality in public life, which ranged from spying to assassination. Gandhi could never agree with Tilak on an ethics of this kind. K.M.Panikkar says: "To Gandhiji it was not sufficient that the ideal should be *Lok Samgraha* or the welfare of all. It was even more important that the means should be ethically right [...] it must be uncontaminated not merely by selfishness but by anything which injures others". Gandhi says: "After many a frank chat with the Lokamanya I had come to see that on some vital matter we could never agree [....] I only know that we fundamentally differed"; "I cannot claim the honour of being the follower of the late Lokamanya [....] I am conscious that my method is not Mr.Tilak's method". According to Gandhi both the end as well as the means to achieve it should be good and only then an action can be said to be good. He further stated that even if one's 'inner voice' tells one to do an evil act one should not do it: "If a voice told a thief, 'kill that girl, cut off her limbs and take away her jewellery', I would not say it was the still small voice within. It would be sheer wickedness".

Ivan Strenski says that the ethic of action in the *Gita* is employed to guide the use of public violence in political matters. The *Gita*, and the *Mahabharata*, of which it forms a portion, are about war. The straightforward literal injunction of the *Gita* is to fight, and to fight to death. Thus Krishna urges the reluctant Arjuna to rally his courage and fight. This will surprise those familiar only with the more 'spiritual' interpretations of the *Gita*.

Tilak's ethics propounded in the *Gitarahasya* is subjective, relative, dubious, ambivalent and machiavellian. He harbours on the idea that violence is a simple thing, a mere performance of caste duty. But violence in any form is self-defeating and it always involves irrationality, however lofty the motives may be. Violence simply works on the principle that 'end justifies the means'. This was the ethics of the Nazis.

Often violence is motivated and pre-meditated and carefully planned. It is irrational in the domain of motivation as well as in the results it produces. The best example for this is the Godhra pogrom of February-March 2002 in the State of Gujarat. Kushwant Singh says that during the Godhra massacre armed mobs were out in different parts of Gujarat with detailed lists of Muslim homes and establishments. Several hundred Muslims were hacked to death or burnt alive, women raped, homes and shops looted and burnt. Not only did the police remain inert, when the army arrived on the scene it was not deployed. Officers who tried to do their duty and foil the plans of the mobs were transferred out. Arundhati Roy says about the Gujarat massacre: "The leaders of the mob had computer-generated cadastral lists marking out Muslim homes, shops, business and even partnerships. They had mobile phones to co-ordinate the action. They had trucks loaded with thousands of gas cylinders, hoarded weeks in advance, which they used to blow up Muslim commercial establishments. They had not just police protection and police connivance, but also covering fire". If Tilak were to be alive today, he would have, in all likelihood, endorsed the communal pogrom of Gujarat which was meticulously planned and executed.

Influence on the Hindutva Movement

In Tilak, Hindu religion invaded the domain of politics. He was an icon of religio-centric politics in his time. But he was eclipsed by Gandhi in the leadership of the Congress Party. This political displacement of Tilak corresponded with what *seemed* the virtually final eclipse of his reading of the *Gita* as well. But it was not so. On 30 January 1948 Nathuram Godse (1912-1949) fired three shots at point blank range at Gandhi. The assassin after firing the shots raised his hand with the gun and called for the police. He voluntarily surrendered to the authorities. The Hindu Mahasabha celebrated the event by distributing sweets. Godse later said that he had done his duty like Arjuna in the Mahabharata whom Krishna advised to kill his own relatives because they were evil. He had also read Tilak's writings.

Godse exhibited a surprisingly serene composure after the murder and showed his legal skill and self-confidence in the way in which he argued his case in English, a language he supposedly did not know well. Ashis Nandy says that it was as if the assassination gave meaning and drive to a life which otherwise was becoming increasingly prosaic. Godse was extremely religious. He read into the *Gita* with his martial background. For him Krishna was speaking to Arjuna about *real battles* and not allegorical battles fought in the inner self. Tilak's ethics of intrinsic goodness of violence had once again come back to life. It was once again seen as a sacred duty of the patriots of the Hindu *rashtra*.

Gandhi was denounced by Hindutva ideologues for preaching and practising the doctrine of *ahimsa* (non-violence) in the most 'perverted form'. He was killed by a Hindu for having undermined and betrayed Hindu India. Gopal Godse, brother of Nathuram Godse says: 'Our motive was not to achieve control of the government; ... we were simply trying to rid the nation of someone who had done and was doing great harm to it. He had consistently insulted the Hindu nation and had weakened it by his doctrine of *ahimsa*". Patrick Nair reports that at Nagpur the RSS have built a shrine in honour of Godse. While visiting Nagpur in the 1980s he wandered into the RSS complex and found a shrine dedicated to Nathuram Godse. It had a plaque with the message that one day when the Hindu nationalists come to power a far more fitting memorial would be erected. Prior to 30 January 1948, there had been five known unsuccessful attempts to kill Gandhi, all of them except one in Maharashtra – the land of Tilak. The first was in Poona in June 1934 when Gandhi was engaged in an anti-untouchability campaign there. The second, in July 1944, at Panchgani where Nathuram Godse, dressed in a Nehru shirt, pyjama and jacket, rushed towards Gandhi brandishing a dagger in his hand and shouting anti-Gandhi slogans. But he was overpowered by the people around Gandhi. The third, in September 1944, at Sevagram which also involved Godse along with some others. The fourth, in June 1946, near Poona when some unknown persons tried to derail the train in which Gandhi was travelling. The fifth, on 20 January 1948 in New Delhi which involved a bomb attack.

The unprecedented growth of the RSS and its affiliates and the upsurge of militancy among the Hindus should be seen as one of the effects of the re-reading of Tilak's interpretation of the *Gita*. Following Tilak's example many Hindutva ideologues and organisations are now giving new interpretations not only to the *Gita* but also to other sacred books of the Hindus like, the *Ramayana* and *Mahabharata* and even *Puranas* in order to rationalise violence as a means to promote Hindu cultural nationalism. Referring to *Mahabharata* – of which the *Gita* forms a part – Rajmohan Gandhi says that the epic is a story of unending revenge and violence.

In his own time Tilak became the guru of V.D.Savarkar (1883-1966), especially in his extreme ideology of nationalism. It was Tilak who recommended the case of Savarkar for a scholarship to go to London for studies. In London Savarkar was busy with production of bombs, eventually sending a manual on this subject back to Tilak, publication of revolutionary pamphlets, books, etc. The founder of the RSS, Keshav Baliram Hedgewar (1889-1940) also came under the influence of Tilak. Another prominent RSS leader who was influenced by Tilak was Balkrishna Shivaram Moonje (1872-1948) the founder of the Bhonsle Military School in Nasik. Madhav Kashinath Damley founder of *Lokhandi Morcha* or *Iron Front*, a Fascist movement, was also a follower of Tilak. Tilak's thoughts have influenced the Hindu Mahasabha, the Jan Sangh and the RSS. The RSS subscribe to Tilak's understanding of *karma-yoga* and the *swayamsevaks* are advised to read the *Gita* regularly. Krishna Kumar writing about the revival of Hindu nationalism in India says: "the RSS was a blossom of the vigorous seed of revivalist nationalism that Tilak had sown". Almost all those convicted in the trial of Gandhi murder case had a connection, past or present with either the Hindu Mahasabha or the RSS and they were believers in violence.

Many Hindutva ideologues make strenuous effort to popularise the view that the Hindu gods and goddesses are 'weapon wielding deities'. In 1966 N.N.Banerjee, president of the Hindu Mahasabha, on the occasion of the golden jubilee of the organisation told the Hindus that all their deities, such as, Siva, Vishnu, Durga, Kali, Kartikeya, Shri Ramachandra, Shri Krishna are warriors and they carry weapons. Hence Hindus need to realise their significance and should become their dynamic worshippers. Aurobindo reminds us that in the *Mahabharata*, Krishna says that God created battle and armour, the sword, the bow and the dagger.

Describing Goddess Kali, V.S.Naipaul says: "Kali, 'the black one', the coal-black aboriginal goddess, surviving in Hinduism as the emblem of female destructiveness, garlanded with human skulls, tongue forever out for fresh blood, eternally sacrificed to but insatiable". Ashis Nandy states that Kali is the new symbol of a treacherous cosmic mother, eager to betray and prone to aggression, fierce, violent, associated with robbers, thieves, thugs, prostitutes, and in some of her incarnations she was associated with certain dangerous diseases. B.Walker says that Kali holds in two of her hands a sword and a dagger and in the other two are severed heads dripping with blood. Her long tongue hangs out of her mouth and blood trickles down her chin and neck as she gorges herself at her cannibal feasts. In one hideous image a headless Kali holds her own severed head, while the mouth greedily drinks the blood spurting from her neck.

Rama of *Ramayana* is depicted as wielding a bow and arrow. In fact, the symbol of the Shiv Sena is Ram's bow and arrow. He is also projected as the national hero of the Hindu nation. Hanuman is the monkey-god who served Rama with steadfast devotion. But he is also a symbol of irrational destruction. He went to Lanka in search of Sita. Before he left he destroyed everything in sight, razing houses and uprooting trees as though they were grass until he was captured by Indrajit, son of Ravana. In a bid to humiliate Hanuman and send him back to Ram, an oil-soaked cloth was tied to his tail and set alight.

But Hanuman, charged through the city and the surrounding countryside causing untold havoc and burning all the crops with his fiery tail. Today Hanuman is the model for the Bajrang Dal activists – the Indian version of the Nazi Stormtroopers (SA, *Sturmabteilung* 'storming department'). Durga Vahini cadets emulate the Goddess Durga, the demon-killing protective mother, who is actually supposed to be the goddess Kali. Many Hindutva ideologues now speak of militant Hinduism as the 'Third Eye' of the Hindu. M.M.Ahluwalia maintains that the Hindu revolutionaries were influenced by the European revolutionaries on the one hand and the militancy of Hindu gods and goddesses and historical heroes on the other. Many Bengali secret societies were inspired by Tilak's interpretation of the *Gita*.

The members of the *Anushilan Samiti* ('disciplinary organisation') took an oath of allegiance to the organisation before an image of Goddess Kali with the *Bhagavadgita* in one hand and a revolver in the other. Aurobindo envisaged *karma yoga* as a means of legitimising violence as a form of sacrifice. He believed in an aggressive Hinduism. According to him open attack, unsparing criticism, the severest satire, the most wounding irony, are all methods perfectly justifiable and indispensable in politics. In 1951 N.C.Chatterjee as president of the Hindu Mahasabha said: "The greatest task of the Mahasabha is to create Hindu character on the basis of the Geetha (sic)". In 1960, V.G.Deshpande in his presidential address of the 45th Annual Session of the All India Hindu Mahasabha spoke of the need to resort to guerrilla and mountain warfare. The *karma yoga* expounded in the *Gita* is practised by the RSS *pracharaks* ('preachers') which is described as a matter of inner sacrifice. They maintain that action, even when violent, can constitute a means of renunciation when it is undertaken without regard to personal advantage and in the service of Hindu nation (*rashtra*) and Hindu *dharma*.

Many Nazis of Germany took inspiration from the *Gita*. For example, Heinrich Himmler (1900-1945), the chief of Hitler's security service (SS, *Schutzstaffel = security guard*) constantly carried with him this sacred book, cited from it, compared Hitler to Lord Krishna and wanted his SS troop to be like the Kshatriya caste of India which saw war as part of their spirituality. Savitri Devi (1905-1982) a staunch Nazi (popularly known as 'Hitler's Priestess') was the first woman writer who regarded Adolf Hitler as a divine incarnation equal of Ram and Krishna in the *Gita*. She justified the elimination of millions of Jews in Nazi Germany by quoting from the *Gita*. Devi also considered the *Schutzstaffel* of Hitler as the incarnation of the Indo-Aryan Kshatriya caste. According to Victor and Victoria Trimondi, the *Gita* spiritualises cruelty (*skralisierung der Grausamkeit*). All imaginable forms of cruelty were practised in the fratricidal war described in the *Gita*. In addition, Hitler envisaged cruelty as a virtue of the new generation of Nazi youth.

Writing in the 1960s K.M.Panikkar said that the *Gita* has become the scripture of the new age, the main foundation on which its ethic, its social doctrines and even its political action depends. The Rama myth is a help to rationalise the aggressiveness and violence of the Shiv Sena, VHP, BJP, RSS, Bajrang Dal and the Sangh Parivar as a whole. Rama is the new icon of the anti-Muslim movement in India as was Shivaji in Tilak's time. *Mahabharata* is seen as a scripture of war. The televising of *Ramayana* (1987-1989 in 91 weekly episodes) and *Mahabharata* (1988-1990 in 94 episodes) helped the Hindu masses to imbibe the spirit of violence from their favourite sacred books, gods and goddesses. Today, the sacred books of Hinduism – which are meant to guide the everyday religious code of the Hindus – are often used to extol violence for a so-called 'greater cause'. The saffronised NCERT school textbook of Social Sciences for Class IX extols revolutionaries like Tilak, Aurobindo, V.D.Savarkar, G.D. Savarkar, Swami Saradhananda, Sister Nivedita, and militant organisations like *Anushilan Samiti* (Bengal), *Yugantar* Party (Bengal, led by Barindra Ghose brother of Aurobindo Ghose), *Abhinav Bharat* (in Maharashtra, led by Savarkar brothers), Baroda Secret Society (Maharashtra), etc.

In 1991 the BJP campaigned vigorously for the extension of a Sunday morning television serial depicting the life of the famous Indian political philosopher, Chanakya or Kautilya (the word 'Kautilya' means 'crookedness and treachery'), the reputed author of *Arthasastra*, a hand book of totalitarian, ruthless and cynical stagecraft characterised by depravity in standards of morality. The serial portrayed Chanakya's struggle to assist Chandra Gupta Maurya (320-297 B.C) in ancient India in a way to suggest its similarities to the struggle waged by the BJP then to seize political power in New Delhi. But those who are familiar with the functioning of the BJP knows that much of its ethics is 'chanakyan' where 'end justifies the means'. Its 'India Shining', 'Feel Good', 'Super Power India' slogans were founded on chanakyan cut-throat ethics of lies, crookedness and ruthlessness with the desire to win 300 seats in the Indian parliament during the general elections of 2004 – a dubious heritage from Tilak's ethics of expediency.

But Tilak interpreted it in the interest of his political expediency and twisted its message to justify violence, extremism and militancy. Today, some Hindutva ideologues consider him as the person who freed the Indian National Congress from the so-called scourge of moderation. Tilak selectively cited from the *Gita* in order to justify his ethical stand and he believed in the intrinsic goodness of violence. This might be the reason why he said that politics is a game of worldly people and not of *sadhus*.

Tilak's experiment of combining religion and politics became a model for the Hindutva ideologues of contemporary India. Communal violence in India today is frequently and almost ubiquitously justified by using Hindu scriptures, especially the *Gita*, *Ramayana* and *Mahabharta*. Many interpret them literally, and indulge in the most eccentric forms violence against their enemies without qualms of conscience.

Arvind Sharma remarks that it was more than a mere curiosity that both Mahatma Gandhi and his assassin Nathuram Godse swore by the *Bhagavadgita*

– one by its figurative interpretation and the other by its literal. S.C. Sen Gupta observes that the *Gita* is patently a call to arms, an exposition of the doctrine of violence when it becomes a duty. B.R. Ambedkar, criticising Hinduism and its the tendency towards violence, observes that the *Gita* is about the justification of war; Krishna offers a philosophical defence of war and killing in war.

During the *rath yatra* of L.K.Advani in 1990, in many places the most common offering was traditional weaponry: arrows, dices, maces, swords, trident and *kripans*. At Jetpur in Gujarat 101 kshatriya youths offered him a bowl containing their blood. No wonder why V.S.Naipaul says: "I think religion is the greatest curse of mankind. It has killed more people, destroyed more property, than any other thing".

TILAK AND GANESH FESTIVALS

Tilak was maybe the main Indian political pioneer who understood the quality of the masses. He developed numerous projects so as to unite individuals. He contended that saint love is at the foundation of nationality, social request and religion. Nehru commented that Tilak was the primary political pioneer of the new India who achieved the masses and drew quality from them.

In 1895 Tilak introduced the Ganapati celebrations. Ganesh is a standout amongst the most prevalent of the divinities adored by the Hindus. The Ganapati development was introduced by Tilak as a counterpoise to the Muslim celebration Muhurram in which Hindus of the lower stations partook. Till then, Ganapati celebrations had nothing of an open character. In any case, Tilak succeeded in changing a straightforward household ceremony into an open festival.

In 1894 Tilak with the assistance of the Natu siblings was in charge of making the celebration an open occasion enduring ten days with music and a sorted out parade including young men from schools, and universities. Melodies were sung in acclaim of Tilak and Shivaji. Young men were occupied with fencing and other physical activities. The Natu siblings showed them sword and single stick activities.

Stanley A. Walport watches that through the Ganapati celebrations Tilak succeeded in uniting the up to this point disregarded urban and laborer bring down classes, influencing them with political melodies and discourses, boring young fellows to walk about town in aggressor gatherings and bestowing to Hinduism a congregational character up to this point obscure to it. Amid the parades they yelled: "O Heroes of Hind" and "Love your Country as God".

Frequently the Ganapati celebrations incited the Muslim people group. Tilak composed articles in a tone which was exceptionally offense to the Muslims, calling the Hindus to refrain from going about as the bearers of the bodies of Hassan and Hussain, that the sobbing stories of the Muslims in their Muharam festivities have nothing in them that would conscious patriotism. In 1894 and 1895 Tilak held exceptional Ganapati gatherings in his own particular house at Poona and at these tunes were sung in which direct Hindus and the British government were condemned, and Tilak affirmed these tunes.

David Smith watches that the love of Ganesh was rehashed in Maharashtra by the immense autonomous pioneer Tilak. Today, the Ganesh celebration is the biggest Hindu open religious execution in Maharashtra. Yogendra K.Malik and V.B. Singh help us that Tilak's utilization to remember the Ganesh celebrations was a case of the utilization of conventional religious images to assemble the Hindus in the reason for Hindu patriotism. As per Walport, with the Ganesh celebrations aggressor Hinduism's first cutting edge framework was conceived.

Shivaji Festivals

Tilak was instrumental in reviving the memory of Shivaji and setting in motion a great national propaganda which culminated in 1895 in the celebration at the chief centres of Brahmin activity in the Deccan of Shivaji's reputed birthday. According to Tilak, the Shivaji festivals serve like manure to the seeds of enthusiasm and the spirit of nationalism. He saw in this festival a peculiar value for the whole country, and argued that it is the duty of everyone to see that this character of the festival is not ignored or misrepresented.

Shivaji festivals at times created tension between the Muslims and the Hindus. Some of the articles that appeared in *Kesari* prove this fact. But Tilak said: "The Shivaji festival is not celebrated to alienate or even to irritate the Mahomedans. [....] We are not against a festival being started in honour of Akbar or any other hero from old Indian history".

The Shivaji festivals were also attempts to consolidate Hindu consciousness and Hindu militancy. Kushwant Singh adds that every time the Ganesh and Shivaji festivals were celebrated there were Hindu-Muslim riots. Walport says that, with the revival of the Shivaji festivals the next link in the organisational chain of militant Hinduism was developed.

Shivaji as a Role Model for Violence as Higher Duty

Shivaji, the Maratha leader, provided a kind of mythological exemplar for Tilak of his ethics of violence as higher duty, whose festivals he ardently promoted, though Mahatma Gandhi considered Shivaji as a misguided patriot. In 1896 Tilak lamented the neglect of the sites associated with the life and death of Shivaji. He said: "That the place of coronation and the tomb of that great man who gave the joy of independence to Maharashtra for two centuries should have been so utterly forgotten by the Marathas is indeed a misfortune". On 24 June 1906 Tilak wrote an article in his *Mahratta* entitled "Is Shivaji not a National Hero?" He called Shivaji '*swadeshi* hero' and argued that "Shivaji is the only hero to be found in Indian history". Tilak also began the modern promotion of Shivaji, as the leader of Maratha independence in Maharashtra. He urged children to read a portion of a historical novel entitled *Ushahkal* dealing with the times of Shivaji. According to him, what makes Shivaji a national hero is the spirit which guided him throughout and not his deeds as such. But history tells us that Shivaji treacherously murdered Afzal Khan. Ivan Strenski reminds us that Tilak's failure to bring about a method of controlled use of force must be seen at least partly as a failure of his political mythology. In a word, the myth of Shivaji sent all the wrong messages to those who might have wished for an ethic of justifiable use of force. Moreover, knowing about other ambivalent features of Tilak's political behaviour, one might conclude that Tilak chose the Shivaji myth precisely *because* it was ambivalent: it permitted him to appeal to chivalrous and heroic elements of the Maratha leader's lofty character, while at the same time permitting him to trade upon some of Shivaji's unsavoury qualities.

Strenski argues that Shivaji's killing of the Mughal general Afzal Khan raises many ethical questions. The 'great chivalric hero' Shivaji arrived with concealed deadly weapons to meet Afzal Khan. At his first opportunity, Shivaji murdered Afzal Khan on the very spot where they had agreed to talk peace. Walport describes the murder of Afzal Khan as follows:

To all outward appearances clad innocently enough, Shivaji approached the Muslim in his plain cloth shirt, but under it he wore a vest of mail, and concealed in his right sleeve was a scorpion-shaped dagger, while the finger tips of his left hand were sheathed with metal tiger claws. The embrace with which he greeted Afzal evoked the death-pang outcry from the Muslim.

What followed was the massacre of Afzal Khan's entire retinue. Now leaderless, the Mughal army dispersed and Shivaji won what Marathi patriots have celebrated as a great victory – a victory won by duplicity and deception. Shivaji's failure to keep his solemn word make him seem cowardly and dishonourable, little better than a sneak thief. Put on to the balance with the rest of Shivaji's deeds, it weighs heavily against permitting any honest reader to see in him an honourable man. Hence, says Strenski, Shivaji cannot be a role model for anyone who wishes to found an ethic of the principled or controlled use of violence.

It has been discovered that many years prior to the killing of Afzal Khan, Shivaji used the pretext of marriage to wrest control of a territory. After promising to marry the daughter of Chandra Rao More, the ruler of Javli, he killed More and took over Javli. Strenski says: "some of Tilak's own most notorious public deeds seem to indicate that his philosophy of political action was informed by the very moral ambivalence that characterises the myth of Shivaji".

Anti Cow-Killing Societies

Tilak started and used Anti-Cow-Killing Society, which in its original form was a religious movement founded on the fact that the Hindus regard the cow as a sacred animal. Unfortunately, his Anti Cow-Killing Society was regarded as a direct movement to provoke Muslims. Tilak did not take part in any anti-cow killing movement as such, but took advantage of the ill-feeling between the Hindus and Muslims for which this movement was a symptom. Tilak took a prominent part in inflaming the minds of Hindus against the Muslims. In several of his articles in *Kesari* he upheld the view that in the anti-cow-killing riots, as in all other outbreaks, the Musalmans were the aggressors. He praised the spirit in which the Hindus had stood up to their assailants when attacked and blamed those who held that when assailed by Muslims the Hindus should flee.

Gymnastic Societies

Tilak maintained that unless Hindus learned to employ force they must expect to be impotent witness of the gradual downfall of their ancient institutions. Therefore, he proceeded to organise Gymnastic Societies in which physical training and the use of more or less primitive weapons were taught in order to develop the martial instincts of the rising generation. The Natu brothers were recognised leaders of Hindu orthodoxy. They carried Tilak's propaganda to schools and colleges proclaiming that unless they learned to employ force the Hindus must expect to be impotent witnesses of the gradual downfall of all their ancient institutions.

His Gymnastic Societies sometimes resorted themselves into juvenile bands of dacoits to swell the coffers of *swaraj*. Young Hindus were taught to use arms and induced to believe it to be their duty to employ them against the enemy. The teaching which he gave or caused to be given to the members of the said societies was of such an evil and demoralising nature that with his approbation the members of some such societies formed themselves into bands of robbers who committed murder and robbery with the object of obtaining money to pursue Tilak's political campaign.

Extremist Journalism

Tilak started two newspapers *Kesari* and *Mahratta*. He wrote incriminating articles to encourage terrorism. In several of his writings he spoke of the cheapness of bombs and the economy with which they could be manufactured. He described the bomb as a charm and an amulet and a legitimate weapon of political reform. He even considered terrorism as an expression of patriotism. He said: "There is an excess of patriotism at the root of the bombs in Bengal". He went so far as to say that the Bengalee murders were 'beneficent murders' so that, in his opinion, there might be a beneficent murderer.

Tilak used his newspapers to incite the Hindus to assert their rights. He vilified the Muslims and the British.

From June through August of 1902, *Kesari* ran a highly provocative series of nine editorials entitled 'Guerrilla Warfare'. Sometimes *Kesari* contained articles on methods of the Russian Revolutionaries and the cult of the bomb in Bengal. He openly advocated Russian methods of retaliation. Writing in *Kesari* on 16 July 1907 he exhorted Indians to follow the Russian methods of political agitation. Tilak also wrote some articles proposing to the government to make gymnastics a compulsory subject in schools

In the *Kesari* of 28 May 1907 he exhorted Indian leaders to emulate the example of Russian democrats in their methods of political agitation. He also spoke of how the Russians managed to evade press censorship. On 27 July 1907 Tilak wrote in *Kesari*: "We find in Mr. Savarkar's book a true echo of the thoughts of Mazzini, his secret and the open attempts to bring about the unification of Italy"; "We find in Mazzini's writings a clear enumeration of the noble principles of democratic politics". When Tilak began *Kesari* and *Mahratta* he had stated that the aim of the two newspapers would be to give a fearless account of the existing condition in the country, to give reviews of Indian books and to give correct estimates of political affairs in Britain. But as is evident, his columns went beyond this scope and promoted extremism and militancy. They became vehicles for his radical political views and ethics of violence.

Militant Activities

Tilak was the founder of the militant revolutionary school in the national movement. He seems to have had connections with the secret societies at Nasik, Bengal and elsewhere. He felt himself strong to capture the Congress organisation in 1907, though it was not successful. The fight between the Moderates and the Extremists carried on in the political arena led to a split in the Indian National Congress. The extremist founded a party of their own. But Tilak said that the extremist of today will be the moderates of tomorrow just as the moderates of today were extremists yesterday. In 1907 at Surat, Tilak and his revolutionary group were expelled from the Congress for their radicalisation of Indian politics, which included also Aurobindo Ghose. The rift was only healed in 1914 when Tilak finalised a pact with the Muslim League for a joint front against the British.

It has been argued that in the murder of Walter Charles Rand and Charles Egerton Ayerst at Nasik, the assassins were only giving effect to Tilak's teachings. He played a leading role in inflaming the minds of the Hindus against the Muslims. During the cow-killing agitation of 1893, which caused disturbances throughout the country and much loss of life and property, He thus showed himself as an open advocate of violence and the cult of physical force.

Sometimes he advocated insurrection and argued that the Boer system of warfare which had been successful against the British, was that which had been adopted by Shivaji against the Muslims. In 1908 Tilak was tried for sedition because of an attempt on the life of Kingsford, a British judge at Muzaffarpur. Though the intention was to murder Kingsford, the assassins missed the target and two ladies were killed. Tilak in his writings supported the bomb throwers. This bomb outrage offered the government a golden chance to arrest Tilak. Tilak was sentenced for six years in prison. Tilak was convicted for inciting disaffection against the British in his writings in Marathi. But he claimed that the English renderings were defective. The trial ended in his incarceration and he was sent to Mandalay (Myanmar) and it was there that he composed his influential commentary on the *Gita* – the *Gitarahasya.*

Anti-Muslim Attitude

Tilak played a prominent part in inflaming the minds of the Hindus against the Muslims. Between 1880 and 1890 throughout India there was an evident antipathy between Hindus and Muslims. There were numerous riots and encounters between the members of the two faiths in many parts of the county. He promoted Ganapati festivals, in the first place, to prevent people from taking part in the Muslim festival Muharram. He was accused of inciting the Hindus to assert their rights to play music in passing before mosques. He even called the Muslims a savage race. He said: "even a savage race like the Mohammedans did not disarm the Hindus while exercising their imperial sway over India".

In High Court of Justice, Kings Bench Division accused Tilak of several crimes. For example, in 1893 during the Hindu-Muslim riots in Bombay Tilak took advantage of the situation to stir up the feeling of the Hindus against the Muslims. He was accused of using the Anti-Cow Killing Societies as a means to provoke the Muslims. According to the report of the Bombay government on 16 July 1918, on the occasion of Shivaji's coronation festival, Tilak presided at a lecture on conscription. In his speech he called the army a mercenary which consisted of Muslims and foreigners. It has been observed that basically, Tilak's anti-Muslim attitude manifested itself in four things: the question of playing music before the mosques, the Ganapati celebrations, the Shivaji movement and the Anti-Cow Killing Societies.

AntiChristian Attitude

Tilak saw Christianity as an enemy of Hinduism. He said: "Now I turn to the forces that are arrayed against us. There are mainly two forces of (1) science and (2) Christianity. If our religion is threatened with any hostile criticism, it comes from these two". Once he took tea in a Christian missionary school and accepted to do penance for it.

Tilak was vehemently opposed to the so-called conversion activities of the Christians. When Pandita Ramabai, a great Sanskrit scholar who became a widow, converted to Christianity and then set up *Sharada Sadan* for educating destitute high-caste widows, Tilak alleged that it was being covertly used to promote conversion to Christianity.

Tilak never really favoured social reforms. On 30 July 1907 he wrote in *Kesari* against Christian involvement in social reform and human rights issues.

He said: Though the correspondence with regard to the abolition of the customs of dedicating minor girls to the gods at Jejuri and Savantwadi is carried on under the leadership of Dr.Bhandarkar, it is the Missionaries who are as a matter of fact at the bottom of the whole affair.

It was they who first brought to the notice of Government that such girls led an immoral life after attaining puberty and that the existing statutory resolutions were quite inadequate to remedy the [sic] evil. [....] It is not at all possible for the people to believe that the above suggestion of the Missionaries originated from disinterested motives. [....] Our hypocritical Missionaries do not seem to know that immorality is not a criminal offence in England and that the value of the chastity of women can be estimated there in damages. The missionaries needlessly interfered in the matter.

Again, referring to Christianity Tilak said: "Our enemies are fast disappearing before the teachings of modern science, take courage and work hard for the final triumph". He envisaged a time when, instead of Christians preaching Christianity in India, Hindus will see their preachers proclaiming *Sanatana Dharma* (Eternal Religion) all over the world.

Critical Attitude towards Buddhism and Jainism

Tilak did not view benevolently the Buddhists and the Jains of India. He praised Adi Sankara of Kaladi who aggressively fought these two religions. Tilak says: "Buddhism flourished and attacks were made on Hindu religion by Buddhists and Jains. After 600 years of chaos rose one great leader, Shankaracharya and he brought together all the common philosophical elements for our religion and proved and preached them in such a way that Buddhism was swept away from the land".

4

Tilak View on Vedas

The Rig-Veda, we have seen, does not contain particular references to a day and a night of six months' span however the inadequacy is more than made up by parallel entries from the Iranian sacred texts. In any case, on account of the sunrise, the long persistent day break with its spinning wonderful qualities, which is the exceptional normal for the North Pole, there is luckily no such trouble.

Ushas, or the Goddess of Dawn, is a critical and most loved Vedic divinity and is commended in around twenty songs of the Rig-Veda and specified more than three hundred times, in some cases in the particular and here and there in the plural. These psalms, as indicated by Muir, are among the most wonderful, — if not the most excellent,— in the whole accumulation; and the divinity, to which they are tended to, is considered by Macdonell to be the most effortless making of Vedic verse, there being not any more enchanting figure in the graphic religious verses of whatever other writing. To put it plainly, Ushas, or the Goddess of Dawn, is portrayed in the Rig-Veda psalms with more than expected completion and what is still more imperative for our motivation is that the physical character of the god is not, at all, darkened by the depiction or the exemplification in the songs.

Here, thusly, we have a fine chance of demonstrating the legitimacy of our hypothesis, by appearing, if conceivable, that the most seasoned depiction of the sunrise is truly Polar in character. From the earlier it doesn't look likely that the Vedic writers could have gone into such delights over the fleeting sunrise of the tropical or the mild zone, or that such a great amount of tension about the coming day break ought to have been revealed, just on the grounds that the Vedic minstrels had no electric light or candles to use amid the short night of under 24 hours. Yet, the first light psalms have not, up 'til now, been analyzed from this point of view. It appears to have been implicitly accepted by all translators of the Vedas, Eastern and Western, that the Ushas of the Rig-

Veda can be no other than the day break with which we are commonplace in the tropical or the calm zone.

That Yaska and Sayana thought so is sufficiently characteristic, however even the Western researchers have taken similar view, likely affected by the hypothesis that the level of Central Asia was the first home of the Aryan race. In this way a few expressions in the day break songs, which would have generally recommended the request with respect to the physical or the cosmic character of the Vedic day break, have been either disregarded, or some way or another clarified away, by researchers, who could surely have tossed all the more light on the subject, had they not been affected by the presumption said above. It is with entries like these that we are here predominantly concerned, and we should in a matter of seconds see that if these are deciphered normally, they completely set up the Polar way of the Vedic first light.

The principal imply, in regards to the long length of the Vedic first light, is acquired from the Aitareya Brahmana, IV, 7. Before beginning the Gavam-ayana yield, there is a long recitation of at least a thousand verses, to be presented by the Hoti minister. This Ashvinashastra, as it is called, is tended to Agni, Ushas and Ashvins, which divinities lead toward the end of the night and the initiation of the day. It is the longest recitation to be recounted by the Hoti and the ideal opportunity for presenting it is after 12 pm, when "the dimness of the night is going to be assuaged by the light of the day break" (Nir. XII, I; Ashv. Shr. Sutra, VI, 5, 8). Similar timeframe is alluded to likewise in the Rig-Veda, VII, 67, 2 and 3. The shastra is long to the point, that the Hoti, who needs to discuss it, is coordinated to revive himself by drinking already softened spread in the wake of giving up thrice a tad bit of it (Ait. Br. IV, 7; Ashv. Shr. Sutra; VI, 5, 3). "He should eat ghee," watches the Aitareya.

Brahmana, "before he begins rehashing. Pretty much as in this world a truck or a carriage goes well if spread (with oil), in this way his rehashing continues well on the off chance that he be spread with ghee (by eating it)." It is obvious that if such a recitation must be done before the ascending of the sun, either the Hoti must begin his errand not long after 12 pm when it is dim, or the span of the day break should then have been adequately long to empower the cleric to complete the recitation in time in the wake of starting to present it on the principal appearance of light not too far off as coordinated. The main supposition is not feasible, as it is explicitly set out that the shastra, is not to be presented until the haziness of the night is mitigated by light.

So between the main appearance of light and the ascent of the sun, there probably been, back then, time enough to present the long commendatory melody of not dregs than a thousand verses. Nay, in the Taittiriya Samhita (II,

1, 10, 3) we are informed that occasionally the recitation of the shastra however initiated at the correct time, finished much sooner than dawn, and all things considered, the Samhita requires that a specific creature yield ought to be performed. Ashvalayana coordinates that in such a case the recitation ought to be proceeded up to dawn by presenting different psalms (Ashv. S.S. VI, 5, 8); while Apastamba (S.S. XIV, 1 and 2), in the wake of saying the yield alluded to in the Taittiriya Samhita, includes that all the ten Mandalas of the Rig-Veda might be discussed, if important, in such a case. It is clear from this that the real ascending of the sun over the skyline was a wonder frequently postponed past desire, back then and in a few places in the Taittiriya Samhita, (II, 1, 2, 4) we are informed that the Devas needed to play out a prayaschitta on the grounds that the sun did not sparkle of course.

Another indication of the long duration of the dawn is furnished by the Taittiriya Samhita, VIII 2. 20. Seven oblations are here mentioned, one to *Ushas* one to *Vyushti* one to *Udeshyat*, one to *Udyat*, one to *Udita* one to *Suvarga* and one to *Loka*. Five of these are evidently intended for the dawn in its five forms. The Taittiriya Brahmana (III, 8, 16, 4) explains the first two, *viz.*, to *Ushas* and *Vyushti*, as referring to dawn and sunrise, or rather to night and day, for according to the Brahmana "*Ushas* is night, and *Vyushti* is day." But even though we may accept this as correct and we take *Ushas* and *Vyushti* to be the representatives of night and day because the former signalizes the end of the night and the latter the beginning of the day, still we have to account for three oblations, *viz.* one to the dawn about to rise (*Udeshyat*,) one to the rising dawn (*Udyat*), and one to the dawn that has risen (*Udita*) the first two of which are according to the Taittiriya Brahmana, to be offered before the rising of the sun. Now the dawn in the tropical zone is so short that the three-fold distinction between the dawn that is about to rise, the dawn that is rising, and one that has risen or that is full-blown (*vi-ushti*) is a distinction without a difference. We must, therefore, hold that the dawn which admitted such manifold division for the practical purpose of sacrifice, was a long dawn. The three-fold division of the dawn does not seem to be unknown to the poets of the Rig-Veda. For, in VIII, 41, 3, Varuna's "dear ones are said to have prospered the three dawns for him," and by the phrase *tisrah danuchitrah* in I, 174, 7, "three dew-lighted" dawns appear to be referred to. There are other passages in the Rig-Veda where the dawn is asked not to delay, or tarry long, lest it might be scorched liked a thief by the sun (V, 79, 9); and in II, 15, 6, the steeds of the dawn are said to be (slow) (*ajavasah*), showing that the people were sometimes tired to see the dawn lingering long on the horizon. But a still more remarkable statement is found in I, 113, 13, where the poet distinctly asserts,‡ "the Goddess Ushas dawned continually or perpetually (*shasvat*) in former days (*pura*);" and the adjective *shashvat-tama* (the most lasting) is applied to the dawn in I, 118, 11. Again the very existence and use of two such words as *ushas* and *vi-ushti* is, by itself, a proof of the long duration of the dawn; for, if the dawn was brief, there was no practical necessity of speaking of the full-blown state (*vi+ushti*) of the dawn as has been done several times in the Rig-Veda.

The expression, *ushasah vi-ushtau*, occurs very often in the Rig-Veda and it has been translated by the phrase, on the flashing forth of the dawn." But no one seems to have raised the question why two separate words, one of which is derived from the other simply by prefixing the preposition *vi*, should be used in this connection. Words are made to denote ideas and if *ushas* and *vi-ushti* were not required to denote two distinct phenomena, no one, especially in those early days, would have cared to use a phrase, which, for all ordinary purposes, was superfluously cumbrous. But these facts, howsoever suggestive, may not be regarded as conclusive and we shall, therefore, now turn to the more explicit passages in the hymns regarding the duration of the Vedic dawn.

The first verse I would quote in this connection is Rig-Veda I, 113, 10: *Kiyati a yat samaya bhavati ya vyushuryashcha nunam vyuchhan Anu purvah kripate vavashana pradidhyana josham anyabhir eti*

The first quarter of the verse is rather difficult. The words are *kiyati yat samaya bhavati*, and Sayana, whom Wilson follows, understands *samaya* to mean "near." Prof, Max Muller translates *samaya* (Gr. *Omos*, Lat, *Simul*,) by "together," "at once" while Roth, Grassmann and Aufrecht take *samaya bhavati* as one expression meaning "that which intervenes between the two." This has given rise to three different translations of the verse: WILSON, (following Sayana): For how long a period is it that the dawns have arisen? For how long a period will they rise? Still desirous to bring us light, Ushas pursues the function of those that have gone before and shining brightly, proceeds with the others (that are to follow).

GRIFFITH, (following Max Muller): — How long a time and they shall be together, — Dawns that have shone and Dawns to shine hereafter? She yearns for former Dawns with eager longing and goes forth gladly shining with the others. MUIR, (following Aufrecht): — How great is the interval that lies between the Dawns which have arisen and those which are yet to rise? Ushas yearns longingly after the former Dawns, and gladly goes on shining with the others (that are to come).

But in spite of those different renderings, the meaning of the verse, so far as the question before us is concerned, can be easily gathered.

There are two sets of dawns, one of, those that have past, and the other of those that are yet to shine. If we adopt Wilson's and Griffith's translations, the meaning is that these two classes of dawns, taken together, occupy such a long period of time as to raise the question, — How long they will be together? In other words, the two classes of dawns, taken together, were of such a long duration that men began to question as to when they would terminate, or pass away.

If, on the other hand, we adopt Aufrecht's translation, a, long period appears to have intervened between the past and the coming dawns; or, in other words, there was a long break or hiatus in the regular sequence of these dawns. In the first case, the description is only possible if we suppose that the duration of the dawns was very long, much longer than what we see in the temperate or the tropical zone; while in the second, a long interval between the past and the present dawns must be taken to refer to a long pause, or night, occurring immediately before the second set of dawns commenced their new course, — a phenomenon which is possible only in the Arctic regions.

Thus whichever interpretation we adopt— a long dawn, or a long night between the two sets of dawns, — the description is intelligible, only if we take it to refer to the Polar conditions previously mentioned. The Vedic passages, discussed hereafter, seem, however, to support Sayana's or Max

Muller's view. A number of dawns is spoken of, some past and some yet to come: and the two groups are said to occupy a very long interval. That seems to be the real meaning of the verse. But without laying much stress on any particular meaning for the present, it is enough for our purpose to show that, even adopting Aufrecht's rendering, we cannot escape from the necessity of making the description refer to the Polar conditions.

The verse in question is the tenth in the hymn, and it may be noticed that in the 13th verse of the same hymn we are told that "in former days, perpetually '*shashvat*' did the Goddess Ushas shine," clearly indicating that the Dawn, in early days, lasted for a long time.

The following verse is, however, still more explicit, and decisive on the point. The seventh Mandala of the Rig-Veda contains a number of dawn-hymns. In one of these (VII, 76), the poet, after stating in the first two verses that the Dawns have raised their banner on the horizon with their usual splendour, expressly tells us, (verse 3), that a period of *several days* elapsed between the first appearance of the dawn on the horizon and the actual rising of the sun that followed it. As the verse is very important for our purpose. O Dawn wast seen not again forsaking (woman), like I have followed Sayana in splitting *jara-iva* of *Samhita* text into *jare+iva*, and not *jarah+iva* as Shakala has done in the *Pada* text; for *jare+iva* makes the simile more appropriate than if we were to compare *ushas* with *jarah*. Literally rendered the verse, therefore, means, "Verily, many were those *days* which were aforetime at the uprising of the sun, and about which, O Dawn! thou wast seen moving on, as towards a lover, and not like one (woman) who forsakes." I take *pari* with *yatah*, meaning that the dawn goes after the days. *Yatah pari*, thus construed, means "after which," or "about which." Sayana takes *pari* with *dadrikshe* and Griffith renders *yatah* by "since." But these constructions do not materially alter the meaning of the second half of the verse, though taking *pari* with *yatah* enables us to take the second line as an adjectival clause, rendering the meaning more plain. In IV, 52, 1, the Dawn is said to shine after her sister (*svasuh pari*), and *pari*, with an ablative, does not necessarily denote "from" in every case but is used in various senses, as, for instance, in III, 5, 10, where the phrase *Bhrigubhyah pari* occurs, and is rendered by Grassmann as equivalent to "for the sake of *Bhrigus*," while Sayana paraphrases *pari* by *paritah* "round about."

In the verse under consideration we can, therefore, take *pari* with *yatah* and understand the expression as meaning "after, about or around which (days)." It must also be borne in mind that there must be an expression to correspond with *jare* in the simile and this we get only if we construe *yatah pari* in the way proposed above. If we now analyze the verse it will be found to be made up of three clauses, one principal and two adjectival. The principal statement asserts that those days were many. The demonstrative "those" (*tani*) is them followed by two relative clauses, *ya prachinam* &c., and, *yatah pari* &c.

The first of these states that the days referred to in the principal clause were those that "*preceded* the rising of the sun." But if the days preceded the rising of the sun, one might think that they were pervaded with darkness. The poet, therefore, further adds, in the second relative clause, that though these days were anterior to the rising of the sun, yet they were such that "the Dawn was seen to move after or about them as after a loner, and not like a woman who forsakes." In short, the verse states in unmistakable terms (1) that many days (*bahulani ahani*) passed between the appearance of the first morning beams and sunrise, and (2) that these days were faithfully attended by the Dawn, meaning that the whole period was one of continuous Dawn, which never vanished during the time. The words as they stand convey no other meaning but this, and we have now to see how far it is intelligible to us.

To the commentators the verse is a perfect puzzle. Thus Sayana does not understand how the word "days" (*ahani*) can be applied to a period of time anterior to sunrise; for, says he, "The word day (*ahah*) is used only to denote such a period of time as is invested with light of the Dawn."

Then, again he is obviously at a loss to understand how a number of days can be said to have elapsed between the first beams of the dawn and sunrise. These were serious difficulties for Sayana and the only way to get over them was to force an unnatural sense upon the words, and make them yield some intelligible meaning. This was no difficult task for Sayana. The word *ahani,* which means "days," was the only stumbling block in his way, and instead of taking it in the sense in which it is ordinarily used, without exception, everywhere in the Rig-Veda, he went back to its root-meaning, and interpreted it as equivalent to "light" or "splendour."

Ahan is derived from the root *ah* (or philologically *dah*), "to burn," or "shine," and *Ahana* meaning "dawn" is derived from the same root. Etymologically *ahani* may, therefore, mean splendours; but the question is whether it is so used anywhere, and why we should here give up the ordinary meaning of the word. Sayana's answer is given above. It is because the word "day" (*ahan*) can, according to him, be applied only to a period after sunrise and before sunset. But this reasoning is not sound, because in the Rig-Veda VI, 9, 1, *ahah* is applied to the dark as well as to the bright period of time, for the verse says, "there is a dark day (*ahah*) and a bright day (*ahah*)." This shows that the Vedic poets were in the habit of using the word *ahah* (day) to denote a period of time devoid of the light of the sun. Sayana knew this, and in his commentary on I, 185, 4, he expressly says that the word *ahah* may include night. His real difficulty was different, *viz.*, the impossibility of supposing that a period of several days could have elapsed between the first appearance of light and sunrise, and this difficulty seems to have been experienced even by Western scholars.

Thus Prof. Ludwig materially adopts Sayana's view and interprets the verse to mean that the splendours of the dawn were numerous, and that they appear either before sunrise, or, if *prachinam* be differently interpreted "in the east" at the rising of the sun. Roth and Grassman seem to interpret *prachinam* in the same way. Griffith translates *ahani* by "mornings" and *prachinam* by "aforetime." His rendering of the verse runs thus: — "Great is, in truth, the number of the mornings, which were aforetime at the sun's uprising; since thou, O Dawn, hast been beheld repairing as to thy love, as one no more to leave him."

But Griffith does not explain what he understands by the expression, "a number of mornings which were aforetime at the sun's uprising."

The case is, therefore, reduced to this. The word *ahan*, of which *ahani* (days) is a plural form, can be ordinarily interpreted to mean (1) a period of time between sunrise and sunset; (2) a nycthemeron, as when we speak of 360 days of the year; or (3) a measure of time to mark a period of 24 hours, irrespective of the fact whether the sun is above or below the horizon, as when we speak of the long Arctic night of 30 days. Are we then to abandon all these meanings, and understand *ahani* to mean "splendours" in the verse under consideration?

The only difficulty is to account for the interval of many days between the appearance of the banner of the Dawn on the horizon and the emergence of the sun's orb over it; and this difficulty vanishes if the description be taken to refer to the dawn in the Polar or Circum-Polar regions. That is the real key to the meaning of this and similar other passages which will be noted hereafter; and in its absence a number of artificial devices have been made use of to make these passages somehow intelligible to us. But now nothing of the kind is necessary. As regards the word "days" it has been observed that we often speak "a night of several days," or a "night of several months" when describing the Polar phenomena. In expressions like these the word "day" or "month" simply denotes a measure of time equivalent to "twenty-four hours," or "thirty days;" and there is nothing unusual in the exclamation of the Rig-Vedic poet that "many were the days between the first beams of the dawn and actual sunrise." We have also seen that, at the Pole, it is quite possible to mark the periods of twenty-four hours by the rotations of the celestial sphere or the circum-polar stars, and these could be or rather must have been termed "days" by the inhabitants of the place.

In the first chapter of the Old Testament we were told that God created the heaven and the earth and also light "on the first day," while the sun was created on the fourth "to divide the day from the night and to rule 'the day." Here the word "day" is used to denote a period of time even before the sun was created; and a *fortiori*, there can be no impropriety in using it to denote a period of time before sunrise. We need not, therefore, affect a hypercritical spirit in examining the Vedic expression in question. If Sayana did it, it was because he did not know as much about the Polar regions as we now do. We have no such excuse and must, therefore, accept the meaning which follows from the natural construction and reading of the sentence.

It is therefore clear that the verse in question (VII, 76, 3) expressly describes a dawn continuously lasting for many days, which is possible only in the Arctic regions. I have discussed the passage at so much length because the history of its interpretation clearly shows how certain passages in the Rig-Veda, which are unintelligible to us in spite of their simple diction, have been treated by commentators, who know not what to make of them if read in a natural way. But to proceed with the subject in hand, we have seen that the Polar dawn could be divided into periods of 24 hours owing to the circuits it makes round the horizon. In such a case we can very well speak of these divisions as so many day-long dawns of 24 hours each and state that so many of them are past and so many are yet to come, as has been done in the verse (I, 113, 10) discussed above.

We may also say that so many day-long dawns have passed and yet the sun has not risen, as in II, 28, 9, a verse addressed to Varuna wherein the poet asks for the following boon from the deity:

Para rina savir adha mat-kritani ma aham rajan anya-kritena bhojam I

Avyushta in nu bhuyasir ushasa a no jivan Varuna tasu shadhi I I

Literally translated this means "Remove far the debts (sins) incurred by me. May I not, O King! be affected by others' doings.

Verily, many dawns (have) not fully (*vi*) flashed forth. O Varuna! direct that we may be alive during them." The first part of this verse contains a prayer usually addressed to Gods, and we have nothing to say with respect to it, so far as the subject in hand is concerned. The only expression necessary to be discussed is *bhuyasih ushasah avyushtah* in third quarter of the verse. The first two words present no difficulty. They mean "many dawns." Now *avyushta* is a negative participle from *vyushta,* which again is derived from *ushta* with *vi* prefixed.

I have referred to the distinction between *ushas* and *vyushti* suggested by the threefold or the five-fold division of the dawn. *Vyushti,* according to the Taittiriya Brahmana, means "day," or rather "the flashing forth of the dawn into sunrise" and the word *a+vi+ushta*, therefore, means "not-fullyflashed-forth into sunrise." But Sayana and others do not seem to have kept in view this distinction between the meanings of *ushas* and *vyushti*; or if they did, they did not know or had not in their mind the phenomenon of the long continuous dawn in the Arctic regions, a dawn, that lasted for several day-long periods of time before the sun's orb appeared on the horizon. The expression, *bhuyasih ushasah avyushtah*, which literally means "many dawns have not dawned, or fully flashed forth," was therefore a riddle to these commentators.

Every dawn, they saw, was followed by sunrise; and they could not, therefore, understand how "many dawns" could be described as "notfully-flashed-forth." An explanation was thus felt to be a necessity and this was obtained by converting, in sense, the past passive participle *avyushta* into a future participle; and the expression in question was translated as meaning, "during the dawns (or days) that have not *yet* dawned " or, in other words, "in days to come." But the interpretation is on the face of it strained and artificial. If future days were intended, the idea could have been more easily and briefly expressed. The poet is evidently speaking of things present, and, taking *vi-ushta* to denote what it literally signifies, we can easily and naturally interpret the expression to mean that though *many* dawns, meaning *many* daylong portions of time during which the dawn lasted, have passed, yet it is not*vyushta,* that is the sun's orb has not yet emerged from below the horizon and that Varuna should protect the worshipper under the circumstances.

There are many other expressions in the Rig-Veda which further strengthen the same view. Thus corresponding to *bhuyasih* in the above passage, we have the adjective *purvih* (many) used in IV, 19, 8 and VI, 28, 1, to denote the number of dawns, evidently showing that numerically more than one dawn is intended. The dawns are again not un-frequently addressed in the plural number in the Rig-Veda, and the fact is wellknown to all Vedic scholars. Thus in I, 92, which is a dawn-hymn, the bard opens his song with the characteristically emphatic exclamation "these (*etah*) are those (*tyah*) dawns (*ushasah*), which have made their appearance on the horizon," and the same expression again occurs in VII, 78, 3. Yaska explains the plural number *ushasah* by considering it to be used only honorifically (Nirukta XII, 7); while Sayana interprets it as referring to the number of divinities that preside over the morn.

The Western scholars have not made any improvement on these explanations and Prof. Max Muller is simply content with observing that the Vedic bards, when speaking of the dawn, did sometimes use the plural just as we would use the singular number! But a little reflection will show that neither of these explanations is satisfactory. If the plural is honorific why is it changed into singular only a few lines after in the same hymn? Surely the poet does not mean to address the Dawn respectfully only at the outset and then change his manner of address and assume a familiar tone.

This is not however, the only objection to Yaska's explanation. Various similes are used by the Vedic poets to describe the appearance of the dawns on the horizon and an examination of these similes will convince any one that the plural number, used in reference to the Dawn, cannot be merely honorific. Thus in the second line of I, 92, 1, the Dawns are compared to a number of "warriors" (*dhrishnavah*) and in the third verse of the same hymn they are likened to "women (*narih*) active in their occupations."

They are said to appear on the horizon like "waves of waters" (*apam na urmayah*) in VI, 64, 1, or like "pillars planted at a sacrifice" (*adhvareshu svaravah*) in IV, 51, 2. We are again told that they work like "men arrayed" (*visho na yuktah*), or advance like "troops of cattle" (*gavam na sargah*) in VII, 79, 2, and IV, 51, 8, respectively. They are described as all "alike" (*sadrishih*) and are said to be of "one mind" (*sanjanante*), or "acting harmoniously" IV, 51, 6, and VII, 76,

5. In the last verse the poet again informs us that they "do not strive against each other" (*mithah na yatante*), though they live jointly in the "same enclosure" (*samane urve*).

Finally in X, 88, 18, the poet distinctly asks the question, "How many fires, how many suns and how many dawns (*ushasah*) are there?" If the Dawn were addressed in plural simply out of respect for the deity, where was the necessity of informing us that they do not quarrel though collected in the same place?

The expressions "waves of waters," or "men arrayed" &c., are again too definite to be explained away as honorific. Sayana seems to have perceived this difficulty and has, probably for the same reason, proposed an explanation slightly different from that of Yaska. But, unfortunately, Sayana's explanation does not solve the difficulty, as the question still remains why the deities presiding over the dawn should be more than one in number. The only other explanation put forward, so far as I know, is that the plural number refers to the dawns on successive days during the year, as we perceive them in the temperate or the tropical zone. On this theory there would be 360 dawns in a year, each followed by the rising of the sun every day. This explanation may appear plausible at the first sight. But on a closer examination t will be found that the expressions used in the hymns cannot be made to reconcile with this theory.

For, if 360 dawns, all separated by intervals of 24 hours, were intended by the plural number used in the Vedic verses, no poet, with any propriety, would speak of them as he does in I, 92, 1, by using the double pronoun *etah* and *tyah* as if he was pointing out to a physical phenomenon before him; nor can we understand how 360 dawns, spread over the whole year, can be described as advancing like "men arrayed" for battle. It is again absurd to describe the 360 dawns of the year as being collected in the "same enclosure" and "not striving against or quarrelling with each other." We are thus forced to the conclusion that the Rig-Veda speaks of a team or a group of dawns, unbroken or uninterrupted by sunlight, so that if we be so minded, we can regard them as constituting a single long continuous dawn. This is in perfect accord with the statement discussed above, *viz.*, that many days passed between the first appearance of light on the horizon and the uprising of the sun (VII, 76, 3).

We cannot, therefore, accept the explanation of consecutive dawns, nor that of Yaska, nor of Sayana regarding the use of the plural number in this case. The fact is that the Vedic dawn represents one long physical phenomenon which can be spoken of in plural by supposing it to be split up into smaller day-long portions. It is thus that we find Ushas addressed sometimes in the plural and sometimes in the singular number. There is no other explanation on which we can account for and explain the various descriptions of the dawn found in the different hymns.

But to clinch the matter, the Taittiriya Samhita, IV, 3, 11, expressly states that the dawns are thirty sisters, or, in other words, they are thirty in number and that they go round and round in five groups, reaching the same appointed place and having the same banner for all. The whole of this *Anuvaka* may be said to be practically a dawn-hymn of 15 verses, which are used as Mantras for the laying down of certain emblematical bricks called the "dawnbricks" on the sacrificial altar. There are sixteen such bricks to be placed on the altar, and the *Anuvaka* in question gives 15 Mantras, or verses, to be used on the occasion, the 16th being recorded elsewhere.

These 15 verses, together with their Brahmana (T.S.V, 3, 4, 7), are so important for our purpose, that I have appended to this chapter the original passages, with their translation, comparing the version in the Taittiriya Samhita with that of the Atharva-Veda, in the case of those verses which are found in the latter. The first verse of the section or the *Anuvaka*, is used for laying down the first dawnbrick and it speaks only of a single dawn first appearing on the horizon. In the second verse we have, however, a couple of dawns mentioned as "dwelling in the same abode." A third dawn is, spoken in the third verse, followed by the fourth and the fifth dawn.

The five dawns are then said to have five sisters each, exclusive of themselves, thus raising the total number of dawns to thirty. These "thirty sisters" (*trimhshat svasarah*) are then described as "going round" (*pari yanti*) in groups of six each, keeping up to the same goal (*nishkritam*). Two verses later on, the worshipper asks that he and his follower should be blessed with the same concord as is observed amongst these dawns. We are then told that one of these five principal dawns is the child of Rita, the second upholds the greatness of Waters the third moves in the region of Surya, the fourth in that of Fire or Gharma, and the fifth is ruled by Saviti, evidently showing that the dawns are not the dawns of consecutive days. The last verse of the *Anuvaka* sums up the description by stating that the dawn, though it shines forth in various forms, is but *one* in reality. Throughout the whole *Anuvaka* there is no mention of the rising of the sun or the appearance of sunlight, and the *Brahmana* makes the point clear by stating, "There was a time, when all this was neither day nor night, being in an undistinguishable state.

It was *then* that the Gods perceived these dawns and laid them down, *then* there was light; therefore, it brightens to him and destroys his darkness for whom these (dawn-bricks) are placed." The object of this passage is to explain how and why the dawn-bricks came to be laid down with these Mantras, and it gives the ancient story of thirty dawns being perceived by the Gods, not on consecutive days, but during the period of time when it was neither night nor day. This, joined with the express statement at the end of the *Anuvaka* that in reality it is but one dawn, is sufficient to prove that the thirty dawns mentioned in the *Anuvaka* were continuous and not consecutive. But, if a still more explicit authority be needed it will be found in the Taittiriya Brahmana, II, 5, 6, 5. This is an old Mantra, and not a portion of the explanatory *Brahmana*, and is, therefore, as good an authority as, any of the verses quoted above. It is addressed to the dawns and means, "These very Dawns are those that first shone forth, the Goddesses make five forms; eternal (*shashvatih*), (they) are not separated (*na avaprijyanti*), nor do (they) terminate (*na gamanti antam*)."

The "five forms" here referred to correspond with the division of 30 dawns into 5 groups of 6 each, made in the Taittiriya Samhita, after the manner of sacrificial *shal-ahas*, or groups of six days; and we are expressly told that the dawns, which make these 5 forms, are continuous, unseparated, or uninterrupted. In the Rig-Veda I, 152, 4, the garment of the lover of the dawns (*lit.* the maidens, *kaninam jaram*) is described as "inseparable" and "wide" (*an-avaprigna* and *vitata*), and reading this in the light of the aforesaid Mantra from the Taittiriya Brahmana we are led to conclude that in the Rig-Veda itself the dawny garment of the sun, or the garment, which the dawns, as mothers, weave for him (cf. V, 47, 6), is considered as "wide" and "continuous." Translated into common language this means that the dawn described in the Rig-Veda was a long and continuous phenomenon. In the Atharva-Veda (VII, 22, 2) the dawns are described as *sachetasah* and *samichih*, which means that they are "harmonious" and "walk together" and not separately.

The first expression is found in the Rig-Veda, but not the second, though it could be easily inferred, from the fact that the dawns are there described as "collected in the same enclosure." Griffith renders *samichih* by "a closely gathered band" and translates the verse thus: "The Bright one hath sent forth the Dawns, a closely gathered band, immaculate, unanimous, brightly refulgent in their homes."

Here all the adjectives of the dawns clearly indicate a group of undivided dawns acting harmoniously; and yet strange to say Griffith, who translates correctly misses the spirit altogether. We have thus sufficient direct authority for holding that it is a "team," or in Griffith's words, "a closely gathered band" of thirty continuous dawns that is described in the Vedic hymns, and not the evanescent dawn of the temperate or the tropical zone, either single or as a series of consecutive dawns. It is interesting to examine how Sayana explains the existence of as many as thirty dawns, before we proceed to other authorities.

In his commentary on the Taittiriya Samhita IV, 3, 11, he tells us that the first dawn spoken of in the first verse in the *Anuvaka*, is the dawn at the beginning of the creation, when everything was undistinguishable according to the *Brahmana*. The second dawn in the second verse is said to be the ordinary dawn that we see every day. So far it was all right; but the number of dawns soon outgrew the number of the kinds of dawn known to Sayana. The third, fourth and fifth verses of the *Anuvaka* describe three more dawns, and Sayana was at last forced to explain that though the dawn was one yet by its Yogic or occult powers it assumed these various shapes! But the five dawns multiplied into thirty sisters in the next verse, and Sayana finally adopted the explanation that thirty separate dawns represented the thirty consecutive dawns of one month. But why only thirty dawns of one month out of 360 dawns of a year should thus be selected in these Mantras is nowhere explained. The explanations, besides being mutually inconsistent, again conflict with the last verse in the *Anuvaka* with the *Brahmana* or the explanation given in the Samhita itself, and with the passage from the Taittiriya Brahmana quoted above.

But Sayana was writing under a firm belief that the Vedic dawn was the same as he and other Vedic scholars like Yaska perceived it in the tropical zone; and the wonder is, not that he has given us so many contradictory explanations, but that he has been able to suggest so many apparently plausible explanations as the exigencies of the different Mantras required. In the light of advancing knowledge about the nature of the dawn at the North Pole, and the existence of man on earth before the last Glacial epoch We should, therefore, have no hesitation in accepting more intelligible and rationalistic view of the different passages descriptive of the dawns in the Vedic literature. We are sure Sayana himself would have welcomed a theory more comprehensive and reasonable than any advanced by him, if the same could have been suggested to him in his own day. Jyotish or astronomy has always been considered to be the "eye of the Veda," and as with the aid of the telescope this eye now commands a wider range than previously, it will be our own fault if we fail to utilize the knowledge so gained to elucidate those portions of our sacred books which are still unintelligible. But to proceed with the subject, it may be urged that it is only the Taittiriya Samhita that gives us the number of the dawns, and that it would not be proper to mix up these statements with the statements contained in the hymns of the Rig-Veda, and draw a conclusion from both taken together. The Taittiriya Samhita treats of sacrificial rites and the Mantras relating to the dawn-bricks may not be regarded as being originally connected. The fact that only some-of these are found in the Atharva-Veda Samhita, might lend some support to this view. But a critical study of the *Anuvaka*, will remove all these doubts.

The "thirty sisters" are not mentioned one by one, leaving it to the hearer, or the reader, to make up the total, and ascertain the final number for himself. The sixth verse in the *Anuvaka* expressly mentions "the thirty sisters" and is, by itself, sufficient to prove that in ancient days the number of dawns was considered to be thirty. But if an authority from the Rig-Veda be still needed, we have it in VI, 59, 6, where Dawn is described as having traversed "thirty steps" (*trimshat padani akramit*). This statement has, as yet, remained unexplained.

"A single dawn traversing thirty steps" is but a paraphrase of the statement refers very probably to the same fact. that "dawns are thirty sisters, keeping to the same goal in their circuits." Another verse which has not yet been satisfactorily explained is the Rig-Veda I, 123, 8. It says "The dawns, alike today and alike tomorrow, dwell long in the abode of Varuna. Blameless, they forthwith go round (*pari yanti*) thirty *yojanas*; each its destined course (*kratum*)." The first half of the verse presents no difficulty. In the second we are told that the dawns go round thirty *yojanas*, each following its own "plan," which is the meaning of *kratu*, according to the Petersberg Lexicon. But the phrase "thirty *yojanas*" has not been as yet satisfactorily explained. Griffith following M. Bergaigne understands it to mean thirty regions or spaces, indicating the whole universe; but there is no authority for this meaning. Sayana, whom Wilson follows, gives an elaborate astronomical explanation. He says that the sun's rays precede his rising and are visible when the sun is below the horizon by thirty *yojanas*, or; in other words, the dawn is in advance of the sun by that distance. When dawns are, therefore, said to traverse thirty *yojanas*, Sayana understands by it the astronomical phenomenon of the dawn illumining a space of thirty *yojanas* in advance of the sun, and, that when the dawn, at one place, is over, it is to be found in another place, occupying a space of thirty *yojanas* in that place. The explanation is very ingenious; and Sayana also adds that the dawns are spoken of in the plural number in the verse under consideration, because the dawns at different places on the surface of the earth, brought on by the daily motion of the sun, are intended.

But unfortunately the explanation cannot stand scientific scrutiny. Sayana says that the sun travels 5,059 *yojanas* round the Meru in 24 hours; and as Meru means the earth and the circumference of the earth is now known to be about 24,377 miles, a *yojana* would be about 4.9, or in round number, about 5 miles. Thirty such *yojanas* will, therefore, be 150 miles; while the first beams of the dawn greet us on the horizon when the sun is not less than 16º below the horizon. Taking one degree equal to 60 miles, 16º would mean 960 miles, a distance far in excess of the thirty *yojanas* of Sayana. Another objection to

Sayana's explanation is that the Vedic bard is evidently speaking of a phenomenon present before him, and not mentally following the astronomical dawns at different places produced by the daily rotation of the earth on its axis. The explanation is again inapplicable to "thirty steps (padani)" of the dawn expressly mentioned in VI, 59, 6. Therefore, the only alternative left is, to take the phrases "thirty *yojanas*," "thirty sisters," and "thirty steps" as different versions of one and the same fact, *viz.*, the circuits of the dawn along the Polar horizon. The phrase "each its destined course" also becomes intelligible in this case, for though thirty dawns complete thirty rounds, each may well be described as following its own definite course.

The words *pari yanti* in the text literally apply to a circular (*pari*) motion, (cf. the words *pari-ukshanam, paristaranam,* &c.); and the same term is used in the Taittiriya Samhita with reference to "thirty sisters." The word *yojana* primarily means "a chariot" (VIII, 72, 6) and then it came to denote "distance to be accomplished with unharnessing the horses," or what we, in the vernacular, call a "*tappa*." Now this *tappa*, or "the journey to be accomplished without unharnessing the horse," may be a day's journey and Prof. Max Muller has in one place interpreted the *yojana* in this way. In V, 54, 5, the Maruts are said "to have extended their greatness as far as the sun extends his daily course," and the word in the original for "daily course" is *yojanum*. Accepting this meaning, we can interpret the expression "the dawns forth with go round (*pari yanti*) thirty *yojanas*" to mean that the dawns complete thirty daily rounds as at the North Pole. That circular motion is here intended is further evident from 111, 61, 3, which says, in distinct terms, "Wending towards the same goal (*samanam artham*), O Newly-born (Dawn)! turn on like a wheel (*ckakramiva a vavritsva*)." Although the word *navyasi* (newly-born) is here in the vocative case, yet the meaning is that the dawn, ever anew or becoming new every day, revolves like a wheel. Now a wheel may either move in a perpendicular plane, like the wheel of a chariot, or in a horizontal plane like the potter's wheel.

But the first of these two motions cannot be predicated of the dawn anywhere on the surface of the earth. The light of the morning is, everywhere, confined to the horizon, as described in the Rig-Veda, VII, 80, 1, which speaks of the dawns as "unrolling the two *rajasi*, which border on each other (*samante*), and revealing all things." No dawn, whether in the rigid, the temperate, or the tropical zone can, therefore, be seen travelling, like the sun, from east to west, over the head of the observer in a perpendicular plane. The only possible wheel-like motion is, therefore, along the horizon and this can be witnessed only in regions near the Pole. A dawn in the temperate or the tropical zone is visible only for a short time on the eastern horizon and is swallowed up, in the same place by the rays of the rising sun.

It is only in the Polar regions that we see the morning lights revolving along the horizon for some day-long periods of time, and if the wheellike motion of the dawn, mentioned in III, 61, 3, has any meaning at all, we must take it to refer to the revolving splendours of the dawn in the Arctic regions previously described. The expressions "reaching the appointed place (*nish-kritam*) day by day" (I, 123, 9), and "wending ever and ever to the same goal" (111, 61, 3) are also illsuited to describe the dawn in latitudes below the Arctic circle, but if we take these expressions to refer to the Polar dawn they become not only intelligible, but peculiarly appropriate, as such a dawn in its daily circuits must come to the point from which it started every twenty-four hours. All these passages taken together, therefore, point only to one conclusion and that is that both the Rig-Veda and the Taittiriya Samhita describe a long and continuous dawn divided into thirty dawn-days, or periods of twenty four hours each, a characteristic found only in the Polar dawn.

There are a number of other p ıssages where the dawn is spoken of in the plural, especially in the case of matutinal deities, who are said to follow or come after not a single dawn but dawns in the plural (I, 6, 3; I, 180, 1; V, 76, 1; VII, 9, 1; VII, 63, 3). These passages have been hitherto understood as describing the appearance of the deities after the consecutive dawns of the year. But now a new light is thrown upon them by the conclusion established above from the examination of the different passages about the dawn in the Rig-Veda, the Taittiriya and the Atharva Veda Samhita.

It may, however, be mentioned that I do not mean to say that in the whole of the Rig-Veda not a single reference can be found to the dawn of the tropical or the temperate zone. The Veda which mentions a year of 360 days is sure to mention the evanescent dawn which accompanies these days in regions to the south of the Arctic circle. A greater part of the description of the dawn is again of such a character that we can apply it either to the long Polar dawn, or to the short-lived dawn of the tropics. Thus both may be said to awaken every living being (I, 92, 9,) or disclose the treasures concealed by darkness (I, 123, 4).

Similarly when dawns of different days are said to depart and come, a new sister succeeding each day to the sister previously vanished (I, 124, 9), we my either suppose that the consecutive dawns of different days are intended, or that a number of day-long dawns, which succeed one another after every 24 hours at the Pole, were in the mind of the poet. These passages do not, therefore, in any way affect the conclusion we have arrived at above by the consideration of the *special* characteristics of the dawns mentioned in the hymns. What we mean to prove is that Ushas, or the Goddess of the first appearance of which formed the subject of so many beautiful hymns in the Vedic literature, is not the evanescent dawn of the tropics but the long continuous and revolving dawn of the pole; and if we have succeeded in proving this from the passages discussed above, it matters little if a pass age or more are found elsewhere in the Rig-Veda, describing the ordinary tropical dawn.

The Vedic Rishis who sang the present hymns, must have been familiar with the tropical dawn if they now and then added a 13th month to secure the correspondence of the lunar and the solar year. But the deity of the Dawn was an ancient deity, the attributes of which had become known to the Rishis by orally preserved traditions, about the primeval home; and the dawn-hymns, as we now possess them, faithfully describe these characteristics. How these old characteristics of the Goddess of Dawn were preserved for centuries is a question to which I shall revert after examining the whole of the Vedic evidence bearing on the Polar theory. For the present we may assume that these reminiscences of the old home were preserved much in the same way as we have preserved the hymns, accent for accent and letter for letter, for the last three or four thousand years.

It will be seen from foregoing discussion that if the dawn-hymns in the Rig-Veda be read and studied in the light of modern scientific discoveries and with the aid of passages in the Atharva Veda and the Taittiriya Samhita and Brahmana they clearly establish the following results:

(1) The Rig-Vedic dawn was so long that *several days* elapsed between the first appearance of light on the horizon and the sunrise which followed it, (VII, 76, 3); or, as described in 11, 28, 9, many dawns appeared one after another before they ripened into sunrise.

(2) The Dawn was addressed in the plural number not honorifically, nor as representing the consecutive dawns of the Year, but because it was made up of *thirty parts* (I; 123, 8; VI, 59, 6; T.S., IV, 3, 11, 6).

(3) Many dawns *lived in the same place, acted harmoniously* and *never quarreled* with each other, IV, 51, 7-9; VII, 76, 5; A.V. VII, 22, 2).

(4) The *thirty parts* of the dawn were *continuous* and *inseparable,* forming "a closely gathered band," or "a group of dawns," (I, 152, 4; T. Br. II, 5, 6, 5; A.V. VII, 22, 2).

(5) These thirty dawns, or thirty parts of one dawn *revolved round and round like a wheel,* reaching the same goal every day, each dawn or part following its own destined course, (I, 123, 8, 9; III, 61, 3; T.S. IV, 3, 11, 6).

These characteristics it is needless to say are possessed only by the dawn at or near the Pole. The last or the fifth especially is to be found only in lands very near the North Pole and not everywhere in the Arctic regions. We may, therefore, safely conclude that the Vedic Goddess of Dawn is Polar in origin. But it may be urged that while th · Polar-dawn lasts from 45 to 60 days, the Vedic dawn is described only as made up of thirty day-long parts, and that the discrepancy must be accounted for before we accept the conclusion that the Vedic dawn is Polar in character. The discrepancy is not, however, a serious one. We have seen that the duration of the dawn depends upon the powers of refraction and reflection of the atmosphere; and that these again vary according to the temperature of the place, or other meteorological conditions. It is, therefore, not unlikely that the duration of the dawn at the Pole, when the climate there was mild and genial, might be somewhat shorter than what we may expect it to be at present when the climate is severely cold. It is more probable, however, that the dawn described in the Rig-Veda is not exactly such a dawn as may be seen by an observer stationed precisely at the North Pole.

As observed previously, the North Pole is a point, and if men lived near the Pole in early days, they must have lived somewhat to the south of this point. Within this tract it is quite possible to have 30 day-long dawns revolving, like a wheel, after the long Arctic night of four or five months; and, so far as astronomy is concerned, there is, therefore, nothing improbable in the description of the Dawn found in the Vedic literature. We must also bear in mind that the Vedic Dawn often tarried longer on the horizon, and the worshippers asked her not to delay lest the sun might search her like an enemy (V, 79, 9).

This shows that though 30 days was the usual duration of the Dawn it was sometimes exceeded, and people grew impatient to see the light of the sun. It was in cases likes these, that Indra, the God who created the dawns and was their friend, was obliged to break the car of the dawn and bring the sun above the horizon (II, 15, 6; X, 73, 6).

There are other places in which the same legend is referred to (IV, 30, 8), and the obscuration of the Dawn by a thunderstorm is, at present, supposed to be the basis of this myth. But the explanation, like others of its kind, is on the face of it unsatisfactory.

That a thunderstorm should occur just at the time of the dawn would be a mere accident, and it is improbable that it could have been made the basis of a legend.

Again, it is not the obscuration, but the delaying of the Dawn, or its tarrying longer on the horizon than usual, that is referred to in the legend, and we can better account for it on the Polar theory, because the duration of dawn, though usually of 30 days, might have varied at different places according to latitude and climatic conditions, and Indra's bolt was thus needed to check these freaks of the Dawn and make way for the rising sun. There are other legends connected with the Dawn and the matutinal deities on which the Polar theory throws quite a new light; but these will be taken up in the chapter on Vedic myths, after the whole direct evidence in support of the theory is examined.

But if the Vedic dawn is Polar in origin, the ancestors of the Vedic bards must have witnessed it, not in the Post-Glacial, but in the Pre-Glacial era; and it may be finally asked why a reference to this early age is not found in the hymns before us?

Fortunately the hymns do preserve a few indications of the time when these long dawns appeared. Thus, in I, 113, 13, we are told that the Goddess Dawn shone perpetually in *former* days (*pura*) and here the word *pura* does not mean the foregone days of this *kalpa*, but rather refers to a by-gone age, or *pura kalpa* as in the passage from the Taittiriya Samhita (I, 5, 7, 5), quoted and discussed in the next chapter.

The word *prathama*, in the Taittiriya Samhita, IV, 3, 11, 1 and the Taittiriya Brahmana, II, 5, 6, 5, does not again mean simply "first in order," but refers to "ancient times," as when Indra's "first" or "oldest" exploits are mentioned in 1, 32, 1, or when certain practices are said to be "first" or "old" in X, 90, 16. It is probable that it was this import of the word *prathama* that led Sayana to propose that the first dawn, mentioned in the Taittiriya Samhita IV, 3, 11, represented the dawn at the beginning of the creation. The Vedic poets could not but have been conscious that the Mantras they used to lay down the dawn-bricks were inapplicable to the dawn as they saw it, and the Taittiriya Samhita (V, 3, 4, 7), which explains the Mantras, clearly states that this story or the description of the dawns is a tradition of old times when the Gods perceived the thirty dawns.

It is not, therefore, correct to say that there are no references in the Vedic hymns to the time when these long dawns were visible. We shall revert to the point later on, when further evidence on the subject will be noticed and discussed. The object of the present chapter was to examine the *duration* of the Vedic dawn, the Goddess of the morning, the subject of so many beautiful hymns in the Rig-Veda, and to show that the deity is invested with Polar characteristics. The evidence in support of this view has been fully discussed; and we shall, therefore, now take up the other Polar and Circum-Polar tests previously mentioned, anti see whether we can find out further evidence from the Rig-Veda to strengthen our conclusions.

LONG DAY AND LONG NIGHT

At the point when a long consis.ent first light of thirty days, or a closelygathered band of thirty day breaks, is appeared to have been explicitly alluded to in the Vedic writing, the taxing night going before such a day break takes after as per normal procedure; and where a difficult night wins, it must have a taxing day to match it amid the year.

The rest of the parcel of the year, in the wake of deducting the time of the taxing night, the taxing day and the long morning and night dusks, would likewise be described by a progression of conventional days and evenings, a day and night together failing to exceed twenty-four hours, however, inside the point of confinement, the day may step by step increase throughout the night at one time and the night over the course of the day at another, delivering an assortment of customary days and evenings of various lengths. Every one of these marvels are so associated cosmically that in the event that one of them is set up, the others take after as an issue of logical induction.

Along these lines, if the long span of the Vedic sunrise is once illustrated, it is, cosmically, superfluous to hunt down additional confirmation with respect to the presence of long days and evenings in the Rig-Veda. Yet, as we are managing a condition of things which existed a few thousand years prior, and with confirmation, which, however generally passed on, has not yet been translated in the way we have done, it is more secure to treat, practically speaking, the previously mentioned cosmic wonders as detached truths, and independently gather prove bearing on every, keeping the galactic association for possible later use till we come to consider the aggregate impact of the entire proof in support of the few actualities said above. I don't intend to infer that there is any vulnerability in the connection of arrangement between the above cosmic actualities. In actuality, nothing can be more sure than such an arrangement. Be that as it may, in gathering and looking at the proof bearing on realities like those under thought, it is constantly fitting by and by to gather however much confirmation and from the greatest number of various perspectives as could reasonably be expected.

In this and the accompanying two sections, we, thusly, propose to look at independently the proof that can be found in the Vedic writing about the taxing day, the taxing night, the quantity of months of daylight and of obscurity, and the character of the year, and check whether it unveils qualities discovered just at, or around, the North Pole. What's more, first in regards to the difficult night, — a night of a few days' span, for example, makes the northern scopes excessively cool or uncomfortable for human residence at present, however which, in interglacial times, seemed to have brought about no further bother than what may come about because of obscurity, long and ceaseless haziness for various days, however, without anyone else, it was not an attractive condition of things, and the end of which more likely than not been enthusiastically searched for by men who needed to experience such experience. There are numerous entries in the Rig-Veda that talk about long and horrendous haziness, in some shape, which shielded the foes of Indra, and to annihilate which Indra needed to battle with the evil spirits or the Dasas, whose fortresses are all said to be covered in this obscurity. Along these lines in I, 32, 10, Vitra, the customary adversary of Indra, is said to be inundated in long dimness (dirgham tamah ashayad Indrashatruh), and in V, 32, 5, Indra is portrayed as having put Shushna who was on edge to battle, in "the obscurity, of the pit" (tamasi harmye), while the following verse discusses asurye tamasi (lit. sunless murkiness), which Max Muller renders by "shocking haziness."

Regardless of these entries the battle amongst Vritra and Indra is thought to be a day by day and not a yearly battle, a hypothesis the legitimacy of which will be analyzed when we go to the examination of Vedic myths. For the present it is adequate to note that the above expressions lose all their appropriateness, if the obscurity, in which the different foes of Indra are said to have thrived, be taken to be the conventional murkiness of twelve, or, best case scenario, of twenty-four hours' span. It was, in actuality, a long and a loathsome or sunless, obscurity, which exhausted every one of the forces of Indra and his partner Gods to overcome.

However, aside from this unbelievable battle, there are different verses in the Rig-Veda which clearly show the presence of a night longer than the longest cis-Arctic night. In any case the Vedic versifiers are seen much of the time conjuring their divinities to discharge them from haziness.

Thus in II, 27, 14, the poet says, "Aditi, Mitra and also Varuna forgive if we have committed any sin against you! May I obtain the wide fearless light, O Indra! May not the long darkness comeover us." The expression in the original for "long darkness" is *dirghah tamisrah*, and means rather an "uninterrupted succession of dark nights (*tamisrah*)" than simply "long darkness." But even adopting Max Muller's rendering given above† the anxiety here manifested for the disappearance of the long darkness is unmeaning, if the darkness never lasted for more than twenty-four hours. In I, 46, 6, the Ashvins are asked "to vouchsafe such strength to the worshipper as may carry him through darkness"; and in VII, 67 a the poet exclaims: "The fire has commenced to burn, the ends of darkness have been seen, and the banner of the Dawn has appeared in the cast!" The expression "ends of darkness" (*tamasah antah*) is very peculiar, and it would be a violation of idiom to take this and other expressions indicating "long darkness" to mean nothing more than long winter nights, as we have them in the temperate or the tropical zone. As stated previously the longest winter night in these zones must be, at best, a little short of twenty-four hours, and even then these long nights prevail only for a fortnight or so. It is, therefore, very unlikely that Vedic bards perpetuated the memory of these long nights by making it a grievance of such importance as to require the aid of their deities to relieve them from it.

There are other passages where the same longing for the end of darkness or for the appearance of light is expressed, and these cannot be accounted for on the theory that to the, old Vedic bards night was as death, since they had no means which a civilized person in the twentieth century possesses, of dispelling the darkness of night by artificial illumination. Even the modern savages are not reported to be in the habit of exhibiting such impatience for the morning light as we find in the utterances of the Vedic bards; and yet the latter were so much advanced in civilization as to know the use of metals and carriages. Again not only men, but Gods, are said to have lived in long darkness. Thus, in X, 124, I, Agni is told that he has stayed "*too long* in the *long* darkness," the phrase used being *jyog eva dirgham tama ashayishtah*. This double phrase *jyog* (long) *dirgham* is still more inappropriate, if the duration of darkness never exceeded that of the longest winter-night. In II, 2, 2, the same deity, Agni, is said to shine during "continuous nights," which, according to Max Muller, is the meaning of the word *kshapah* in the original. The translation is no doubt correct, but Prof. Max Muller does not explain to us what he means by the phrase "continuous nights." Does it signify a succession of nights uninterrupted by sun-light? or, is it only an elegant rendering, meaning nothing more than a number of nights?

The learned translator seems to have narrowly missed the true import of the phrase employed by him. But we need not depend on stray passages like the above to prove that the long night was known in early days. In the tenth Mandala of the Rig-Veda we have a hymn (127) addressed to the Goddess of night and in the 6th verse of this hymn Night is invoked to "become easily fordable" to the worshipper (*nah sutara bhava).* In the Parishishta, which follows this hymn in the Rig-Veda and which is known as *Ratri-sukta* or *Durga-stava*, the worshipper asks the Night to be favourable to him, exclaiming "May we reach the other side in safety!

May we reach the: other side in safety!"† In the Atharva-Veda, XIX, 47, which is a reproduction, with some variations, of the above Parishishta, the second verse runs thus. "Each moving thing finds rest in her (Night), *whose yonder boundary is not seen, nor that which keeps her separate.* O spacious, darksome night! May we, uninjured, reach the end of thee, reach, O thou blessed one, thine end!" And in the third verse of the 50th hymn of the same book the worshippers ask that they may pass uninjured in their body, "through each succeeding night, (*ratrim ratrim*)." Now a question is naturally raised why should every one be so anxious about safely reaching the other end of the night? And why should the poet exclaim that "its yonder boundary is nor seen, nor what keeps it separate?" Was it because it was an ordinary winter night, or, was it because it was the long Arctic night? Fortunately, the Taittiriya Samhita preserves for us the oldest traditional reply to these questions and we need not, therefore, depend upon the speculations of modern commentators. In the Taittiriya Samhita I, 5, 5, 4, we have a similar Mantra or prayer addressed to Night in these words:— "O Chitravasu! let me safely reach thy end.. A little further (I, 5, 7, 5), the Samhita itself explains this Mantra, or prayer thus: — "Chitravasu is (means) the night; in old times (*pura*), the Brahmans (priests) were afraid that it (night) would not dawn." Here we have an express Vedic statement, that in old times, the priests or the people, felt apprehensions regarding the time when the night would end. What does it signify? If the night was not unusually long, where was the necessity for entertaining any misgivings about the coming dawn?

Sayana, in commenting on the above passage, has again put forward his usual explanation, that nights in the winter were long and they made the priest apprehensive in regard to the coming dawn. But here we can quote Sayana against himself, and show that he has dealt with this important passage in an off hand manner. It is well-known that the Taittiriya Samhita often explains the Mantras, and this portion of the Samhita is called Bramana, the whole of the Taittiriya Samhita being made up in this way of Mantras and the Brahmana, or prayers and their explanations or commentary mixed up together. The statement regarding the apprehensions of the priests about the coming dawn, therefore, falls under the Brahmana portion of the Samhita. Now the contents of the Brahmans are usually classified by Indian divines under the ten following heads —

(1) *Hetu* or reason;

(2) *Nirvachana*, or etymological explanation;

(3) *Ninda*, or censure;

(4) *Prashamsa*, or praise;

(5) *Samshaya*, or doubt;

(6) *Vidhi*, or the rule;

(7) *Parakriya*, or others' doings;

(8) *Pura-kalpa*, or ancient rite or tradition;

(9) *Vyavadharana-kalpana* or determining the limitations;

(10) *Upamana*, an apt comparison or simile.

Sayana in his introduction to the commentary on the Rig-Veda mentions the first nine of these, and as an illustration of the eighth, *Pura-kalpa*, quotes the explanatory passage from the Taittiriya Samhita, I, 5, 7, 5, referred to above. According to Sayana the statement, "In former times the priests were afraid that it would not dawn," therefore, comes under *Pura-kalpa*, or ancient traditional history found in the Bramanas. It is no *Arthavada*, that is, speculation or explanation put forth by the Brahmana itself. This is evident from the word *pura* which occurs in the Samhita text, and which shows that some piece of ancient traditional information is here recorded.

Now if this view is correct; a question naturally arises why should ordinary long winter nights have caused such apprehensions in the minds of the priests only "in former times," and why should the long darkness cease to inspire the same fears in the minds of the present generation. The long winter nights in the tropical and the temperate zone are as long today as they were thousands of years ago, and yet none of us, not even the most ignorant, feels any misgiving about the dawn which puts an end to the darkness of these long nights. It may, perhaps, be urged that in ancient times the bards had not acquired the knowledge necessary to predict the certain appearance of the dawn after a lapse of some hours in such cases.

But the lameness of this excuse becomes at once evident when we see that the Vedic calendar was, at this time, so much advanced that even the question of the equation of the solar and the lunar year was solved with sufficient accuracy Sayana's explanation of winter nights causing misgivings about the coming dawn must, therefore, be rejected as unsatisfactory. It was not the long winter-night that the Vedic bards were afraid of in former ages. It was something else, something very long, so long that, though you knew it would not last permanently, yet, by its very length, it tired your patience and made you long for, eagerly long for, the coming dawn.

In short, it was the long night of the Arctic region, and the word *pura* shows that it was a story of former ages, which the Vedic bards knew by tradition, I have shown elsewhere that the Taittiriya Samhita must be assigned to the Kittika period.

We may, therefore, safely conclude that at about 2500 B.C., there was a tradition current amongst the Vedic people to the effect that in former times, or rather in the former age, the priests grew so impatient of the length of the night, the yonder boundary of which was not known, that they fervently prayed to their deities to guide them safely to the other end of that tiresome darkness. This description of the night is inappropriate unless we take it to refer to the long and continuous Arctic night.

Let us now see if the Rig-Veda contains any direct reference to the long day, the long night, or to the Circumpolar calendar, besides the expressions about long darkness or the difficulty of reaching the other boundary of the endless night noticed above. We have seen before that the Rig-Vedic calendar is a calendar of 360 days, with an intercalary month, which can neither be Polar nor Circumpolar. But side by side with it the Rig-Veda preserves the descriptions of days and nights, which are not applicable to the cis-Arctic days, unless we put an artificial construction upon the passages containing these descriptions. Day and night is spoken of as a couple in the Vedic literature, and is denoted by a compound word in the dual number.

Thus we have *Ushasa-nakta* (I, 122, 2), Dawn and Night; *Naktoshasa* (I, 142, 7), Night and Dawn; or simply *Ushasau* (I, 188, 6) the two Dawns; all meaning a couple of Day and Night. The word *Aho-ratre* also means Day and Night; but it does not occur in the Rig-Veda, though Aitareya Brahmana (II, 4) treats it as synonymous with *Ushasa-nakta*. Sometimes this pair of Day and Night is spoken of as two sisters or twins; but whatever the form in which they are addressed, the reference is usually unambiguous. Now one of the verses which describes this couple of Day and Night is III, 55, 11.

The deity of the verse is *Aho-ratre*, and it is admitted on all hands that it contains a description of Day and Night. It runs thus:

Nana chakrate yamya vapumshi tayor anyad rochate krishnam anyat |

Shyavi cha yad arushi cha swasarau mahad devanam asuratvam ekam ||

The first three quarters or feet of this verse contain the principal statements, while the fourth is the refrain of the song or the hymn.

Literally translated it means: — "The twin pair (females) make many forms; of the two one shines, the other (is) dark; two sisters (are) they, the dark (*shyavi*), and the bright (*arushi*). The great divinity of the Gods is *one* (unique)." The verse looks simple enough at the first sight, and simple it is, so far as the words are concerned. But it has been misunderstood in two important points. We shall take the first half of the verse first. It says "the twin pair make many forms; of the two one shines and the other is dark." The twin pair are Day and Night, and one of them is bright and the other dark. So far, therefore, there is no difficulty. But the phrase "make many forms" does not seem to have been properly examined or interpreted. The words used in the original verse are *nana chakrate vapumshi*, and they literally mean "make many bodies or forms." We have thus a twofold description of the couple; it is called the shining and the dark and also described as possessed of many forms. In I, 123, 7, the couple of Day and Night is said to be *vishurupe*; while in other places the adjective: *virupe* is used in the same sense.

It is evident, therefore, that the "bodies" or "forms" intended to be denoted by these words must be different from the twofold character of the couple as shining and dark and if so, the phrases *vishurupe virupe* or *nana vapumshi* used in connection with the couple of Day and Night must be taken to mean something different from "bright and dark," if these expressions are not to be considered as superfluous or tautological. Sayana interprets these phrases as referring to different colours (*rupa*), like black, white, *&c.*, and some of the Western scholars seem to have adopted this interpretation. But I cannot see the propriety of assigning different colours to Day and Night. Are we to suppose that we may have sometimes green-violet, yellow or blue days and nights? Again though the word *rupa* lends itself to this construction, yet *vapumshi* cannot ordinarily be so understood. The question does not, however, seem to have attracted the serious attention of the commentators; so that even Griffith translates *vishurupe* by "unlike in hue" in I, 123, 7. The *Naktoshasa* are described as *virupe* also in I, 113, 3, but there too Sayana gives the same explanation. It does not appear to have occurred to any one that the point requires any further thought. Happily, in the case of Rig.

I, 113, 3, we have, however, the advantage of consulting a commentator older than Sayana. The verse occurs in the *Uttararchika* of Sama-Veda (19, 4, 2, 3), Madhava in his *Vivarana,* a commentary on the Sama-Veda explains *virupe* thus:— "In the *Dakshinayana* during the year there is the increase of night, and in the *Uttarayana* of day." Madhava's *Vivarana* is a scarce book, and I take the above quotation from an extract from his commentary given in a footnote to the Calcutta edition of the Sama-Veda Samhita, with Sayana's commentary, published by Satyavrata Samashrami, a learned Vedic scholar of Calcutta. It is not known who this Madhava is, but Pandit Satyavrata states that he is referred to by Durga, the commentator of Yaska. We may, therefore, take Madhava to be an old commentator, and it is satisfactory to find that he indicates to us the way out of the difficulty of interpreting the phrases *vishurupe* and *virupe* occurring so many times in Rig-Veda, in connection with the couple of Day and Night.

The word "form" (*rupa*) or body (*vapus*) can be used to denote the extent, duration, or length of days and nights, and *virupe* would naturally denote the varying *lengths* of days and nights, *in addition* to their colour which can be only twofold, dark or bright. Taking our clue from Madhava, we may, therefore, interpret the first half of the verse as meaning "The twin pair assume various (*nana*) lengths (*vapumshi*); of the two one shines and the other is dark." But though the first half may be thus interpreted, another difficulty arises, as soon as we take up the third quarter of the verse.

It says, "Two sisters are they, the dark (*shyavi*) and the bright (*arushi*)." Now the question is whether the two sisters (*svasarau*) here mentioned are the same as,, or different from, the twin paii (*yamya*) mentioned in the first half of the verse. If we take them as identical, the third *pada* or quarter of the verse becomes at once superfluous. If we take them as different, we must explain how and where the two pairs differ. The commentators have not been able to solve the difficulty, and they have, therefore, adopted the course of regarding the twins (*yamya*) and the sisters (*svasara*) as identical, even at the risk of tautology. It will surely be admitted that this is not a satisfactory course, and that we ought to find a better explanation, if we can. This is not again the only place where two distinct couples of Day and Night are mentioned. There is another word in the Rig-Veda which denotes a pair of Day and Night. It is *Ahani*, which does not mean "two days" but Day and Night, for, in VI, 9, 1, we are expressly told that "there is a dark *ahah* (day) and a bright *ahah* (day)." *Ahani*, therefore, means a couple of Day and Night, and we have seen that *Ushasa-nakta* also means a couple of Day and Night. Are the two couples same or different? If *Ahani* be regarded as synonymous with *Ushasa-nakta* or *Aho-ratre*, then the two couples would be identical; otherwise different. Fortunately, Rig. IV, 55, 3, furnishes us with the means of solving this difficulty.

There *Ushasa-nakta* and *Ahani* are separately invoked to grant protection to the worshipper and the separate invocation clearly proves that the two couples are two separate dual deities, though each of them represents a couple of Day and Night. Prof. Max Muller has noticed this difference between *Ushasa-nakta* and *Ahani* or the two *Ahans* but he does not seem to have pushed it to its logical conclusion. If all the 360 days and nights of the year were of the same class as with us, there was no necessity of dividing them into two representative couples as *Ushasa-nakta* and *Ahani*. The general description "dark, bright and of various lengths," would have been quite sufficient to denote all the days and nights of the year.

Therefore, if the distinction between *Ushasa-nakta* and *Ahani*, made in IV, 55, 3, is not to be ignored, we must find out an explanation of this distinction; and looking to the character of days and nights at different places on the surface of the earth from the Pole to the Equator the only possible explanation that can be suggested is that the year spoken of in these passages was a circum-Polar year, made up of one long day and one long night, forming one pair, and a number of ordinary days and nights of various lengths, which, taking a single day and night as the type can be described as the second couple, "bright, dark and. of varying lengths." There is no other place on the surface of the earth where the description holds good. At the Equator, we have only equal days and nights throughout the year and they can be represented by a single couple "dark and bright, but always of the same length." In fact, instead of *virupe* the pair would be *sarupe*. Between the Equator and science of Language, Vol. II, p. 534 the Arctic Circle, a day and night together never exceed twenty-four hours, though there may be a day of 23 hours and a night of one hour and *vice versa*, as we approach the Arctic Circle.

In this case, the days of the year will have to be represented by a typical couple, "dark and night, but of various lengths, *virupe*." But as soon as we cross the Arctic Circle and go into "The Land of the Long Night," the above description requires to be amended by adding to the first couple, another couple of the long day and the long night, the lengths of which would vary according to latitude. This second couple of the long day and the long night, which match each other, will have also to be designated as *virupe*, with this difference, however, that while the length of days and nights in the temperate zone would vary at the same place, the length of the long night and the long day would not vary at one and the same place but only at different latitudes. Taking a couple of Day and Night, as representing the days and nights of the year, we shall have, therefore, to divide the different kinds of diurnal changes over the globe into three classes:

(i) At the Equator, — A *single* couple; dark and bright but always of the *same* form, or length (*sarupe*).

(ii) Between the Equator and the Arctic Circle, — A *single* couple; dark and bright, but of *various* forms, or lengths, (*virupe*).

(iii) Between the Arctic Circle and the Pole, — *Two* couples; each dark and bright, but of *various* forms or lengths (*virupe*).

At the Pole, there is only one day and one night of six months each. Now if we have an express passage in the Rig-Veda (IV, 55, 3) indicating two different couples of Day and Night *Ushasa-nakta* and

Ahani, it is evident that the *ahoratre* represented by them are the days and nights of the Circum-Polar regions, and of those alone. In the light of IV, 55, 3, we must, therefore, interpret III, 55, 11, quoted above, as describing two couples, one of the twin pair and the other of two sisters. The verse must, therefore, be translated:

"The twin pair (the first couple) make many forms (lengths); of the two one shines and the other is dark. Two sisters are they the *shyavi* or the, dark and *arushi* or the bright (the second couple)." No part of the verse is thus rendered superfluous, and the whole becomes far more comprehensible than otherwise.

We have seen that days and nights are represented by two distinct typical couples in the Rig-Veda *Ushasa-nakta* and *Ahani*; and that if the distinction is not unmeaning we must take this to be the description of the days and nights within the Arctic Circle. Whether *Ahani* means a couple of Day and Night distinct from *Ushasa-nakta* in every place where the word occurs, it is difficult to say. But that in some places, at least, it denotes a peculiar couple of the Day and Night, not included in, and different from, *Ushasa-nakta* is evident from IV, 55, 3. Now if *Ahani* really means the couple of the long day and the long night, as distinguished from the ordinary days and nights, there is another way in which these two couples can be differentiated from each other. The ordinary days and nights follow each other closely the day is succeeded by the night and the night by the day; and the two members of the couple, representing these days and nights, cannot be described as separated from each other.

But the long night and the long day, though of equal duration do not follow each other in close succession. The long night occurs about the time when the sun is at the winter solstice, and the long day when he is at the summer solstice; and these two solstitial points are separated by 180°, being opposite to each other in the ecliptic. This character of *Ahani* seems to have been traditionally known in the time of the *Aranyakas*. Thus the Taittiriya Aranyaka, I, 2, 3, in discussing the personified year, first says that the Year has one head, and two different mouths, and then remarks that all his is "seasoncharacteristic," which the commentator explains by stating that the Year-God is said to have two mouths because it has two *Ayanas*, the northern and the southern, which include the seasons. But the statement important for our purpose is the one which follows next. The Aranyaka continues "To the right and the left side of the Year-God (are) the bright and the dark (days)" and the following verse refers to it: — "Thy one (form) is bright, thy another sacrificial (dark), two *Ahans* of different forms, though art like *Dyau*. Thou, O Self-dependent! protectest all magic powers, O Pushan! let thy bounty be here auspicious." The verse, or the Mantra, here referred to is Rig. VI, 58, 1. Pushan is there compared to Dyau and is said to have two forms, dark and bright, like the *Ahani*.

These dark and bright forms of *Ahani* are said to constitute the right and left side of the Year-God, that is, the two opposite parts of the body of the personified year. In other words the passage clearly states that the dark and the bright part of *Ahani*, do not, follow each other closely, but are situated on the diametrically opposite sides of the year. This can only be the case if the couple of Day and Night, represented by *Ashani*, be taken to denote the long night and the long day in the Arctic regions. There the long night is matched by the long day and while the one occurs when the sun is at the wintersolstice, the other occurs when he is at the summer-solstice. The two parts of *Ahani* are, therefore, very correctly represented as forming the right and the left side of the Year-God, in the *Aranyaka,* and the passage thus materially supports the view about the nature of *Ahani* mentioned above.

Lastly, we have express passage in the Rig-Veda where a long day is described. In V, 54, 5, an extended daily course (*dirgham yojanam*) of the sun is mentioned and the Maruts are said to have extended their strength and greatness in a similar way. But the most explicit statement about the long day is found in X, 138, 3. This hymn celebrates the exploits of Indra, all of which are performed in aerial or heavenly regions. In the first verse the killing of Vritra and the releasing of the dawns and the waters are mentioned; and in the second the sun is said to have been made to shine by the same process. The third verse is as follows:

Vi suryo madhye amuchad ratham divo vidad dasaya pratimanam aryah |
Dridhani Pipror asurasya mayinah Indro vyasyach chakrivam Rijishvana ||

The fourth, fifth and the sixth verses all refer to the destruction of Vritra's forts, the chastisement of Ushas and placing of the moons in the heaven. But the third verse quoted above is alone important for our purpose. The words are simple and easy and the verse may be thus translated "The sun unyoked his car in the midst of heaven; the Arya found a counter-measure (*pratimanam*) for the Dasa. Indra, acting with Rijishvan, overthrew the solid forts of Pipru, the conjuring Asura. "It is the first half of the verse that is relevant to our purpose.

The sun is said to have unyoked his car, not at sunset, or on the horizon, but in the midst of heaven, there to rest for some time. There is no uncertainty about it, for the words are so clear; and the commentators have found it difficult to explain this extraordinary conduct of the sun in the midway of the heavens. Mr. Griffith says that it is, perhaps an allusion to an eclipse, or to the detention of the sun to enable the Aryans to complete the overthrow of their enemies.

Both of these suggestions are, however, not satisfactory. During a solar eclipse the sun being temporarily hidden by the moon is invisible wholly or partially and is not besides stationary. The description that the sun unyoked his car in the mid-heaven cannot, therefore, apply to the eclipsed sun. As regards the other suggestion, *viz.,* that the sun remained stationary for a while to allow his favourite race, the Aryans, to overthrow their enemies, it seems to have had its origin in the Biblical passage (Joshua, X, 12, 13), where the sun is said to have stood still, at the word of Joshua, until the people had avenged themselves upon their enemies. But there is no authority for importing this Biblical idea into the Rig-Veda.

Indra's exploits are described in a number of hymns in the Rig-Veda, but in no other hymn he is said to have made the sun stand still for the Aryans. We must, therefore, reject both the explanations suggested by Griffith. Sayana gets over the difficulty by interpreting the phrase, *ratham vi amuchat madhye divah*, as meaning that "the sun loosened (*viamuchat*) his carriage, that is, set it free to travel, towards the middle (*madhye*) of heaven, (*ratham prasthanaya vimuktavan*)." Sayana's meaning, therefore, is that when Indra obtained compensation from Vritra, he let loose the chariot of the sun to travel towards the midst of the sky. But the construction is evidently a strained one. The verb *vi* much is used in about a dozen places in the Rig-Veda in relation to horses, and everywhere it means to "unharness," "unyoke," or "separate the horses from the carriage for rest," and even Sayana has interpreted it in the same way.

Thus *vimuchya* is explained by him as *rathat vishlishya* in I, 104, 1, and *rathat vi-muchya* in III, 32, 1, and *rathat visrijya* in X, 160, 1, (also compare I, 171, 1; I, 177, 4; VI, 40, 1).

The most natural meaning of the present verse would, therefore, be that the "sun unyoked his carriage." But even supposing that *vi much* can be interpreted to mean "to loosen for travel," the expression would be appropriate only when there is an antecedent stoppage or slow motion of the sun. The question why the sun stopped or slackened his motion in the midst of the sky would, therefore, still remain unsolved. The phrase *divah madhye* naturally means "*in* the midst of the sky," and cannot be interpreted to mean "*towards* the mid-heaven." Of course if the sun was below the horizon, we may describe him as having loosened his horses for travel as in V, 62, 1; but even there the meaning seems to be that the horses rested at the place. In the present case the sun is already in the midst of heaven, and we cannot take him below the horizon without a palpable distortion of meaning. Nor can we properly explain the action of retaliation (*pratimanam*), if we accept Sayana's interpretation. We must, therefore, interpret the first half of the verse to mean that "the sun unyoked his carriage in the midst of heaven."

There is another passage in the Rig-Veda which speaks of the sun halting in the midst of heaven. In VII, 87, 5, the king Varuna is said to have made "the golden (sun) rock like a swing in the heaven" (*chakre divi prenkham hiranmayam*), clearly meaning that the sun swayed backwards and forwards in the heaven being visible all the time, (*cf.* also VII, 88, 3).

The idea expressed in the present verse is exactly the same, for even within the Arctic regions the sun will appear as swinging only during the long continuous day, when he does not go below the horizon once every twenty-four hours. There is, therefore, nothing strange or uncommon in the present verse which says that, "the sun unyoked his carriage for some time in the midst of the sky;" and we need not be impatient to escape from the natural meaning of the verse. A long halt of the sun in the midst of the heaven is here clearly described, and we must take it to refer to the long day in the Arctic region. The statement in the second line further supports the same view. European scholars appear to have been misled, in this instance, by the words *Arya* and *Dasa*, which they are accustomed to interpret as meaning the Aryan and the non-Aryan race. But though the words may be interpreted in this way in some passages, such is not the case everywhere.

The word *Dasa* is applied to Indra's enemies in a number of places. Thus Shambara is called a *Dasa* (IV, 30, 14,) and the same adjective is applied to Pipru in VIII, 32, 2, and to Namuchi in V, 30, 7. Indra is said to inspire fear into the *Dasa* in X, 120, 2 and in II, 11, 2 he is described as having rent the *Dasa* who considered himself immortal. In the verse under consideration Indra's victory over Pipru is celebrated, and we know that Pipru is elsewhere called a *Dasa*. It is, therefore, quite natural to suppose that the words *Arya* and *Dasa* in the above verse, refer to Indra and Pipru, and not to the Aryan and the non-Aryan race. The exploits described are all heavenly, and it jars with the context to take a single sentence in the whole hymn as referring to the victory of the Aryan over the non-Aryan race. There is again the word *Pratimana* (*lit.* countermeasure), which denotes that what has been done is by way of retaliation, a sort of counter-poise or counterblast, with a view to avenge the mischief done by *Dasa*. A battle between the Aryans and the non-Aryans cannot be so described unless a previous defeat of the Aryans is first alluded to. The plain meaning of the verse, therefore, is that the sun was made to halt in the midst of the sky, producing a long day, and Indra thus found a counter-poise for *Dasa* his enemy.

For we know that darkness is brought on by the *Dasa*, and it is he who brings on the long night; but if the *Dasa* made the night long, Indra retaliated or counter-acted by making the day as long as the night of the *Dasa*. The long night of the Arctic regions is, we have seen, matched by the long day in those regions, and the present verse expresses the same idea of matching the one by the other. There is no reference to the victory of the Aryan race over the non-Aryans, or anything of that kind as supposed by Western scholars. Sayana, who had no historic theories to mislead him, has rightly interpreted *Arya* and *Dasa* in this verse as referring to Indra and his enemy; but he, in his turn, has misinterpreted as shown above, the first half of the verse in regard to the sun's long halt in the midst of the sky. The misinterpretation of the: second hemistich conies from Western scholars, like Muir who interprets *Arya* as meaning the

Aryans and *Dasa,* the non-Aryans. This shows how in the absence of the true key to the meaning of a passage, we may be led away by current theories, even where the words are plain and simple in themselves.

We thus-see that the Rig-Veda speaks of two different couples of Day and Night, one alone of which represents the ordinary days and nights in the year and the second, the *Ahani,* is a distinct couple by itself, forming, according to the Taittiriya Aranyaka, the right and the left hand side of the Year, indicating the long Arctic day and night. The Taittiriya Samhita again gives us in clear terms a tradition that in the former age the night was so long that men were afraid it would not dawn. We have also a number of expressions in the Rig-Veda denoting "long nights" or "long and ghastly darkness" and also the "long journey" of the sun. Prayers are also offered to Vedic deities to enable the worshipper to reach safely the end of the night, the "other boundary of which is not known." Finally we have an express text declaring that the sun halted in the midst of the sky and thereby retaliated the mischief brought on by Dasa's causing the long night. Thus we have not only the long day and the long night mentioned in the Rig-Veda, but the idea that the two match, each other is also found therein, while the Taittiriya Aranyaka tells us that they form the opposite sides of Year-God. Besides the passages proving the long duration of the dawn, we have, therefore, sufficient independent evidence to hold that the long night in the Arctic regions and its counterpart the long day were both known to the poets of the Rig-Veda and the Taittiriya Samhita distinctly informs us that it was a phenomenon of the former (*pura*) age.

I shall close this chapter with a short discussion of another Circum-Polar characteristic, I mean the southern course of the sun. It is previously stated, that the sun can never appear overhead at any station in the temperate or the frigid zone and that an observer stationed within these zones in the northern hemisphere will see the sun to his right hand or towards the south, while at the North Pole the sun will seem to rise from the south. Now the word *dakshina* in Vedic Sanskrit denotes both the "right hand" and the "south" as it does in other Aryan languages; for, as observed by Prof. Sayce, these people had to face the rising sun with their right hands to the south, in addressing their gods and hence Sanskrit *dakshina,* Welsh *dehau* and Old Irish *des* all mean at once "right hand" and "south." With this explanation before us, we can now understand how in a number of passages in the Rig-Veda Western scholars translate *dakshina* by "right side," where Indian scholars take the word to mean "the southern direction." There is a third meaning of *dakshina, viz.,* "largess" or "guerdon," and in some places the claims of rich largesses seem to have been pushed too far. Thus when the suns are said to be only for *dakshinavats* in

I, 125, 6, it looks very probable that originally the expression had some reference to the southern direction rather than to the gifts given at sacrifices. In III, 58, I, Surya is called the son of *Dakshina* and even if *Dakshina* be here taken to mean the Dawn, yet the question why the Dawn was called *Dakshina* remains, and the only explanation at present suggested is that *Dakshina* means "skilful" or "expert." A better way to explain these phrases is to make them refer to the southerly direction; and after what has been said above such an explanation will seem to be highly probable.

It is, of course, necessary to be critical in the interpretation of the Vedic hymns, but I think that we shall be carrying our critical spirit too far, if we say that in no passage in the Rig-Veda *dakshina* or its derivatives are used to denote the southerly direction (I, 95, 6; II, 42, 3).

Herodotus informs us (IV, 42) that certain Phoenician mariners were commanded by Pharaoh Neco, king of Egypt, to sail round Libya (Africa) and return by the Pillars of Hercules (Straits of Gibraltar). The mariners accomplished the voyage and returned in the third year. But Herodotus disbelieves them, because, on their return they told such (to him incredible) stories, that in rounding Libya they saw the sun to their right. Herodotus could not believe that the sun would ever appear in the north; but the little thought that what was incredible to him would itself be regarded as indisputable evidence of the authenticity of the account in later days. Let us take a lesson from this story, and not interpret *dakshina*, either by "right-hand side" or by "largess," in every passage in the Rig-Veda.

There may not be distinct passages to show that the sun, or the dawn, came from the south. But the very fact that Ushas is called *Dakshina* (I, 123, 1; X, 107, 1), and the sun, the son of *Dakshina* (III, 58, 1), is itself very suggestive, and possibly we have here phrases which the Vedic bards employed because in their days these were old and recognized expressions in the language. Words, like fossils, very often preserve the oldest ideas or facts in a language; and though Vedic poets may have forgotten the original meaning of these phrases, that is no reason why we should refuse to draw from the history of these words such conclusions as may legitimately follow from it.

The fact that the north is designated by the word *ut-tara,* meaning "upper" and the south by *adha-ra,* meaning "lower," also points to the same conclusion; for the north cannot be overhead or "upper" except to an observer at or near the North Pole. In later literature, we find a tradition that the path of the sun lies through regions which are lower (*adha*) than the abode of the Seven Rishis, or the constellation of Ursa Major. That ecliptic lies to the south of the constellation is plain enough, but it cannot be said to be *below* the constellation, unless the zenith of the observer is in the constellation, or between it and the North Pole, a position, possible only i n the case of an observer in the Arctic region.

I have already quoted a passage from the Rig-Veda, which speaks of the Seven Bears (*Rikshah*), as being placed on high in the heavens (*uchchah*). But I have been not able to find out any Vedic authority for the tradition that the sun's path lies below the constellation of the Seven Bears. It has also been stated previously that mere southerly direction of the sun, even if completely established, is not a sure indication of the observer being within the circum-polar region as the sun will appear to move always to the south of the observer even in the temperate zone. It is, therefore, not necessary to pursue this point further. It has been shown that the Rig-Veda mentions the long night and the long day and we shall see in the next chapter that the months and the seasons mentioned in this Old Book fully accord with the theory we have formed from the evidence hitherto discussed.

MONTHS AND SEASONS

Starting with the tradition about the half yearly night of the Gods found everywhere in Sanskrit literature, and also in the Avesta, we have found direct references in Rig-Veda to a long continuous dawn of thirty days, the long day and the long night, when the sun remained above the horizon or went below it for a number of 24 hours; and we have also seen that the Rig-Vedic texts describe these things as events of a bye-gone age. The next question, therefore, is — Do we meet in the Vedas with similar traces of the Arctic condition of seasons months or years? It is stated previously that the calendar current at the time of the Vedic Samhitas was different from the Arctic calendar. But if the ancestors of the Vedic people ever lived near the North Pole, "we may," as observed by Sir Norman Lockyer with reference to the older Egyptian calendar, "always reckon upon the conservatism of the priests of the temples retaining the tradition of the old rejected year in every case." Sir Norman Lockyer first points out how the ancient Egyptian year of 360 days was afterwards replaced by a year of 365 days; and then gives two instances of the traditional practice by which the memory of the old year was preserved. "Thus even at Philæ in later times," says he "in the temple of Osiris, there were 360 bowls for sacrifice, which were filled daily with milk by a specified rotation of priests. At Acanthus there was a perforated cask into which one of the 360 priests poured water from the Nile daily." And what took place in Egypt, we may expect to have taken place in Vedic times. The characteristics of an Arctic year are so unlike those of a year in the temperate zone, that if the ancestors of the Vedic people ever lived within the Arctic regions, and immigrated southwards owing to glaciation, an adaptation of the calendar to the altered geographical and astronomical conditions of the new home was a necessity, and must have been effected at the time. But in making this change, we may, as remarked by Sir Norman Lockyer, certainly expect the conservative priests to retain as much of the old calendar as possible, or at least preserve the traditions of the older year in one form or another especially in their sacrificial rites.

Indo-European etymological equations have established the fact that sacrifices, or rather the system of making offerings to the gods for various purposes, existed from the primeval period, and if so, the system must have undergone great modifications as the Aryan races moved from the Arctic to the temperate zone. I have shown elsewhere that calendar and sacrifice, especially the annual *sattras*, are closely connected, and that in the case of the annual *sattras*, or the sacrificial sessions which lasted for one year, the priests had in view, as observed by Dr. Haug,† the yearly course of the sun. It was the duty of these priests to keep up sacrificial fire, as the Parsi priests now do and to see that the yearly rounds of sacrifices were performed at proper times (*ritus*). The sacrificial calendar in the Arctic home must, however, have been different from what it came to be afterwards; and happily many traces of this calendar are still discoverable in the sacrificial literature of Vedic times, proving that the ancient worshippers or sacrificers of our race must have lived in circum-polar regions. But before discussing this evidence, it is necessary to briefly describe the points wherein we might expect the ancient or the oldest sacrificial system to differ from the one current in Vedic times.

In the Samhitas and Brahmans, the annual *sattras*, or yearly sacrificial sessions, are said to extend over twelve months. But this was impossible within the Arctic region where the sun goes below the horizon for a number of days or months during the year, thereby producing the long night. The oldest duration of the annual *sattras*, if such *sattras* were ever performed within the Polar regions, would, therefore, be shorter than twelve months. In other words, an annual *sattra* of *less* than twelve months would be the chief distinguishing mark of the older sacrificial system, as contrasted with the later annual *sattra* of twelve months. It must also be borne in mind that the number of the months of sunshine and darkness cannot be the same everywhere in the Circum-Polar regions. At the Pole the sun is alternately above and below the horizon for six months each. But as all people cannot be expected to be stationed precisely at the Pole, practically the months of sunshine will vary from seven to eleven for the inhabitants of the Arctic region, those nearest to the North Pole having seven month's sunshine, while those living father south from the Pole having the sun above their horizon for eight, nine or ten months according to latitude. These periods of sunshine would be made up of the long Arctic day at the place and a succession of ordinary days and nights closely following each other; and sacrificial sessions would be held, or principal business transacted, and important, religious and social ceremonies performed only during this period. It would, so to say, be a period of action, as contrasted with the long night, by which it was followed.

The long dawn following the long night, would mark the beginning of this period of activity; and the Arctic sacrificial year would, practically, be made up, only of these months of sunshine. Therefore, the varying number of the months of sunshine would be the chief peculiarity of the Arctic sacrificial calendar, and we must bear it in mind in examining the traces of the oldest calendar in the Rig-Veda, or other Samhitas.

A dawn of thirty days, as we measure days, implies a position so near the North Pole, that the period of sunshine at the place could not have been longer than about seven months, comprising, of course, a long day of four or five months, and a succession of regular days and nights during the remaining period; and we find that the Rig-Veda does preserve for us the memory of such months of sunshine.

We refer first to the legend of Aditi, or the seven Adityas (suns), which is obviously based on some natural phenomenon. This legend expressly tells us that the oldest number of Adityas or suns was seven, and the same idea is independently found in many other places in the Rig-Veda. Thus in IX, 114, 3, seven Adityas and *seven* priests are mentioned together, though the names of the different suns are not given therein. In II, 27 1, Mitra, Aryaman, Bhaga, Varuna, Daksha and Amsha are mentioned by name as so many different Adityas but the seventh is not named. This omission does not, however, mean much, as the septenary character of the sun is quite patent from the fact that he is called *saptashva* (seven-horsed, in V, 45, 9, and his "seven-wheeled" chariot is said to be drawn by "seven bay steeds" (I, 50, 8), or by a single horse "with seven names" in I, 164, 2. The Atharva Veda also speaks of "the seven bright rays of the sun" (VII, 107, 1); and the epithet *Aditya,* as applied to the sun in the Rig-Veda, is rendered more clearly by *Aditeh putrah* (Aditi's son) in A.V. XIII, 2, 9. Sayana, following Yaska, derives this sevenfold character of the sun from his seven rays, but why solar rays were taken to be seven still remain unexplained, unless we hold that the Vedic bards had anticipated the discovery of seven prismatic rays or colours, which were unknown even to Yaska or Sayana. Again though the existence of seven suns may be explained on this hypothesis, yet it fails to account for the death of the eighth sun, for the legend of Aditi (Rig. X,

72, 8-9) tells us, "Of the eight sons of Aditi, who were born from her body, she approached the gods with seven and cast out Martanda.

With seven sons Aditi approached (the gods) in the former age (*purvyam yugam*); she brought thither Martanda again for birth and death." The story is discussed in various places in the Vedic literature and many other attempts, unfortunately all unsatisfactory, have been made to explain it in a rational and intelligent way. Thus in the Taittiriya Samhita, VI, 5, 61 *f*. the story of Aditi cooking a *Brahmaudana* oblation for the gods, the Sadhyas, is narrated. The remnant of the oblation was given to her by the gods, and four Adityas were born to her from it. She then cooked a second oblation and ate it herself first; but the Aditya born from it was an imperfect egg. She cooked a third time and the Aditya Vivasvat, the progenitor of man, was born. But the Samhita does not give the number and names of the eight Adityas and this omission is supplied, by the Taittiriya Brahmana (I, 1, 9, 1*f*).

The Brahmana tells us that Aditi cooked the oblation four times and each time the gods gave her the remnant of the oblation. Four pairs of sons were thus born to her; the first pair was Dhati and Aryaman, the second Mitra and Varuna, the third Amsha and Bhag and the fourth Indra and Vivasvat. But the Brahmana does not explain why the eighth son was called Martanda and cast away. The Taittiriya Aranyaka, I, 13, 2-3, (cited by Sayana in his gloss on Rig. II, 27, 1, and X, 72, 8) first quotes the two verses from the Rig-Veda (X, 72, 8 and 9 which give the legend of Aditi but with a slightly different reading for the second line of the second verse. Thus instead, of *tvat punah Martandam a abharat* (she *brought again* Martanda thither for birth and death), the Aranyaka reads *tat para Martandam a abharat* (she *set aside* Martanda for birth and death). The Aranyaka then proceeds to give the names of the eight sons, as Mitra, Varuna, Dhatri, Aryaman, Amsha, Bhaga, Indra and Vivasvat. But no further explanation is added, nor are we told which of these eight sons represented Martanda. There is, however, another passage in the Aranaka (I, 7, 1-6) which throws some light on the nature of these Adityas.

The names of the suns here given are different. They are: Aroga, Bhraja, Patara, Patanga, Svarnara, Jyotishimat, Vibhasa and Kashyapa; the last of which is said to remain, constantly at the great mount Meru, permanently illumining that region. The other seven suns are said to derive their light from Kashyapa and to be alone visible to man. We are then told that these seven suns are considered by some Acharyas to be the seven manifestations of the *Pranas*, or the vital powers in man; while others are said to hold the opinion that they are the types of seven officiating priests (*ritvijah*).

A third explanation is then put forward, *viz.*, that the distinction of seven suns is probably based on the different effects of sun's rays in different months or seasons, and in support of it a Mantra, or Vedic verse, *Dig-bhraja ritrun karoti;* (resorting to, or shining in, different regions) they (make the seasons), is quoted. I have not been able to find the Mantra in the existing Samhitas, nor does Sayana give us any clue to it, butt simply observes "the different features of different seasons cannot be accounted for, except by supposing them to have been caused by different suns; therefore, different suns must exist in different regions." But this explanation is open to the objection (actually raised by Vaishampayana), that we shall have, on this theory, to assume the existence of thousands of suns as the characteristics of the seasons are so numerous. The Aranyaka admits, to a certain extent the force of this objection, but says — *ashtau to vyavasitah,* meaning that the number eight is settled by the text of the scripture, and there is no further arguing about it.

The Shatapatha Brahmana, III, 1, 3, 3, explains the legend of Aditi somewhat on the same lines. It says that seven alone of Aditi's sons are styled *Devah Adityah* (the gods Adityas) by men, and that the eighth Martanda was born undeveloped, whereupon the Aditya gods created man and other animals out of him. In two other passages of the Shatapath Brahmana, VI, 1, 2, 8, and XI, 6, 3, 8, the number of dityas Ais, however, given as twelve. In the first (VI, 1, 2, 8) they are said to have sprung from twelve drops generated by Prajapati and then placed in different regions (*dikshu*); while in second (XI, 6, 3, 8) these twelve Adityas are identified with the twelve months of the year.

The number of Adityas is also given as twelve in the Upanishads: while in the post-Vedic literature they are everywhere said to be twelve, answering to the twelve months of the year. Muir, in his Original Sanskrit Texts Volumes IV and V, gives most of these passages, but offers no explanation as to the legend of Aditi, except such as is to be found in the passages quoted. There are many different speculations or theories of Western Scholars regarding the nature and character of Aditi, but as far as the number of Adityas is concerned, I know of no satisfactory explanation as yet suggested by them. On the contrary the tendency is, as observed by Prof. Max Muller, to regard the number, seven or eight, as unconnected with any solar movements. A suggestion is made that eight Adityas may be taken to, represent the eight cardinal points of the compass, but the death or casting away of the eighth Aditya seals the fate of this explanation, which thus seems to have been put forward only to be rejected like Martanda, the eighth Aditya.

We have here referred to, or quoted, the texts and passages bearing on Aditi's legend. or the number of Adityas at some length, in order to show how we are apt to run into wild speculations about the meaning of a simple legend when the key to it is lost: That the twelve Adityas are understood to represent the twelve month-gods in later Vedic literature is evident from the passage in the Shatapatha Brahmana (XI, 6, 3, 8 = Bih. Arn. Up. III, 9, 5) which says, "There are twelve months of the year; these are the Adityas." With this explanation before us, and the belief that different seasonal changes could be explained only by assuming the existence of different suns, it required no very great stretch of imagination to infer that if twelve Adityas now represent the twelve months of the year, the seven Adityas must have once (*purvyam yugam*) represented the seven months of the year. But this explanation, reasonable though it was, did not commend itself, or we might even say, occur to Vedic scholars, who believed that the home of the Aryans lay somewhere in Central Asia. It is, therefore, satisfactory to find that the idea of different suns producing different months is recognized so expressly in the Taittiriya Aranyaka, which quotes a Vedic text, not now available, in support thereof and finally pronounces in favour of the theory, which regards the seven suns as presiding over seven different heavenly regions and thereby producing different seasons, in spite of the objection that it would lead to the assumption of thousands of suns — an objection, which the Aranyaka disposes of summarily by observing that eight is a settled number and that we have no right to change it. That this explanation is the most probable of all is further evident from Rig. IX, 114, 3, which says "There are seven sky-regions (*sapta dishah*), with their different suns (*nana suryah*), there are seven Hotis as priests, those who are the seven gods, the Adityas, — with them. O Soma! protect us." Here *nana suryah* is an adjective which qualifies *dishah* (*sapta*), and the correlation between seven regions and seven suns is thus expressly recognized.

Therefore, the simplest explanation of Aditi's legend is that she presented to the gods, that is, brought forth into heavens, her seven sons, the Adityas, to form the seven months of sunshine in the place. She had an eighth son, but he was born in an undeveloped state, or, was, what we may call, stillborn; evidently meaning that the eighth month was not a month of sunshine, or that the period of darkness at the place commenced with the eighth month. All this occurred not in this age, but in the previous age and the words *purvyam yugam* in X, 72, 9, are very important from this point of view. The word *yuga* is evidently used to denote a period of time in the first and second verses of the hymn, which refer to the former age of the gods (*devanam purvye yuge*) and also of later age (*uttare yuge*). Western scholars are accustomed to interpret *yuga* to mean "a generation of men" almost in every place where the phrase is met with; and we shall have to consider the correctness of this interpretation later on. For the purpose of this legend it is enough to state that the phrase *purvyam yugam* occurs twice in the hymn and that where it first occurs (in verse 2), it clearly denotes "an early age" or "some division of time."

Naturally enough we must, therefore, interpret it in the same way where it occurs again in the same hymn, *viz.* in the verse describing the legend of Aditi's seven sons. The sun having seven rays, or seven horses, also implies the same idea differently expressed. The seven months of sunshine, with their different temperatures, are represented by seven suns producing these different results by being differently located, or as having different kinds of rays, or as having different chariots, or horses, or different wheels to the same chariot. It is one and the same idea in different forms, or as the Rig-Veda puts it, "one horse with seven names" (I, 164, 2).

A long dawn of thirty days indicates a period of sunshine for seven months, and we now see that the legend of Aditi is intelligible only if we interpret it as a relic of a time when there were seven flourishing month-gods, and the eighth was either still-born, or cast away. *Martanda* is etymologically derived from *marta* meaning "dead or undeveloped," (being connected with *mrita,* the past participle of *mri* to die) and *anda,* an egg or a bird; and it denotes a dead sun, or a sun that has sunk below the horizon, for in Rig. X, 55, 5, we find the word *mamara* (died) used to denote the setting of the daily sun.

The sun is also represented as a bird in many places in the Rig-Veda (V, 47, 3; X, 55, 6; X, 177, 1; X, 189, 3). A cast away bird (*Martanda*) is, therefore, the sun that has set or sunk below the horizon, and whole legend is obviously a reminiscence of the place where the sun shone above the horizon for seven months and went below it in the beginning of the eighth. If this nature of the sun-god is once impressed on the memory, it cannot be easily forgotten by any people simply by their being obliged to change their residence; and thus the sevenfold character of the sun-god must have been handed down as an old tradition, though the Vedic people lived later on in places presided over by the twelve Adityas.

That is how ancient traditions are preserved everywhere, as, for instance, those relating to the older year in the Egyptian literature, previously referred to. We have seen above that the peculiar characteristic of the Arctic region is the *varying* number of the months of sunshine in that place.

It is not, therefore, enough to say that traces of a period of seven months' sunshine are alone found in the Rig-Veda. If our theory is correct, we ought to find references to periods of eight, nine or ten months' sunshine along with that of seven months either in the shape of traditions, or in some other form; and fortunately there are such references in the Rig-Veda, only if we know where to look for them. We have seen that the sun's chariot is said to be drawn by seven horses, and that this seven-fold character of the sun has reference to the seven suns conceived as seven different monthgods.

There are many other legends based on this seven-fold division, but as they do not refer to the subject under discussion, we must reserve their consideration for another occasion. The only fact necessary to be mentioned in this place is that the number of the sun's horses is said to be not only *seven* (I, 50, 8), but also ten in IX, 63, 9; and if the first be taken to represent seven months, the other must be understood to stand for ten months as well. We need not, however, depend upon such extension of the legend of seven Adityas to prove that the existence of nine or ten months of sunshine was known to the poets of the Rig-Veda. The evidence, which I am now going to cite, comes from another source, I mean, the sacrificial literature, which is quite independent of the legend of the seven Adityas.

The Rig-Veda mentions a number of ancient sacrificers styled "our fathers" (II, 33, 13; VI, 22, 2), who instituted the sacrifice in ancient times and laid down, for the guidance of man, the path which he should, in future, follow. Thus the sacrifice offered by Manu, is taken as the type and other sacrifices are compared with it in I, 76, 5. But Manu was not alone to offer this ancient sacrifice to the gods. In X, 63, 7, he is said to have made the first offerings to the gods along with the seven Hotis; while Angiras and Yayati are mentioned with him as ancient sacrificers in I, 31, 17, Bhigu and Angiras in VIII, 43, 13, Atharvan and Dadhyanch in I, 80, 16 and Dadhyanch, Angiras, Atri and Kanva in I, 139, 9.

Atharvan by his sacrifices is elsewhere described, as having first extended the paths, whereupon the sun was born (I, 83, 5), and the Atharvans, in the plural, are styled "our fathers" (*nah pitarah*) along with Angirases, Navagvas and Bhgus in X, 14, 6. In II, 34, 12, Dashagvas are said to have been the first to offer a sacrifice; while in X, 92, 10 Atharvan is spoken of, as having established order by sacrifices, when the Bhigus showed themselves as gods by their skill. Philologically the name of Atharvan appears as Athravan, meaning a fire-priest, in the Avesta, and the word Angiras is said to be etymologically connected with the Greek *Aggilos*, a "messenger" and the Persian *Angara* "a mounted courier." In the Aitareya Brahmana (III, 34) Angirases are said to be the same as Angarah, "burning coals or fire," (Cf. Rig. X. 62, 5). Whether we accept these etymologies as absolutely correct or not, the resemblance between the different words sufficiently warrants the assumption that Atharvan and Angiras must have been the ancient sacrificers of the whole Aryan race and not merely of the Vedic people. Therefore, even though Manu, Atharvan, Angiras be not the names of particular individuals, still there can be little doubt that they represented families of priests who conducted, if not originated the sacrifices in primeval times, that is, before the Aryan separation, and who, for this reason, seem to have attained almost divine character in the eyes of the poets of the

Rig-Veda. They have all been described as more or less connected with Yama in X, 14, 3-6; but it does not follow therefrom that they were all Yama's agents or beings without any human origin.

For, as stated above, there are a number of passages in which they are described as being the *first* and the *most ancient* sacrificers of the race; and if after their death they are said to have gone to Yama and become his friends and companions, that does not, in any way, detract from their human character. It is, therefore, very important in the history of the sacrificial literature to determine if any traditions are preserved in the Rig-Veda regarding the duration of the sacrifices performed by these ancient ancestors of the Vedic people (*nah purve pitarah*, VI, 22, 2), in times before the separation of the Aryan people, and see if they lend any support to the theory of an early Circum-Polar home.

Now so far as my researches go, I have not been able to find any Vedic evidence regarding the duration of the sacrifices performed by Manu, Atharvan, Bhrigu, or any other ancient sacrificers, except he Angirases. There is an annual *sattra* described in the Shrauta Sutras, which is called the *Angirasam-ayanam*, and is said to be a modification of the *Gavam ayanam*, the type of all yearly *sattras*. But we do not find therein any mention of the duration of the *sattra* of the Angirases. The duration of the *Gavam ayanam* is, however, given in the Taittiriya Samhita, and will be discussed in the next chapter. For the present, we confine ourselves to *sattra* of the Angirases, and have to see if we can find out other means for determining its duration. Such a means is, fortunately, furnished by the Rig-Veda itself. There are two *chief* species of the Angirases (*Angiras-tama*), called the Navagvas and the Dashagvas, mentioned in the Rig-Veda (X, 62, 5 and 6). These two classes of ancient sacrificers are generally mentioned together, and the facts attributed to the Angirases are also attributed to them. Thus, the Navagvas are spoken of as "our ancient fathers," in VI. 22, 2, and as "our fathers" along with Angirases and Bhrigu in X, 14, 6. Like the Angirases, the Navagvas are also connected with the myth of Indra overthrowing Vala, and of Sarma and Panis (I, 62, 3 and 4; V, 29, 12; V, 45, 7; X, 108, 8). In one of these Indra if described as having taken their assistance when he rent the rock and Vala (I, 62, 4); and in V, 29, 12, the Navagvas are said to have praised Indra with songs and broken open the firmly closed stall of the cows. But there are only two verses in which the duration of their sacrificial session is mentioned.

Thus V, 45, 7 says, "Here, urged by hands, hath loudly rung the press-stone, with which the Navagvas sang (sacrificed) for *ten months*"; and in the eleventh verse of the same hymn the poet says, "I place upon (offer to) the waters your light-winning prayers wherewith the Navagvas completed their *ten months.*" In II, 34, 12, we again read, "They, the Dashagvas brought out (offered) sacrifice first of all. May they favour us at the flashing forth of the dawn": while in IV, 51, 4, the Dawns are said "to have dawned richly on the Navagva Angira, and on the seven-mouthed Dashagva," evidently showing that their sacrifice was connected with the break of the Dawn and lasted only for *ten months*. What the Navagvas or the Dashagvas accomplished by means of their sacrifices is further described in V, 29, 12, which says, "The Navagvas and the Dashagvas, who, had offered libations of Soma, praised Indra with songs; labouring (at it) the men laid open the stall of kine though firmly closed;" while in III, 39, 5, we read "Where the friend (Indra), with the friendly energetic Navagvas, followed up the cows on his knees, there verily with ten Dashagvas did Indra find the sun dwelling in darkness (*tamasi kshiyantam*)." In X, 62, 2 and 3, the Angirases, of whom the Dashagvas and Navagvas were the principle species (*Angiras-tama*, X, 62, 6), are however, said to have themselves performed the feat of vanquishing Vala, rescuing the cows and bringing out the sun, at the end of the year (*pari vatsare Valam abhindan*); but it obviously means that they helped Indra in achieving it at the end of the year.

Combining all these statements we can easily deduce (1) that the Navagvas and the Dashavgas completed their sacrifices in *ten months*, (2) that these sacrifices were connected with the early flush of the Dawn; (3) that the sacrificers helped Indra in the rescue of the cows from Vala at the *end of the year*; and (4) that at the place where Indra wept in search for the cows, he discovered the sun "dwelling in darkness."

Now we must examine a little more closely the meaning of these four important statements regarding the Navagvas and the Dashagvas. The first question that arises in this connection is —What is meant by their sacrifices being completed in ten months, and why did they not continue sacrificing for the whole year of twelve months? The expression for 'ten months' in the original is *dasha masah*, and the wards are so plain that there can be no doubt about their import. We have seen that the Navagvas used to help Indra in releasing the cows from the grasp of Vala, and in X, 62, 2 and 3, the Angirases are said to have defeated Vala *at the end of the year*, and raised the sun to heaven. This exploit of Indra, the Angirases, the Navagvas and the Dashagvas, therefore, clearly refers to the *yearly* rescue of the sun, or the cows of the morning, from the dark prison into which they are thrown by Vala; and the expression "Indra found the sun, dwelling in darkness," mentioned above further supports this view. In I, 117, 5, the Ashvins are said to have rescued Vandana, like some bright buried gold, "like one asleep in the lap of Nir-riti (death), like the sun dwelling in darkness (*tamasi kshiyantam*)."

This shows that the expression "dwelling in darkness," as applied to the sun, means that the sun was hidden or concealed below the horizon so as not to be seen by man. We must, therefore, hold that Indra killed or defeated Vala at the end of the year, in a place of darkness, and that the Dashagvas helped Indra by their songs at the time. This might lead any one to suppose that the Soma libations offered by the Navagvas and the Dashagvas for ten months, were offered during the time when war with Vala was waging. But the Vedic idea is entirely different. For instance the morning prayers are recited before the rise of the sun, and so the sacrifices to help Indra against Vala had to be performed *before* the war. Darkness or a dark period, of ten months is again astronomically impossible anywhere on the globe, and as there cannot be ten months of darkness the only other alternative admissible is that the Dashagvas and the Navagvas carried on their ten months' sacrifice during the period of sunshine. Now if this period of sunshine had extended to twelve months, there was no reason for the Dashagvas to curtail their sacrifices and complete them in ten months. Consequently the only infer nce we can draw from the story of the Navagvas and the Dashagvas is that they carried on their sacrifices during ten months of sunshine and after that period the sun went to dwell in darkness or sank below the horizon, and Indra, invigorated by the Soma libations of the Dashagvas, then entered into the cave of Vala, rent it open, released the cows of the morning and brought out the sun at the end of the old and the beginning of the new year, when the Dashagvas again commenced their sacrifices after the long dawn or dawns. In short, the Dashagvas and the Navagvas, and with them all the ancient sacrificers of the race, live in a region where the sun was above the horizon for ten months, and then went down producing a long yearly night of two months' duration. These ten months, therefore, formed the *annual* sacrificial session, or the calendar year, of the oldest sacrificers of the Aryan race and we shall see in the next chapter that independently of the legend of the Dashagvas this view is fully supported by direct references to such a session in the Vedic sacrificial literature.

The etymology of the words Navagva and Dashagva leads us to the same conclusion. The words are formed by prefixing *nava* and *dasha* to *gva*. So far there is no difference of opinion. But Yaska (XI, 19) takes *nava* in *navagva* to mean either "new" or "charming," interpreting the word to mean "those who have charming or new career (*gva*, from *gam* to go)." This explanation of Yaska is, however, unsatisfactory, inasmuch as the Navagvas and the Dashagvas are usually mentioned together in the Rig-Veda, and this close and frequent association of their names makes it necessary for us to find out such an etymological explanation of the words as would make Navagva bear the same relation to *nava* as Dashagva may have to *dasha*. But *dasha* or rather *dashan*, is a numeral signifying "ten" and cannot be taken in any other sense therefore, as observed by Prof. Lignana, *nava* or rather *navan* must be taken to mean "nine."

The meaning of *gva* (*gu+a*) is, however, yet to be ascertained. Some derive it from *go*, a cow, and others from *gam*, to go. In the first case the meaning would be "of nine cows" or "of ten cows"; while in the second case the words would signify "going in nine" or "going in ten," and the fact that the Dashagvas, are said to be ten in III, 39, 5, lends support to the latter view. But the use of the words Navagva and Dashagva, sometimes even in the singular number as an adjective qualifying a singular noun, shows that a group or a company of nine or ten men, is not, at any rate, always intended.

Thus in VI, 6, 3, the rays of Agni are said to be *navagvas*, while Adhrigu is said to be *dashagva* in VIII, 12, See his Essay on "The Navagvas and the Dashagvas of the Rig-Veda" in the Proceedings of the 7th International Congress of Orientalists, 1886, pp. 59-68. The essay is in Italian and I am indebted to the kindness of Mr. Shrinivas Iyengar B.A., B.L., High Court Pleader, Madras, for a translation of the same. 2, and Dadhyanch *navagva* in IX, 108, 4. We must, therefore, assign to these epithets some other meaning, and the only other possible explanation of the numerals "nine" and "ten" is that given by Sayana, who says (Comm. on Rig. I, 62, 4), "The Angirases are of two kinds, the Navagvas or those who rose after completing *sattra* in nine months, and the Dashagvas or those who rose after finishing the *sattra* in ten months." We have seen that in the Rig-Veda V, 45, 7 and 11, the Navagvas are said to have completed their sacrifices in ten months.

Sayana's explanation is therefore, fully warranted by these texts, and very probably it is based on some traditional information about the Dashagvas. Prof. Lignana of Rome, suggests that the numerals *navan* and *dashan* in these names should be taken as referring to the period of gestation, as the words *nava-mahya* and *dasha-mahya* occur in the Vendidad, V, 45, (136), in the same sense.

Thus interpreted Navagva would mean "born of nine months," and Dashagva "born of ten months." But this explanation is highly improbable, inasmuch as we cannot first suppose that a number of persons were born prematurely in early times, and secondly that it was specially such persons that attained almost divine honours.

The usual period of gestation is 280 days or ten lunar months (V, 78, 9), and those that were born a month earlier cannot be ordinarily expected to live long or to perform feats which wou d secure them divine honours. The reference to the Vendidad proves nothing, for there the case of a still-born child after a gestation of 1, 2, 3, 4, 5, 6, 7, 8, 9 or 10 months is under consideration, and Ahura Mazda See his Essay in the Proceedings of the 7th international Congress of the Orientalists, pp. 59-68. enjoins that the house where such as a still-born child is brought forth should be cleaned and sanctified in a special way. Prof. Lignana's explanation again conflicts with the Vedic texts which say that the Dashagvas were ten in number (III, 39, 5), or that the Navagvas sacrificed only for ten months (V, 47, 5) Sayana's explanation is, therefore, the only one entitled to our acceptance.

I may here mention that the Rig-Veda (V, 47, 7 and 11) speaks of ten months' sacrifice only in connection with the Navagvas, and does not mention any sacrifice of *nine* months. But the etymology of the names now helps us in assigning the ten months' sacrifice to the Dashagvas and the nine month's to the Navagvas. For *navan* in Navagva is only a numerical variation for *dashan* in Dashagva, and it follows, therefore, that what the Dashagvas did by tens, the Navagvas did by nines.

There is another circumstance connected with the Angirases which further strengthens our conclusion, and which must, therefore, be stated in this place.

The Angirases are sometimes styled the *Virupas*. Thus in III, 53, 7, the Angirases are described as "*Virupas, and sons of heaven*"; and the name Virupa once occurs by itself as that of a single being who sings the praises of Agni, in a stanza (VIII, 75, 6) immediately following one in which Angiras is invoked, showing that Virupa is here used as a synonym for Angiras. But the most explicit of these references is X, 62, 5 and 6. The first of these verses states that the Angirases are *Virupas*, and they are the sons of Agni; while the second describes them along with the Navagva and the Dashagva in the following terms, "And which Virupas were born from Agni and from the sky; the Navagva or the Dashagva, as the best of the Angirases (*Angiras-tama*), prospers in the assemblage of the gods." Now *Virupas* literally means "of various forms" and in the above verses it seems to have been used as an adjective qualifying Angirases to denote that there are many species of them. We are further told that the Navagvas and the Dashagvas were the most important (*Angiras-tamah*) of these species. In the last chapter I have discussed the meaning of the adjective *Virupa* as applied to a couple of Day and Night and have shown, on the authority of Madhava, that the word, as applied to days and Nights, denotes their duration, or the period of time over which they extend.

Virupas in the present instance appears to be used precisely in the same sense. The Navagvas and the Dashagvas were no doubt the most important of the early sacrificers, but these too were not their only species. In other words they were not merely "nine-going," and "ten-going," but "various-going" (*virupas*), meaning that the duration of their sacrifices was sometimes shorter than nine and sometimes longer than ten months.

In fact a *Sapta-gu* (seven-going) is mentioned in X, 47, 6, along with Brihaspati, the son of Angiras, and it seems to be used there as an adjective qualifying Brihaspati; for Brihaspati is described in another place (IV, 50, 4) as *saptasya* (seven-mouthed), while the Atharva-Veda IV, 6, 1, describes the first Brahmana, Brihaspati, as dashasya or ten-mouthed. We have also seen that in IV, 51, 4, the Dashagva is also called "seven-mouthed."

All these expressions can be satisfactorily explained only by supposing that the Angirases were not merely "nine-going" or "tengoing," but *virupas* or "various going," and that they completed their sacrifices within the number of months for which the sun was above the horizon at the place where these sacrifices were performed.

It follows, therefore, that in, ancient times the sacrificial session lasted from seven to ten months; and the number of sacrificers (*Hotris*) corresponded with the number of the months, each doing his duty by rotation somewhat after the manner of the Egyptian priests previously referred to.

These sacrifices were over when the long night commenced, during which Indra fought with Vala and vanquished him by the end of the year (*parivatsare*, X, 62, 2). The word *parivatsare* (at the end of the year) is very suggestive and shows that the year closed with the long night.

Another reference to a period of ten months' sunshine is found in the legend of Dirghatamas whom the Ashvins are said to have saved or rescued from a pit, into which he was thrown, after being made blind and infirm. I have devoted a separate chapter later on to the liscussion of Vedic legends. But I take up here the legend of Dirghatamas because we have therein an express statement as to the life of Dirghatamas, which remarkably corroborates the conclusion we have arrived at from the consideration of the story of the Dashagvas.

The story of Dirghatamas is narrated in the Mahabharata, Adiparvan, Chap. 104. He is said to be the son of Mamata by Utathya, and born blind through the curse of Brihaspati his uncle. He was, however, married and had several sons by Pradveshi. The wife and the sons eventually became tired of feeding the blind Dirghatamas (so called because he was born blind), and the sons abandoned him afloat on a worn-out raft in the Ganges.

He drifted on the waters for a long time and distance, when at last the king Bali picked him up. Dirghatamas then had several sons born to him from a *dasi* or a female slave, and also from the wife of Bali, the sons of Bali's wife becoming kings of different provinces.

In the Rig-Veda Dirghatamas is one of the proteges of the Ashvins, and about 25 hymns in the first Mandala are ascribed to him. He is called Mamateya, or the son of Mamata in I, 152, 6, and Uchathya's offspring in I, 158, 4. In the latter hymn he invokes the Ashvins for the purpose of rescuing him from the ordeals of fire and water to which he was subjected by the Dasa Traitana. In I, 147, 3 and IV, 4, 13, Agni is, however, said to have restored to Dirghatamas his eyesight.

But the statement need not surprise us as the achievements of one deity are very often ascribed to another in the Rig-Veda. Dirghatamas does not stand alone in being thus rescued by the Ashvins. Chyavana is spoken of as another protege of the Ashvins, and they are said to have restored him to youth. Vandana and a host of others are similarly mentioned as being saved, rescued, cured, protected or rejuvenated by the Ashvins.

All these achievements are new understood as referring to the exploit of restoring to the sun his decayed power in the winter. But with the expression "like the sun dwelling in darkness" before us, in the legend of Vandana (I, 117, 5), we must make these legends refer not merely to the decayed power of the sun in winter, but to his actual sinking below the horizon for some time. Bearing this in mind, let us try to see what inference we can deduce, so far as the subject in hand is concerned, from the legend of Dirghatamas. The statement in the myth or legend, which is most important for our purpose, is contained in I, 158, 6. The verse may be literally translated as follows: — "Dirghatamas, the son of Mamata, having grown decrepit in the tenth *yuga*, becomes a Brahman charioteer of the waters wending to their goal." The only expressions which require elucidation in this verse are "in the tenth *yuga*," and "waters wending to their goal." Otherwise the story is plain enough.

Dirghatamas grows old in the tenth *yuga*, and riding on waters, as the Mahabharata story has it, goes along with them to the place which is the goal of these waters. But scholars are not agreed as to what *yuga* means. Some take it to mean a cycle of years, presumably five as in the Vedanga-Jyotisha, and invest Dirghatamas with infirmity at the age of fifty.

The Petersburg Lexicon would interpret *yuga*, wherever it occurs in the Rig-Veda, to mean not, "a period of time," but "a generation," or "the relation of descent from a common stock"; and it is followed by Grassmann in this respect. According to these scholars the phrase "in the tenth *yuga*" in the above verse would, therefore, signify "in the tenth generation" whatever that may mean. Indeed, there seems to be a kind of prejudice against interpreting *yuga* as meaning "a period of time" in the Rig-Veda, and it is therefore, necessary to examine the point at some length in this place.

That the word *yuga* by itself means "a period of time" or that, at any rate, it is one of its meanings goes without saying. Even the Petersburg Lexicon assigns this meaning to *yuga* in the Atharva Veda VIII, 2, 21; but so far as the Rig-Veda is concerned *yuga* according to it, must mean "descent," or "generation," or something like it, but never "a period of time." This is especially the case, with the phrase *Manusha yuga*, or *Manushya yugani*, which occurs several times in the Rig-Veda. Western scholars would everywhere translate it to mean "generations of men," while native scholars, like Sayana and Mahidhara; take it to refer to "mortal ages" in a majority of places. In some cases (I, 124, 2; I, 144, 4) Sayana, however, suggests as an alternative, that the phrase may be understood to mean "conjunction" or "couples (*yuga*) of men"; and this has probably given rise to the interpretation put upon the phrase by Western scholars.

Etymologically the word *yuga* may mean "conjunction" or "a couple" denoting either (1) "a couple of day and night," or (2) "a couple of months" *i.e.* "a season," or (3) "a couple of fortnights" or "the time of the conjunction of the moon and the sun," *i.e.* "a month." Thus at the beginning of the Kali-Yuga the planets and the sun were, it is supposed, in conjunction and hence it is said to be called a *yuga*.

It is also possible that the word may mean "a conjunction, or a couple, or even a generation of men." Etymology, therefore, does not help us in determining which of these meanings should be assigned to the word *yuga* or the phrase, *Manusha yuga* in the Rig-Veda, and we must find out some other means for determining it. The prejudice we have referred to above, appears to be mainly due to the disinclination of the Western scholars to import the later Yuga theory into the Rig-Veda.

But it seems to me that the caution has been carried too far, so far as almost to amount to a sort of prejudice. Turning to the hymns of the Rig-Veda, we find as remarked by Muir, the phrase *yuge yuge* used at least in half a dozen places (III, 26, 3; VI, 15, 8; X, 94, 12, &c.), and it is interpreted by Sayana to mean a period of time. In III, 33, 8, and X, 10, we have *uttara yugani* "later age," and in X, 72, 1, we read *uttare yuge* "in a later age"; whilst in the next two verses we have the phrases *Devanam purve yuge* and *Devanam prathame yuge* clearly referring to the later and earlier ages of the gods.

The word *Devanam* is in the plural and *yuga* is in the singular, and it is not therefore possible to take the phrase to mean "generations of gods." The context again clearly shows that a reference to time is intended, for the hymn speaks of the creation and the birth of the gods in early primeval times. Now if we interpret *Devanam yugam* to mean "an age of gods," why should *manushya yugani* or *manusha yuga* be not interpreted to mean "human ages," is more than I can understand. There are again express passages in the Rig-Veda where *manusha yuga* cannot be taken to mean "generations of men." Thus in V, 52, 4, which is a hymn to Maruts, we read *Vishve ye manusha yuga panti martyam rishah*. Here the verb *panti* (protect), the nominative *vishve ye* (all those), and the object is *martyam* (the mortal man), while *rishah* (from injury), in the ablative, denotes the object against which the protection is sought.

So far the sentence, therefore, means "All those who protect man from injury"; and now the question is, what does *manusha yuga* mean? If we take it to mean "generations of men" in the objective case it becomes superfluous, for *martyam* (man) is already the object of *panti* (protect). It is, therefore, necessary to assign to *manusha yuga* the only other meaning we know of, *viz.*, "human ages" and take the phrase as an accusative of time.

Thus the interpreted the whole sentence means "All those, who protect man from injury during human ages." No other construction is more natural or reasonable than this; but still Prof.

Max Muller translates the verse to mean "All those who protect the generations of men, who protect the mortal from injury," in spite of the fact that this is tautological and that there is no conjunctive particle in the texts (like *cha*) to join what according to him are the two objects of the verb "protect."

Mr. Griffith seems to have perceived this difficulty, and has translated, "Who all, through ages of mankind, guard mortal man from injury." Another passage which is equally decisive on this point, is X, 140, 6. The verse is addressed to Agni, and people are said to have put him in front to secure his blessings. It is as follows:

Ritavanam mahisham vishva-darshatam agnim sumnaya dadhire puro janah |
Shrut-karnam saprathas-taman tva gira daivyam manusha yuga ||

Here *ritavanam* (righteous), *mahisham* (strong), *vishvadarshatam* (visible to all), *agnim* (Agni, fire), *shrut-karnam* (attentive eared), *saprathas-taman* (most widely-reaching), *tva* (thee) and *daivyam* (divine) are all in the accusative case governed by *dadhire* (placed), and describe the qualities of Agni. *Janah* (people) is the nominative and *dadhire* (placed) is the only verb in the text. *Sumnaya* (for the welfare) denotes the purpose for which the people placed Agni in front (*puro*) and *gira* (by praises) is the means by which the favour of Agni, is to be secured.

If we, therefore, leave out the various adjectives of Agni, the verse means, "The people have placed Agni (as described) in front for their welfare, with praises."

The only expression that remains is *manusha yuga,* and it can go in with the other words in a natural way only as an accusative of time. The verse would then mean "The people have placed Agni (as described), in front for their welfare, with praises, during human ages."

But Griffith takes *yuga* to mean "generations," and supplying a verb of his own; translates the last part of the verse thus: "Men's generations magnify (Agni) with praise-songs (*gira*)." This shows what straits, we are reduced to if we once make up our mind not to interpret *manusha yuga* to mean "a period of time," for the word "magnify" does not exist in the original.

This verse also occurs in the Vajasaneyi Samhita (XII, 111), and Mahidhara there explains *manusha yuga* to mean "human ages," or "periods of time" such as fortnights. We have, therefore, at least two passages, where *manusha yuga,* must, according to the recognized rules of interpretation, be taken to mean "periods of time," and not "generations of men," unless we are prepared to give up the natural construction of the sentence.

There are no more passages in the Rig-Veda where *manusha yuga,* occurs in juxtaposition with words like *janah* or *martyam,* so as to leave no option as regards the meaning to be assigned to *yuga.* But if the meaning of a phrase is once definitely determined even from a single passage, we can safely understand the phrase in the same sense in other passages, provided the meaning does not conflict there with the context. That is how the meaning of many a Vedic word has been determined by scholars like Yaska, and we are not venturing on a new path in adopting the same process of reasoning in the present case.

But if *manusha yuga* means "human ages" and not "human generations," we have still to determine the exact duration of these ages. In the Atharva-Veda, VIII, 2, 21, which says, "We allot to thee, a hundred, ten thousand years, two, three or four *yugas,*" the word *yuga* obviously stands for a period of time, not shorter than ten thousand years.

But there are grounds to hold that in the early days of the Rig-Veda *yuga* must have denoted a shorter period of time, or, at least, that was one of its meanings in early days. The Rig-Veda often speaks of "the first" (prathama) dawn, or "the first of the coming" (*ayatinam prathama*) dawns (Rig. I, 113, 8; 123, 2; VII, 76, 6; X, 35, 4); while "the last" (*avama*) dawn is mentioned in VII, 71, 3, and the dawn is said to have the knowledge of the *first* day in I, 123, 9. Now, independently of what I have said before about the Vedic dawns, the ordinal numeral "first" as applied to the dawn is intelligible only if we suppose it to refer to the first dawn of the year, or the dawn on the first day of the year, somewhat like the phrase "first night" (*prathama ratrih*) used in the Brahmans.

The "first" (*prathama*) and the "last" (*avama*) dawn must, therefore, be taken to signify the beginning and the end of the year in those days; and in the light of what has been said about the nature of the Vedic dawns in the fifth chapter, we may safely conclude that the "first" of the dawns was no other than the first of a set or group of dawns that appeared at the close of the long night and commenced the year.

Now this "first dawn" is described as "wearing out human ages" (*praminati manushya yugani*) in I, 124, 2, and I, 92, 11; while in I, 115, 2, we are told that "the pious or godly men extend the *yugas*," on the appearance of the dawn (*yatra naro devayanto yugani vitanvate*).

European scholars interpret *yuga* in the above passages to mean "generations of men." But apart from the fact that the phrase *manusha yuga* must be understood to mean "human ages" in at least two passages discussed above, the context in I, 124, 2 and I, 92, 11 is obviously in favour of interpreting the word *yuga*, occurring therein, as equivalent to a period of time. The dawn is here described as commencing a new course of heavenly ordinances, or holy sacrifices (*daivyani vratani*), and setting in motion the *manushya yugani*, obviously implying that with the first dawn came the sacrifices, as well as the cycle of time known as "human ages" or that "the human ages" were reckoned from the first dawn.

This association, of *manusha yuga*, or "human ages," with the "first dawn" at once enables us to definitely determine the length or duration of "human ages"; for if these ages (*yugas*) commenced with the first dawn of the year, they must have ended on the last (*avama*) dawn of the year. In other words *manusha yuga* collectively denoted the whole period of time between the first and the last dawn of the year, while a single *yuga* denoted a shorter division of this period.

Apart from the legend of Dirghatamas, we have, therefore, sufficient evidence in the Rig-Veda to hold that the world, *yuga* was used to denote a period of time, shorter than one year, and that the phrase *manusha yuga* meant "human ages" or "the period of time between the first and the last dawn of year" and not "human generations."

The statement that "Dirghatamas grew old in the *tenth yuga*" is now not only easy to understand, but it enables us to determine, still more definitely, the meaning of *yuga* in the days of the Rig-Veda.

For, if *yuga* was a part of *manusha yuga*, that is, of the period between the first and the last dawn of the year, and the legend of Dirghatamas a solar legend, the statement that "Dirghatamas grew old in the tenth *yuga*" can only mean that "the sun grew old in the tenth *month*." In other words, ten *yugas* were supposed to intervene between the first and the last dawn, or the two termini, of the year; and as ten days or ten fortnights would be too short, and ten seasons too long a period of time to lie between these limits, the word *yuga* in the phrase *dashame yuge*, must be interpreted to mean "a month" and nothing else. In short, Dirghatamas was the sun that grew old in the tenth month, and riding on the aerial waters was borne by them to their goal, that is, to the ocean (VII, 49, 2) below the horizon.

The waters here referred to are, in fact, the same over which the king Varuna is said to rule, or which flow by his commands, or for which he is said to have dug out a channel (VII, 49, 1-4; II, 28 4; VII, 87, 1) and so cut out a path for Surya, and which being released by Indra from the grass of Vritra, bring on the sun (I, 51, 4). Prof. Max Muller, in his *Contributions to the Science of Mythology* (Vol. II, pp. 583-598), has .shown that most of the achievements of the Ashvins can be rationally explained by taking them as referring to the decaying sun.

The legend of Dirghatamas is thus only a mythical representation of the Arctic sun, who ascends above the "bright ocean" (VII, 60, 4,), becomes visible for *manusha yuga* or ten months, and then drops again into the nether waters.

What these waters are and how their nature has been long misunderstood will be further explained in a subsequent chapter, when we come to the discussion of Vedic myths. Suffice it to say for the present that the legend of Dirghatamas, interpreted as above, is in full accord with the legend of the Dashagvas who are described as holding their sacrificial session only for ten months.

I have discussed here the meaning of *yuga* and *manusha yuga* at some length, because the phrases have been much misunderstood, in spite of clear passages showing that "a period of time" was intended to be denoted by them.

These passages (V, 52, 4; X, 140, 6) establish the fact that *manusha yuga* denoted "human ages," and the association of these ages with the "first dawn" (I, 124, 2; I, 115, 2) further shows that the length of a *yuga* was regarded to be shorter than a year. The mention of the tenth *yuga* finally settles the meaning of *yuga* as "one month."

That is how I have arrived at the meaning of these phrases, and I am glad to find that I have been anticipated in my conclusions by Prof. Rangacharya of Madras, on different grounds. In his essay on the *yugas*, he discusses the root meaning of *yuga*, and, taking it to denote "a conjunction," observes as follows, "The phases of the moon being so readily observable, it is probable that, as suggested by Professor Weber, the idea of a period of time known as a *yuga* and depending upon a conjunction of certain heavenly bodies, was originally derived from a knowledge of these phases.

The Professor (Weber) further strengthens his supposition by referring to a passage cited in the Shadvimsha Brahmana (IV, 6) wherein the four *yugas* are still designated by their more ancient names and are con necked with the four lunar phases to which they evidently owe their origin." Mr. Rangacharya then refers to *darsha*, the ancient name for the conjunction of the sun and moon, and concludes, "There is also old mythological or other evidence which leads us to conclude that our forefathers observed many other kinds of interesting celestial conjunctions; and in all probability the earliest conception of a *yuga* meat the period from, new moon to new moon," that is, one lunar month.

The passage stating that it was the first dawn that set the cycle of *manusha yuga* in motion is already quoted above; and if 'we compare this statement with Rig. X, 138, 6, where Indra after killing Vritra and producing the dawn and the sun, is said "to have set the ordering of the months in the sky," it will be further evident that the cycle of the time which began with the first dawn was a cycle of months.

We may, therefore, safely conclude that *manusha yuga* represented, in early days, a cycle of months during which the sun was above the horizon, or rather that period of sunshine and action when the ancestors of the Aryan race held their sacrificial sessions or performed other religious and social ceremonies.

There are many other passages in the Rig-Veda which support the same view. But *manusha yuga* being everywhere interpreted by Western scholars to mean "human generations or tribes," the real meaning of these passages has become obscure and unintelligible.

Thus in VIII, 46, 12, we have. "All (sacrificers), with ladles lifted, invoke that mighty Indra for *manusha yuga*; and the meaning evidently is that Soma libations were offered to Indra during the period of human ages.

But taking *manusha yuga*; to denote "human tribes," Griffith translates "All races of mankind invoke &c." a rendering, which, though intelligible, does not convey the spirit of the original. Similarly, Agni is said to shine during "human ages" in VII, 9, 4. But there too the meaning "human tribes" is unnecessarily foisted upon the phrase. The most striking illustration of the impropriety of interpreting *yuga* to mean "a generation" is, however, furnished by Rig. II, 2, 2. Here Agni is said to shine for *manusha yuga* and *kshapah*. Now *kshapah* means "nights" and the most natural interpretation would be to take *manusha yuga* and *kshapah* as allied expressions denoting a period of time.

The verse will then mean: "O Agni! thou shinest during human ages and nights." It is necessary to mention "nights" because though *manusha yuga* is a period of sunshine, including a long day and a succession of ordinary days and nights, yet the long or the continuous night which followed *manusha yuga* could not have been included in the latter phrase. Therefore, when the whole period of the solar year was intended, a compound expression like "*manusha yuga* and the continuous nights" was necessary and that is the meaning of the phrase in II, 2, 2. But Prof. Oldenberg, following Max Muller, translates as follows "O Agni! thou shinest on human tribes, on continuous nights."

Here, in the first place, it is difficult to understand what "shining on human tribes" means and secondly if *kshapah* means "continuous nights," it could mean nothing except "the long continuous night," and if so, why not take *manusha yuga* to represent the period of the solar year, which remains after the long night is excluded from it? As observed by me before, Prof. Max Muller has correctly translated *kshapah* by "continuous nights," but has missed the true meaning of the expression *manusha yuga* in this place. A similar mistake has been committed with respect to IV, 16, 19, where the expression is *kshapah madema sharadas cha purvih*.

Here, in spite of the accent, Max Muller takes *kshapah* as accusative and so does Sayana. But Sayana correctly interprets the expression as "May we rejoice for many autumns (seasons) and nights."

"Seasons and nights" is a compound phrase, and the particle *cha* becomes unmeaning if we split it up and take nights (*kshapah*) with one verb, and seasons (*sharadah*) with another. Of course so long as the Arctic theory was unknown the phrase "seasons and nights" or "*manusha yuga* and nights" was unintelligible inasmuch as nights were included in the seasons or the *yugas*. But Prof. Max Muller has himself suggested the solution of the difficulty by interpreting *kshapah* as "continuous nights" in II, 2, 2; and adopting this rendering, we can, with greater propriety, take seasons and nights together, as indicated by the particle *cha* and understand the expression to mean a complete solar year including the long night.

The addition of *kshapah* to *manusha yuga*, therefore, further supports the conclusion that the phrase indicated a period of sunshine as stated above. There are many other passages in translating which unnecessary confusion or obscurity has been caused by taking *manusha yuga* to mean human tribes; but a discussion of these is not relevant to the subject in hand.

An independent corroboration of the conclusion we have drawn from the legends of the Dashagvas and Dirghatamas is furnished by the number of seasons mentioned in certain Vedic texts. A period of sunshine of ten months followed by along night of two months can well be described as five seasons of two months each, followed by the sinking of the sun into the waters below the horizon; and as a matter of fact we find the year so described in I, 164, 12, a verse which occurs also in the Atharva Veda (IX, 9, 12) with a slight variation and in the Prashnopanishad I, 11. It may be literally translated as follows: — "The five-footed (*pancha-padam*) Father of twelve forms, they say, is full of watery vapours (*pursihinam*) in the farther half (*pare ardhe*) of the heaven. These others again say (that) He the far-seeing (*vichakshanam*) is placed on the six-spoked (*shadare*) and seven-wheeled (car), in the nearer (*upare* scil. *ardhe*) half of the heaven." The adjective "far-seeing" is made to qualify "sevenwheeled" instead of "He" in the Atharva Veda, (*vichakshane*) being in the locative case while Shankaracharya in his commentary on the Prashnopanishad splits *upare* into two words *u* and *pare* taking *u* as an expletive. But these readings do not materially alter the meaning of the verse. The context everywhere clearly indicates that the yeargod of twelve months (*akriti* X, 85, 5) is here described.

The previous verse in the hymn (Rig. I, 164) mentions "The twelve-spoked wheel, in which 720 sons of Agni are established," a clear reference to a year of twelve months with Tao days and nights. There is, therefore, no doubt that the passage contains the description of the year and the two halves of the verse, which are introduced by the phrases "they say'" and "others say," give us two opinions about the nature of the year-god of twelve forms.

Let us now see what these opinions are. Some say that the year-god is five-footed (*pancha-padam*), that is divided into five seasons; and the others say that he has a six-spoked car, or six seasons.

It is clear from this that the number of seasons was held to be five by some and six by others in early days. Why should there be this difference of opinion? The Aitareya Brahmana I, 1, (and the Taittiriya Samhita I, 6, 2, 3) explains that the two seasons of *Hemanta* and *Shishir* together made a joint season, thereby reducing the number of seasons from six to five.

But this explanation seems to be an afterthought, for in the Shatapatha Brahmana, XIII, 6, 1, 10, *Varsha* and *Sharad* are compounded for this purpose instead of *Hemanta* and *Shishir*. This shows that in the days of the Taittiriya Samhita and the Brahmans it was not definitely known or settled which two seasons out of six should be compounded to reduce the number to five; but as five seasons were sometimes mentioned in the Vedas, some explanation was felt to be necessary to account for the smaller number and such explanation was devised by taking together *any two* consecutive seasons out of six and regarding them as one joint season of four months.

But the explanation is too vague to be true; and we cannot believe that the system of compounding airy two seasons according to one's choice was ever followed in practice. We must, therefore, give up the explanation as unsatisfactory and see if the verse from the Rig-Veda, quoted above, enables us to find out a better explanation of the fact that the seasons were once held to be five. Now the first half of this verse describes the five-footed father as full of watery vapours in the farther part of heaven, while the year of sixspoked car is said to be far-seeing.

In short, *purishinam* (full of, or dwelling in waters) in the first line appears to be a counterpart of *vichakshanam* (far-seeing) in the second line. This is made clear by the verses which follow. Thus the 13th verse in the hymn speaks of "the five-spoked wheel" as remaining entire and unbroken though ancient; and the next or the 14th verse says that "the unwasting wheel with its felly revolves; the ten draw (it) yoked over the expanse.

The sun's eye goes covered with rajas (aerial vapour); all worlds are dependent on him." Comparing this with the 11th verse first quoted, it may be easily seen that *purishinam* (full of watery vapours) and *rajasa avritam* (covered with rajas) are almost synonymous phrases and the only inference we can draw from them is that the five-footed year-god or the sun event to dwell in watery vapours *i.e.,* became invisible, or covered with darkness and (rajas), for some time in the farther part of the heaven.

The expression that "The ten, yoked, draw his carriage," (also cf. Rig. IX, 63, 9) further shows that the five seasons were not made by combining any two consecutive seasons out of six as explained in the Brahmans (for in that case the number of horses could not be called ten), but that a real year of five seasons or ten months was here intended.

When the number of seasons became increased to six, the year-god ceased to be *purishin* (full of waters) and became *vichakshanam* or far-seeing. We have seen that the sun, as represented by Dirghatamas, grew old in the tenth month and riding on aerial waters went into the ocean.

The same .idea is expressed in the present verse which describes two different views about the nature of the year, one of five and the other of six seasons and contrasts their leading features with each other. Thus *pare ardhe* is contrasted with *upare ardhe* in the second line, *pancha-padam* (compare *pacnhare* in the next verse, *i.e.* Rig-Veda I. 164, 13) with *shad-are,* and *purishinam* with *vichakshanam*. In short, the verse under consideration describes the year either (1) as five-footed, and lying in waters in the farther part of heaven, or (2) as mounted on a six-spoked car and far-seeing in the nearer part of the heaven. These two descriptions cannot evidently apply to seasons in one and the same place, and the artifice of combining two consecutive seasons cannot be accepted as a solution of the question. Five seasons and ten months followed by the watery residence of the sun or dark nights, is what is precisely described in the first half of this passage (I, 164, 12), and, from what has been said hitherto, it will be easily seen that it is the Arctic year of ten months that is here described.

The verse, and especially the contrast between*purishinam* and *vichakshanam*, does not appear to have attracted the attention it deserves. Bu in the light of the Arctic theory the description is now as intelligible as any.

The Vedic bards have here preserved for us the memory of a year of five seasons or ten months, although their year had long been changed into one of twelve months. The explanation given in the Brahmans are all so many *post-facto* devices to account for the mention of five seasons in the Rig-Veda, and I do not think we are bound to accept them when the fact of five seasons can be better accounted for.

I have remarked before that in searching for evidence of ancient traditions we must expect to find later traditions associated with them, and Rig. I, 164, 12, discussed above, is a good illustration of this remark. The first line of the verse, though it speaks of five seasons, describes the year as twelve-formed; while the second line, which deals with a year of six seasons or twelve months, speaks of it as "seven-wheeled," that is made up of seven months or seven suns, or seven rays of the sun.

This may appear rather inconsistent at the first sight; but the history of words in any language will show that old expressions are preserved in the language long after they have ceased to denote the ideas primarily expressed by them.

Thus we now use coins for exchange, yet the word "pecuniary" which is derived from *pecus* = cattle, is still retained in the language; and similarly, we still speak of the rising of the sun, though we now know that it is not the luminary that rises, but the earth, by rotating round its axis, makes the sun visible to us. Very much in the same way and by the same process, expressions like *saptashva* (seven horsed) or *sapta-chakra* (seven-wheeled), as applied to the year or the sun, must have become recognized and established as current phrases in the language before the hymns assumed their present form, and the Vedic bards could not have discarded them even when they knew that they were not applicable to the state of things before them. On the contrary, as we find in the Brahmans every artifice, that ingenuity could suggest, was tried to make these old phrases harmonize with the state of things then in, vogue, and from the religious or the sacrificial point of view it was quite necessary to do so.

But when we have to examine the question from a historical stand-point, it is our duty to separate the relics of the older period from facts or incidents of the later period with which the former are sometimes inevitably mixed up; and if we analyze the verse in question (I, 164, 12) in this way we shall clearly see in it the traces of a year of ten months and five seasons.

The same principle is also applicable in other cases, as, for instance, when we find the Navagvas mentioned together with the seven *vipras* in VI, 22, 2. The bards, who gave us the present version of the hymns, knew of the older or primeval state of things only by traditions, and it is no wonder if these traditions are occasionally mixed up with later events. On the contrary the preservation of so many traditions of the primeval home is itself a wonder, and it is this fact, which invests the oldest Veda with such peculiar importance from the religious as well as the historical point of view.

To sum up there are clear traditions preserved in the Rig-Veda, which show that the year once consisted of seven months or seven suns, as in the legend of Aditi's sons, or that there were ten months of the year as in the legend of the Dashagvas or Dirghatamas; and these cannot be accounted for except on the Arctic theory.

These ten months formed the sacrificial session of the primeval sacrificers of the Aryan race and the period was denominated as *manusha yuga* or human ages, an expression much misunderstood by Western scholars. The sun went below the horizon in the tenth of these *yugas* and Indra fought with Vala in the period of darkness which followed and at the end of the year, again brought back the sun "dwelling in darkness" during the period. The whole year of twelve months was thus made up of *manusha yuga* and continuous nights, and, in spite of the fact that the Vedic bards lived later on in places where the sun was above the horizon for twelve months, the expression "*manusha yuga* and *kshapah* (nights)" is still found in the Rig-Veda. It is true that the evidence discussed in this chapter is mostly legendary; but that does not lessen its importance in any way, for it will be seen later on that some of these traditions are Indo-European in character. The tradition that the year was regarded by some to have been made up only of five seasons, or that only *ten* horses were yoked to the chariot of the sun, is again in full accord with the meaning of these legends; and it will be shown in the next chapter that in the Vedic literature there are express statements about a sacrificial session of ten months, which are quite independent of these traditions, and which, therefore, independently prove and strengthen the conclusions deduced from the legends discussed in this chapter.

THE COWS' WALK

The legend of the Dashagvas, who completed their sacrifices during ten months, is not the only relic of the ancient year preserved in the sacrificial literature. The Pravargya ceremony, which is described in the Aitareya Brahmana (I, 18-12), furnishes us with another instance, where a reference to the old year seems to be clearly indicated. Dr. Haug, in his translation of the Aitareya Brahmana, has fully described this ceremony in a note to I, 18. It lasts for three days and precedes the animal and the Soma sacrifice, as no one is allowed to take part in the Soma feast without having undergone this ceremony. The whole ceremony symbolizes the revival of the sun or the sacrificial ceremony (*yajna*), which, for the time being, is preserved as seed in order that it may grow again in due time (Ait. Br. I, 18). Thus one of the chief implements used in the ceremony is a peculiar earthen pot called *Gharma* or *Mahavira*.

Placing it on the Vedic altar the Adhvaryu makes a circle of clay called *khara*, because it is made of earth brought on the back of a donkey to the sacrificial ground. He places the pot on the circle and heats it so as to make it quite hot (*gharma*). It is then lifted by means of two *shaphas* (two wooden pieces), and then milking a cow, the milk is poured into the heated pot and mixed with the milk of a goat whose kid is dead. After this has been done, the contents of the *Mahavira* are thrown into the Ahavaniya fire. But all the contents of the pot are not thus thrown away, for the Hotri is described as eating the remainder of the contents of the *Gharma*, which are said to be full of honey, full of sap, full of food and quite hot. The Aitareya Brahmana (I, 22) gives us a rational of this ceremony as follows "The milk in the vessel is the seed. This seed (in the shape of milk) is poured in Agni (fire) as the womb of the gods for production, for Agni is the womb of the gods."

This explanation proves the symbolic nature of the ceremony, and shows that the sun, the sacrifice or the year is thus preserved as seed for time, and then revived at the proper season. The Mantra or the verse, which is recited on the occasion of pouring the milk into the *Mahavira* is taken from the Rig-Veda VIII, 72 (61) 8, and it is very likely that the verse was selected not simply on account of mere verbal correspondence. The hymn, where the verse occurs, is rather obscure. But the verse itself, as well as the two preceding verses (VIII, 72 (61), 6-7-8) present no verbal difficulty and may be translated as follows:

"6. And now that mighty and great chariot of his with horses (as well as) the line of his chariot is seen."

"7. The seven milk the one, and the two create the five, on the ocean's loud-sounding bank."

"8. With the ten of Vivasvat, Indra by his three-fold hammer, caused the heaven's bucket to drop down."

Here, first of all, we are told that his (sun's) chariot, the great chariot with horses has become visible, evidently meaning that the dawn has made its appearance on the horizon. Then the seven, probably the seven *Hotris*, or seven rivers, are said to milk this dawn and produce the two. This milking is a familiar process in the Rig-Veda and in one place the cows of the morning are said to be milked from darkness (I, 33, 10). The two evidently mean day and night and as soon as they are milked, they give rise to the five seasons. The day and the night are said to be the two mothers of Surya in III, 55, 6, and here they are the mothers of the five seasons. What becomes after the expiry of the seasons is, described in the eighth verse. It says that with the ten of Vivasvat, or with the lapse of ten months, Indra with his three-fold hammer shook down the heavenly jar. This means that the three storing places of the aerial waters (VII, 101, 4) were all emptied into the ocean at this time and along with it the sun also went to the lower world, for sunlight is described to be three-fold in (VII, 101, 2 and Sayana there quotes the Taittiriya Samhita (II, 1, 2, 5), which says that the sun has three lights; the morning light being the *Vasanta,* the midday the *Grishma,* and the evening the *Sharad*. The verse, therefore, obviously refers to the three-fold courses of waters in the heaven and the three-fold light of the sun and all this is said to come to an end with the ten of Vivasvat The sun and the sacrifice are then preserved as seed to be re-generated some time after, — a process symbolized in the Pravargya ceremony. The idea of the sun dropping from heaven is very common in the sacrificial literature.

Thus in the Aitareya Brahmana (IV, 18) we read, "The gods, being afraid of his (sun's) falling *beyond* them being turned upside down, supported him by placing above him the highest worlds"; and the same idea is met with in the Tandya Brahmana (IV, 5, 9, 11). The words "falling beyond" (*parachas atipatat*) are very important, inasmuch as they show that the sun dropped into regions that were en the yonder side. One of the Ashvin's protege is also called Chyavana, which word Prof. Max Muller derives from *chyu* to drop.

The Ashvins are said to have restored him to youth, which, being divested of its legendary form, means the rehabilitation of the sun that had dropped into the nether world. The Pravargya ceremony, which preserves serves the seed of the sacrifice, is, therefore, only one phase of the story of the dropping sun in the sacrificial literature and the verses employed in this ceremony, if interpreted in the spirit of that ceremony, appear, as stated above, to indicate an older year of five seasons and ten months.

But the Mantras used in the Pravargya ceremony are not so explicit as one might expect such kind of evidence to be. Therefore, instead of attempting to give more evidence of the same kind, — and there are many such facts in the Vedic sacrificial literature,— I proceed to give the direct statements about the duration of the annual *Sattras* from the well-known Vedic works. These statements have nothing of the legendary character about them and are, therefore, absolutely certain and reliable. It has been stated before that institution of sacrifice is an old one, and found amongst both the Asiatic and the European branches of the Aryan race. It was, in fact the main ritual of the religion of these people and naturally enough every detail concerning the sacrifices was closely watched, or accurately determined by the priests, who had the charge of these ceremonies. It is true that in giving reasons for the prevalence of a particular practice, these priests sometimes indulged in speculation; but the details of the sacrifice were facts that were settled in strict accordance with custom, and tradition, whatever explanations might be given in regard to their origin. But sometimes the facts were found to be so stubborn as to, defy any explanation, and the priests had to content themselves with barely recording the practice, and adding that "such is the practice from times immemorial." It is with such evidence that we have now to deal in investigating the duration of the annual *Sattras* in ancient times.

There are many annual *Sattras* like *Adityanam-ayanam, Angirasam-ayanam, Gavam-ayanam,* &c. mentioned in the Brahmans and the Shrauta Sutras; and, as observed by Dr. Haug, they seem to have been originally established in imitation of the sun's yearly course. They are the oldest of the Vedic sacrifices and their duration and other details have been all very minutely and carefully noted down in the sacrificial works.

All these annual *Sattras* are not, however, essentially different from each other, being so many different varieties or modifications, according to circumstances, of a common model or type, and the *Gavam-ayanam* is said to be this type; (*vide*, com. on Ashv. S.S. II, 7,). Thus in the Aitareya Brahmana (IV, 17) we are told that "They hold the *Gavam-ayanam*, that is, the sacrificial session called the Cows' walk. The cows are the Adityas (gods of the months). By holding the session called the Cows' walk they also hold the *Adityanam-ayanam* (the walk of the Adityas)." If we, (therefore, ascertain the duration of the *Gavam-ayanam*, the same rule would apply to all other annual *Sattras* and we need not examine the latter separately. This *Gavam-ayanam*, or the Cows' walk, is fully described in three places. Once in the Aitareya Brahmana and twice in the Taittiriya Samhita.

We begin with the Aitareya Brahmana (IV, 17), which describes the origin and duration of the *Sattra* as follows: "The cows, being desirous of obtaining hoofs and horns, held (once) a sacrificial session. In the tenth month (of their sacrifice) they obtained hoofs and horns. They said, 'We have obtained fulfilment of that wish for which we underwent the initiation into the sacrificial rites.

Let us rise (the sacrifice being finished).' Those that arose, are these, who have horns. Of those, who, however, sat (continued the session) saying, 'Let us finish the year,' the horns went off on account of their distrust. It is they, who are hornless (*tuparah*). They (continuing their sacrificial session) produced vigour (*urjam*). Thence after (having been sacrificing for twelve months and) having secured all the seasons, they rose (again) at the end. For they had produced the vigour (to reproduce horns, hoofs, &c. when decaying). Thus the cows made themselves beloved by all (the whole world), and are beautified (decorated) by all."

Here it is distinctly mentioned that the cows first obtained the fulfilment of their desire in ten months, and a number of them left off sacrificing further. Those, that remained and sacrificed for two months more, are called "distrustful," and they had to suffer for their distrust by forfeiting the horns they had obtained. It is, therefore, clear, that this yearly *Sattra*, which in the Samhitas and Brahmans is a *Sattra* of twelve months in imitation of the sun's yearly course, was once completed in ten months. Why should it be so? Why was a *Sattra*, which is annual in its very nature and which now lasts for twelve months, once completed in ten months? How did the sacrificers obtain all the religious merit of a twelve months' sacrifice by sacrificing for ten months only? These are very important questions; but the Aitareya Brahmana neither raises them, nor gives us any clue to their solution. If we, however, go back to the Taittiriya Samhita, the oldest and most authoritative work on the sacrificial ceremonies, we find the questions distinctly raised. The Samhita expressly states that the *Gavam-ayanam* can be completed in *ten* or *twelve* months, according to the choice of the sacrificer; but it plainly acknowledges its inability to assign any reason how a *Sattra* of twelve months could be completed in ten, except the fact that "it is an old practice sanctioned by immemorial usage." These passages are very important for our purpose, and I give below a close translation of each.

The first occurs in the Taittiriya Samhita (VII. 5, 1, 1-2), and may be rendered as follows: "The cows held this sacrificial session, desiring that 'being hornless let horns grow unto us.' Their session lasted (for) ten months. Then when the horns grew (up) they rose saying, We have gained.' But those, whose (horns) were not grown, they rose after completing the year, saying 'We have gained.' Those, that had their horns grown, and those that had not, both rose saying 'We have gained.' Cow's session is thus the year (year session). Those, who know this, reach the year and prosper verily. Therefore, the hornless (cow) moves (grazes) pleased during the two rainy months. This is what the *Sattra* has achieved for her. Therefore, whatever is done in the house of one performing the yearly *Sattra* is successfully, timely and properly done.

This account slightly differs from that given in the Aitareya Brahmana. In the Samhita the cows whose session lasted for twelve months, are said to be still hornless; but instead of getting vigour (*urjam*), they are said to have obtained as a reward for their additional sitting, the pleasure of comfortable grazing in the two rainy months, during which as the commentator observes, the horned cows find their horns an impediment to graze freely in the field, where new grass has grown up. But the statement regarding the duration of the *Sattra viz.*, that it lasted for *ten* or *twelve* months, is the same both in the Samhita and in the Brahmana.

The Samhita again takes up the question in the next *Anuvaka* (VII, 5, 2, 1-2), and further describes the cows' session as follows: "The cows held this sacrificial session, being hornless (and) desiring to obtain horns. Their session lasted (for) ten months; then when the horns grew (up), they said, 'We have gained, let us rise, we have obtained the desire for which we sat (commenced the session).'

Half, or as many, of them as said, 'We shall certainly sit for the two twelfth (two last) months, and rise after completing the year,' (some of them had horns in the twelfth month by trust, (while) by distrust those that (are seen) hornless (remained so). Both, that is, those who got horns, and those who obtained vigour (*urjam*), thus attained their object. One who knows this, prospers, whether rising (from the sacrifice) in the tenth month or in the twelfth. They indeed go by the path (*padena*); he going by the path indeed attains (the end). This is that successful *ayanam* (session). Therefore, it is *go-sani* (beneficial to the cows)."

This passage, in its first part repeats the story given in the previous *anuvaka* of the Samhita and in the Aitareya Brahmana with slight variations. But the latter part contains two important statements: firstly that whether we complete the sacrifice within ten months or twelve months the religious merit or fruit obtained is the same in either case, for both are said to prosper equally; and secondly this is said, to be the case because it is the "*path*" or as Sayana explains "an immemorial custom." The Samhita is, in fact, silent as to the reason why an annual *sattra* which ought to, and as a matter of fact does, now last for twelve months could be completed in ten months; and this reticence is very remarkable, considering how the Samhita sometimes indulges in speculations about the origin of sacrificial rites.

Any how we have two facts clearly established, (1) that at the time of the Taittiriya Samhita the *Gavam-ayanam* the type of all annual *Sattras* could be completed in ten months; and (2) that no reasons was known at the time, as to why a *Sattra* of twelve months could be thus finished in ten, except that it was "an immemorial custom." The Tandya Brahmana IV, 1, has a similar discussion about *Gavamayanam,* and clearly recognizes its twofold characters so far as its duration is concerned. Sayana and Bhatt Bhaskara, in their commentaries on the Taittiriya Samhita, cannot therefore, be said to have invented any new theory of their own as regards the double duration of the annual *Sattra*.

We shall discuss later on what is denoted by "cows" in the above passages. At present we are concerned with the duration of the *Sattra*; and if we compare the above matter-of-fact statements in the Samhita about the double duration of the annual *Sattra* with the legend of the Dashagvas sacrificing for ten months, the conclusion, that in ancient times the ancestors of the Vedic Aryas completed their *annual* sacrificial session in *ten months*, becomes irresistible. This duration of the *Sattra* must have been changed and all such *Sattras* made to last for twelve months when the Vedic people came to live in regions where such an annual session was impossible. But conservatism in such matters is so strong that the old practice must have outlived the change in the calendar, and it *had* to be recognized as an alternative period of duration for this *Sattra* in the Samhitas. The Taittiriya Samhita has thus to record the alternative period, stating that it is an ancient practice, and I think it settles the question, so far as the duration of these *Sattras* in ancient times is concerned. Whatever reasons we may assign for it, it is beyond all doubt that the oldest annual *Sattras* lasted only for ten months.

But the Taittiriya Samhita is not alone in being thus unable to assign any reason for this relic of the ancient calendar, or the duration of the annual *Sattra*. We still designate the twelfth month of the European solar year as *December* which word etymologically denotes the tenth month, (Latin *decem*, Sans. *dashan*, ten; and *ber* Sans. *vara*, time or period), and we all know that Numa added two months to the ancient Roman year and made it of twelve months. Plutarch, in his life of Numa records another version of the story, *viz.*, that Numa according to some, did not add the two months but simply transferred them from the end to the beginning of the year.

But the names of the months clearly show that this could not have been the case, for the enumeration of the months by words indicating their order as the fifth or *Quintilis* (old name for July), the sixth or *Sixtilis*, (old name for August), the seventh or *September* and so on the rest in their order, cannot, after, it is once begun, be regarded to have abruptly stopped at *December*, allowing only the last two months to be differently named. Plutarch has, therefore, rightly observed that "we have a proof in the name of the last (month) that the Roman year contained, at first ten months only and not twelve." But if there was any doubt on the point, it is now removed by the analogy of the *Gavam-ayanam* and the legends of the Dashagvas and Dirghatamas. Macrobius (*Saturnal Lib*. I. Chap. 12) confirms the story of Numa's adding and not simply transposing, two months to the ancient year of ten months. What the Avesta has to say on this subject we shall see later on where traditions about the ancient year amongst the other Aryan races will also be considered.

Suffice it to say for the present that, according to tradition, the ancient Roman year consisted only of ten months, and like the duration of the *Gavamayanam*, it was subsequently changed into a year of twelve months; and yet, so far as I know, no reason has yet been discovered, why the Roman year in ancient times was considered to be shorter by two months. On the contrary, the tendency is either to explain away the tradition some how as inconvenient, or to ignore it altogether as incredible. But so long as the word December is before us and we know how it is derived, the tradition cannot be so lightly set side.

The Encyclopaedia Britannica (*s.v.* calendar) records the ancient tradition that the oldest Roman year of Romulus was of ten months of 304 days and observes "it is not known how the remaining days were disposed of." If, with all the resources of modern science at our command, we have not yet been able to ascertain why the oldest Roman year was of ten months only and how the remaining days were disposed of, we need not be surprised if the Taittiriya Samhita refrained from speculating on the point and contented itself with stating that such was the "*path*" or the old custom or practice handed down from generation to generation from times immemorial.

The Arctic theory, however, now throws quite a new light on these ancient traditions, Vedic as well as Roman; and if we take the *Gavamayanam* of ten months and the old Roman year of ten months as relics of the period when the ancestors of both these races lived together within the circum-polar regions, there is no difficulty of explaining how the remaining days were disposed of. It was the period of the long night, — a time when Indra fought with Vala, to regain the cows imprisoned by the latter and Hercules killed the giant Cacus, a three-headed fire-vomiting monster, who had carried off Hercules' cows and hid them in a cave, dragging them backwards in order that the foot-marks might not be traced.

When the Aryan people migrated southwards from this ancient home they had to change this calendar to suit their new home by adding two more months to the old year. But the traces of the old calendar could not be completely wiped off, and we have still sufficient evidence, traditional or sacrificial, to warrant us in holding that a year of ten months followed by a night of two months was known in the Indo-Germanic period — a conclusion, which is further confirmed by Teutonic myths and legends, gas explained by Prof. Rhys, whose views will be found summarized in a subsequent chapter.

The Taittiriya Samhita and the Aitareya Brahmana speak of the *Gavamayanam* as being really held by the cows. Was it really a session of these animals?

Or was it something else? The Aitareya Brahmana, we have seen, throws out a suggestion that "the cows are the Adityas," that is the month-gods, and the Cows' session is really the session of the monthly sun-gods. Comparative mythology now fully bears out the truth of this remarkable suggestion put forward by the Brahmana. Cows, such as we meet them in the mythological legends, represent days and nights of the year, not only in the Vedic but also in the Greek mythology; any we can, therefore, now give a better account of the origin of this sacrificial session than that it was a session of bovine animals for the purpose of obtaining horns.

Speaking of cows in the Aryan mythology, Prof. Max Muller in his *Contributions to the Science of Mythology* (Vol. II. p. 761) writes as follows: "There were thus three kinds of cows, the real cows, the cows in the dark cloud (rain = milk), and the cows stepping forth from the dark stable of the night (the rays of the morning). These three are not always easy to distinguish in the Veda; nay, while we naturally try to distinguish between them, the poets themselves seem to delight in mixing them up.

In the passage quoted above (I, 32, 11), we saw how the captive waters were compared to cows that had been stolen by Pani (*niruddhah apah Panina iva gavah*), but what is once compared in the Veda is soon identified. As to the Dawn, she is not only compared to a cow, she is called the cow straight out. Thus when we read, R.V. I. 92, 1.

These dawns have made a light on the eastern half of the sky, they brighten their splendour, the bright cows approach, the mothers, the cows, *gavah*, can only be the dawns themselves, the plural of dawn being constantly in the Veda used where we should use the singular. In R.V. 1, 93, 4, we read that 'Agnishomau deprived Pani of his cows and found light for many.' Here again the cows are the dawns kept by Pani in the dark stable or cave of the night, discovered by Sarama and delivered every morning by the gods of light." "We read in R.V. I, 62, 3, that Brihaspati split the rock and found the cows." "Of Indra it is said, II, 19, 3, that he produced the sun and found the cows; of Brihaspati, II, 24, 3, that he drove out the cows, that he split the cave by his word, that he hid the darkness, and lighted up the sky. What can be clearer? The Maruts also, II, 34, 1, are said to uncover the cows and Agni. V, 14, 4, is praised for killing the friends, for having overcome darkness by light, and having found the cows, water and the sun."

"In all these passages we find no *iva* or *na*, which would indicate that the word cow was used metaphorically. The dawns or days as they proceed from the dark stable, or are rescued from evil spirits, are spoken of directly as the cows. If they, are spoken of in the plural, we find the same in the case of the

Dawn (*ushas*) who is often conceived as many, as in II, 28, 2, *upayane ushasam gomatinam*, 'at the approach of the dawns with their cows.' From that it required but a small step to speak of the one Dawn as the mother of the cows, IV, 52, 2, *mata gavam*."

"Kuhn thought that these cows should be understood as the red clouds of the morning. But clouds are not always present at sunrise, nor can it well be said that they are carried off and kept in prison during the night by the powers of darkness."

"But what is important and settles the point is the fact that these cows or oxen of the dawn or of the rising sun occur in other mythologies also and are there clearly meant for days. They are numbered as 12 × 30, that is, the thirty days of the 12 lunar months. If Helios has 350 oxen and 350 sheep, that can only refer to the days and to the nights of the year, and would prove the knowledge of a year of 350 days before the Aryan separation."

Thus the cows in mythology are the days and nights, or dawns, that are imprisoned by Pani, and not real living cows with horns. Adopting this explanation and substituting these metaphorical cows for *gavah* in the *Gavam-ayanam*, it is not difficult to see that underneath the strange story of cows holding a sacrificial session for getting horns, there lies concealed the remarkable phenomenon, that, released from the clutches of Pani, these cows of days and nights walked on for ten months, the oldest duration of the session known as Cows, walk. In plain language this means, if it means anything, that the oldest Aryan year was one of ten months followed by the long night, during which the cows were again carried away by the powers of darkness. We have seen that the oldest Roman year was of ten months, and the Avesta, as will be shown later on, also speaks of ten months' summer prevailing in the Airyana Vaejo before the home:was invaded by the evil spirit, who brought on ice and severe winter in that place. A year of ten months with a long night of two months may thus be taken to be known before the Aryan separation, and the references to it in the Vedic literature are neither isolated nor imaginary. They are the relics of ancient history, which have been faithfully preserved in the sacrificial literature of India, and if they were hitherto misunderstood it was because the true key required for their solution was as yet unknown.

But as stated in the previous chapter, a year in the circum-polar region will always have a varying number of the months or sunshine according to latitude. Although, therefore, there is sufficient evidence to establish the existence of, a year of ten months, we cannot hold that it was the only year known in ancient times. In fact we have seen that the legend of Aditi indicates the existence of the seven months of sunshine; and a band of thirty continuous dawns supports the same conclusion. But it seems that a year of ten months of sunshine was more prevalent, or was selected as the mean of the different varying years. The former view is rendered probable by the fact that of the Angirases of various forms (*virupas*) the Navagvas and the Dashagvas are said to be the principal or the most important in the Rig-Veda (X, 62, 6), But whichever view we adopt, the existence of a year of seven, eight, nine, ten or eleven months of sunshine follows as a matter of course, if the ancient Aryan home was within the Arctic circle. Prof. Max Muller, in his passage quoted above, points out that the old Greek year probably consisted of 350 days, the 350 oxen of Helios representing the days, and 350 sheep representing the nights.

He also notices that in German mythology 700 gold rings of Wieland, the smith, are spoken of, and comparing the number with 720 sons of Agni mentioned in I, 164, 11, he draws from it the conclusion that a year of 350 days is also represented in the German mythology. This year is shorter by ten days than the civil year of 360 days, or falls short of the full solar year by 15 days. It is, therefore, clear that if a year of 350 days existed before the Aryan separation, it must have been followed by a continuous night of ten days; while where the year was of 300 days, the long night extended over 60 days of 24 hours each. We shall thus have different kinds of long nights; and it is necessary to see if we can collect evidence to indicate the longest duration of the night known before the Aryan separation.

Speaking of the cows or oxen of Helios, as stated in the passage quoted above, Prof. Max Muller goes on to observe: "The cows or oxen of Helios thus receive their background from the Veda, but what is told of them by Homer is by no means clear. When it is said that the companions of Odysseus consumed the oxen of Helios, and that they thus forfeited their return home, we can hardly take this in the modern sense of consuming or wasting their days, thought it may be difficult to assign any other definite meaning to it. Equally puzzling is the fable alluded to in the Homeric hymn that Hermes stole the oxen of Apollon and killed two of them. The number of Apollon's oxen is given as fifty (others give the number as 100 cows, twelve oxen and one bull), Which looks like the number of weeks in the lunar year, but why Hermes should be represented as carrying off the whole herd and then killing to, is difficult to guess, unless we refer it to the two additional months in a cycle of four years."

In the light of the Arctic theory the puzzle here referred to is solved without any difficulty. The stealing away or the carrying off of the cows need not now he taken to mean simple wasting of the days in the modern sense of the word; nor need we attribute such stories to the "fancy of ancient bards and story tellers." The legend or the tradition of stealing consuming, or carrying off the cows or oxen is but another form of stating that so many days were lost, being swallowed up in the long night that occurred at the end of the year and lasted, according to latitude, for varying period of time. So long as everything was to be explained on the theory of a daily struggle between light and darkness, these legends were unintelligible. But as soon as we adopt the Arctic theory the whole difficulty vanishes and what was confused and puzzling before becomes at once plain and comprehensible. In the Vedic mythology cows are similarly said to be stolen by Vritra or Vala, but their number is nowhere given, unless we regard the story of Jijrashva (the Red-horse) slaughtering 100 or 101 sheep and giving them to a she-wolf to devour (I, 116, 16; 117, 18), as a modification of the story of stealing the cows.

The Vedic sacrificial literature does, however, preserve for us an important relic; besides the one above noted, of the older calendar and especially the long night. But in this case the relic is so deeply buried under the weight of later explanations, adaptations and emendations, that we must here examine at some length the history of the Soma sacrifices in order to discover the original meaning of the rites which are included under that general name. That the Some sacrifice is an ancient institution is amply proved by parallel rites in the Parsi scriptures; and whatever doubt we may have regarding the knowledge of Soma in the Indo. European period, as the word is not found in the European languages, the system of sacrifices can be clearly traced back to the primeval age.

Of this sacrificial system,, the Soma sacrifice may, at any rate, be safely taken as the oldest representative, since it forms the main feature of the ritual of the Rig-Veda and a whole Mandala of 114 hymns in the Rig-Veda is dedicated to the praise of Soma. A careful analysis of the Soma sacrifice may, therefore, be expected to disclose at least partially, the nature of the oldest sacrificial system of the Aryan race; and we, therefore, proceed to examine the same. The chief characteristic of the Soma sacrifice, as distinguished from other sacrifices, is, as the name indicates, the extraction of the Soma juice and the offering thereof to gods before drinking it. There are three libations of Soma in a day, one in the morning, one in midday and the last in the evening, and all these are accompanied by the chanting of hymns during the sacrifice. These Soma sacrifices, if classed according to their duration, fall under three heads; (1) those that are performed in a single day, called *Ekahas*, (2) those that are performed in more than one and less than thirteen days called *Ahinas*, and (3) those that take thirteen or more than 13 days and may last even for one thousand years, called *Sattras*. Under the first head we have the Agnishtoma, fully described in the Aitareya Brahmana (III, 39-44), as the key or the type of all the sacrifices that fall under this class. There are six modifications of Agnishtoma, *viz.*, Ati-agnishtoma, Ukthya, Shodashi, Vajapeya, Atiratra and Aptoryama, which together with Agnishtoma, form the seven parts, kinds or modifications of the Jyotishtoma, sacrifice, (Ashv. S.S. VI, 11, 1). The modification chiefly consists in the number of hymns to be recited at the libations, or the manner of recitation, or the number of the *Grahvas* or Soma-cups used on the occasion. But with these we are not at present concerned. Of the second class of Soma sacrifices, the *Dvadashaha* or twelve days' sacrifice is celebrated both as *Ahina* and *Sattra* and is considered to be very important. It is made up of three *tryahas* (or three days' performances, called respectively *Jyotis, Go,* and *Ayus*), the tenth day and the two Atiratras (Ait. Br. IV, 23-4).

The nine days' performance (three *tryahas*) is called *Nava-ratra*. Side by side with this, there are, under this head, a number of Soma sacrifices extending over two nights or three nights, four nights, up to twelve nights, called *dvi-ratra, tri-ratra* and so on (Tait. Sam. VII, 1, 4; VII, 3, 2. Ashv. Shr. Sut. X and XI; Tan. Bra. 20, 11, 24, 19). In the third class we have the annual *Sattras* and of these the *Gavam-ayanam* is the type.

Some *Sattras* which come under this class are described as extending over 1,000 years and a discussion is found in sacrificial works as to whether the phrase one thousand years signifies 1,000 real years, or whether it stands for 1,000 days. But we may pass it over as unnecessary for our purpose. The annual *Sattras* are the only important *Sattras* of this class, and to understand their nature we must see what a *shalaha* means. The word literally denotes a group of six days (*shat* + *ahan*) and is used to denote six days' performance in the sacrificial literature. It is employed as a unit to measure a month in the same way as we now use a week, a month being made up of five *shalahas*. The *shalaha*, in its turn, consists of the daily sacrifices called *Jyotis, Go, Ayus* and the same three taken in the reverse order as *Ayus, Go* and *Jyotis*. Every *shalaha*, therefore, begins and ends with a Jyotishtoma (Ait. Br. IV, 15).

The *shalaha* is further distinguished into *Abhiplava* and *Prishthya*, according to the arrangement of the stomas or songs sung at the Soma libations. An annual *Sattra* is in the main, made up of a number of *shalahas* joined with certain special rites at the beginning, the middle and the close of the *Sattra*. The central day of the *Sattra* is called *Vihuvan*, and stands by itself, dividing the *Sattra* into two equal halves like the wings of a house (Tait. Br. I, 2, 3, 1); and the rites in the latter half of the session or after the *Vihuvan* day are performed in an order which is the reverse of that followed in forming the ceremonies in the first half of the sacrifice. The model annual *Sattra* (the *Gavam-anayam*) thus; consists of the following parts:

Parts	Days
1. The introductory Atiratra	1
2. The Chaturvimsha day, otherwise called the Arambhaniya (Ait. Br. IV, 12), or the Prayaniya (Tand. Br. IV. 2), the real beginning of the *Sattra*	1
3. Four Abhiplava, followed by one Prishthya shalaha each month; continued in this way for five months	150
4. Three Abhiplava and one Prishthya shalaha	24
5. The Abhijit day	1
6. The Three Svara-Saman days	3
7. *Vishnuvan* or *the Central day* which stands by itself *i.e.,* not counted in the total of the *Sattra* days	
8. The three Svara-Saman days	3
9. The Vishvajit day	1
10. One Prishthya and three Abhiplava shalahas	24
11. One Prishthya and four Abhiplava shalahas each month continued in this way for four months	120
12. Three Abhiplava shalahas, one Go-shtoma, one Ayu-shtoma, and one Dasharatra (the ten days of Dvadashaha), making up one month	30
13. The Mahavrata day, corresponding to the Chaturvimsha day at the beginning	1
14. The concluding Atiratra	1
Total days:	360

It will be seen from the above scheme that there are really a few sacrificial rites which are absolutely fixed and unchangeable in the yearly *Sattra*. The two Atiratras, the introductory and the concluding, the Chaturvimsha and the Mahavrata day, the Abhijit and the Vishvajit, the three Svara-Saman days on either side of Vishuvan, the Vishuvan itself, and the ten days of Dvadashaha, making up 22 days in all exclusive of Vishuvan, are the only parts that have any specialty about them. The rest of the days are all made up by *Abhiplava* and *Prishthya* shalahas which therefore constitute what may be called the elastic or the variable part of the yearly *Sattra*.

Thus if we want a *Gavam-ayanam* of ten months, we have only to strike off five *shalahas* from the parts marked 3 and 11 in the above scheme. The *Adityanam-ayanam* is another modification of the above scheme in which amongst other changes, the *shalahas* are all *Abhiplava*, instead of being a combination of *Abhiplava* and *Prishthya*; while if all the *shalahas* are *Prishthya*, along with some other changes, it becomes the *Angirasam-ayanam*. All these modifications do not however, touch the total number of 360 days. But there were sacrificers, who adopted the lunar year of 354 days and therefore, omitted 6 days from the above scheme and their *Sattra* is called the *Utsarginam-ayanam* (Tait. Sam. VII, 5, 7, 1, Tandya Brah. V, 10). In short, the object was to make the *Sattra* correspond with the year adopted, civil or lunar, as closely as possible. But these points are not relevant to our purpose.

The Brahmans and the Shrauta Sutras give further details about the various rites to be performed on the Vishuvan, the Abhijit and the Vishvajit or the Svara-Saman day. The Aitareya Aranyaka describes the Mahavrata ceremony; while the Atiratra and the Chaturvimsha are described in the fourth book of the Aitareya Brahmana. The Chaturvimsha is so called because the *stoma* to be chanted on that day is twenty-four-fold. It is the real beginning of the *Sattra* as the Mahavrata is its end. The Aitareya Brahmana (IV, 14) says, "The Hotri pours forth the seed. Thus he makes the seed (which is poured forth) by means of the Mahavrata day produce off-spring. For seed if effused every year is productive." This explanation shows that like the Pravargya ceremony, the Mahavrata was intended to preserve the seed of the sacrifice in order that it might germinate or grow at the proper time. It was a sort of link between the dying and the coming year and appropriately concluded the annual *Sattra*. It will be further seen that every annual *Sattra* had an Ati-ratra at each of its ends and that the Dvadashaha, or rather the ten days thereof, formed an important concluding part of the *Sattra*.

The above is only a brief description, a mere outline of the scheme of the annual *Sattras* mentioned in sacrificial works, but it is sufficient for our purpose. We can see from it that a civil year of 360 days formed their basis, and the position of the Vishuvan was of great importance inasmuch as the ceremonies after it were performed in the reverse order. I have shown elsewhere what important inferences can be drawn from the position of the Vishuvan regarding the calendar in use at the time when the scheme was settled. But we have now to consider of times which preceded the settlement of this scheme, and for that purpose we must describe another set of Soma sacrifices included under the general class of *Sattras*. It has been stated above that side by side with the Dvadashaha, there are *Ahina* sacrifices of two nights, three nights, etc. up to twelve nights. But these sacrifices do not stop with the twelve nights' performance. There are thirteen nights', fourteen nights', fifteen nights', and so on up to one hundred nights' sacrifice called *Trayodasha-ratra*, *Chaturdasha-ratra* and so on up to *Shataratra*.

But since the *Ahina* has been defined to be a sacrifice extending over not more than twelve or less than thirteen days, all the night-sacrifices extending over a period longer than twelve-nights are included in the third class, *viz.*, the *Sattras*. If we, however, disregard this artificial division, it will be found that along with the *Ekaha*, the *Dvadashaha* and the annual *Sattras*, there is a series of, what are termed, the night-sacrifices or *sattras* extending over a period of time from two to one hundred *nights*, but not further. These night-sacrifices or *Ratri-sattras* are mentioned in the Taittiriya Samhita, the Brahmans and the Shrauta Sutras in clear terms and there is no ambiguity about their nature, number, or duration. The Taittiriya Samhita in describing them often uses the word *Ratrih* (nights) in the plural, stating, that so and so was the first to institute or to perceive so many nights meaning so many nights' sacrifice, (*vimshatim ratrih*, VII. 3, 9, 1; *dvatrimshatam ratrih* VII, 4, 4, 1). According to the principle of division noted above all night-sacrifices of less than thirteen nights' duration will be called *Ahina*, while those extending over longer time up to one hundred nights will come under *Sattras*; but this is, as remarked above, evidently an artificial division, and one, who reads carefully the description of these sacrifices, cannot fail to be struck by the fact that we have here a series of night-sacrifices from two to a hundred nights, or if we include the *Ati-ratra* in this series, we have practically a set of hundred nightly Soma sacrifices, though, according to the principle of division adopted, some may fall under the head of *Ahina* and some under that of *Sattras*.

Now an important question in connection with these *Sattras* is why they alone should be designated "*night-sacrifices*" (*ratri-kratus*), or "*night-sessions*" (*ratri-sattras*)? and why their number should be one hundred? or, in other words, why there are no *night*-sattras of longer duration than one hundred nights? The Mimamsakas answer the first part of the question by asking us to believe that the word "night" (*ratrih*) is really used to denote a day in the denomination of these sacrifices (Shabara on Jaimini VIII, 1, 17).

The word *dvi-ratra* according to this theory means two days' sacrifice, and *shata-ratra* a hundred days' sacrifice. This, explanation appears very good at the first sight, and as a matter of fact it has been accepted by all writers on the sacrificial ceremonies. In support of it, we may also cite the fact that as the moon was the measurer of time in ancient days, the night was then naturally more marked then the day, and instead of saying "so many days" men often spoke of "so many nights," much in the same way as we now use the word "fort-night." This is no doubt good so far as it goes; but the question is why should there be no Soma sacrifices of a longer duration than one hundred nights? and, why a gap, a serious gap, is left in the series of Soma sacrifices after one hundred nights *Sattra* until we come to the annual *Sattra* of 360 days? Admitting that "night" means "day," we have Soma sacrifices lasting from 1 to 100 days; and if so where was the harm to complete the series until the yearly *Sattra* of 360 days was reached? So far as I know, no writer on sacrificial ceremonies has attempted to answer this question satisfactorily. Of course adopting the speculative manner of the Brahmans we might say that there are no Soma sacrifices of longer than one hundred nights' duration, because the life of a man cannot extend beyond a hundred years (Tait. Br. III, 8, 16, 2).

But such an explanation can never be regarded as satisfactory, and the Mimamsakas, who got over one difficulty by interpreting "night" into "day," have practically left this latter question untouched, and therefore, unsolved.

In short, the case stands thus: The sacrificial literature mentions a series of 99 or practically one hundred Soma sacrifices, called the "night-sacrifices"; but these do not form a part of any annual *Sattra* like the *Gavam-ayanam*, nor is any reason assigned for their separate existence, nor is their duration which never exceeds a hundred nights, accounted for. Neither the authors of the Brahmans nor those of the Shrauta Sutras much less Sayana and Yaska give us any clue to the solution of this question; and the Mimamsakas, after explaining the word "night" occurring in the names of these sacrifices as equal to "day" have allowed these night-sacrifices to remain as an isolated group in the organized system of Soma sacrifices. Under these circumstances it would no doubt appear presumptuous for any one to suggest an explanation, so many centuries after what may be called the age of the *Sattras*.

But I feel the Arctic theory which, we have seen, is supported by strong independent evidence, not only explains but appropriately accounts for the original existence of this isolated series of a hundred Soma sacrifices; and I, therefore, proceed to give my view on the point.

It seems to me that if the word *ratri* in *Ati-ratra* is still understood to mean "night," and that if the *Ati-ratra* sacrifice is even now performed during the night, there is no reason why we should not similarly interpret the same word in *Dvi-ratra*, *Tri-ratra* &c. up to *Shata-ratra*. The objection, that the Soma juice is not extracted during the night, is more imaginary than real; for as a matter of fact Soma libations are made in the usual way, during the *Ati-ratra* sacrifice. The *Ati-ratra* sacrifice is performed at the beginning and the end of every *Sattra*; and all the three libations of Soma are always offered during the three turns, or *paryayas*, of the night. The Aitareya Brahmana (IV, 5), in explaining the origin of this sacrifice, tells us that the Asuras had taken shelter with the night and the Devas, who had taken shelter with the day, wanted to expel them from the dark region. But amongst the Devas, Indra alone was found ready and willing to undertake this task; and entering into darkness, he with the assistance of Metres, turned the Asuras out of the first part of the night by the first Soma libation, while by means of the middle turn (*paryaya*) of passing the Soma-cup, the Asuras were turned out of the middle part and by the third turn out of the third or the last part of the night.

The three Soma libations, here spoken of, are all made during the night and the Brahmana further observes that there is *no other deity save Indra and the Metres* to whom they are offered (Cf. Apas. Sh. Su. XIV, 3, 12).

The next section of the Brahmana (IV, 6) distinctly raises the question, "How are the Pavamana Stotras to be chanted for the purification of the Soma juice provided for the night, whereas such Sutras refer only to the day but not to the night?" and answers it by stating that the Stotras are the same for the day and the night. It is clear from this that Soma juice was extracted and purified at night during *Ati-ratra* sacrifice and Indra was the *only* deity to whom the libations were offered in order to help him in his fight with the Asuras, who had taken shelter with the darkness of the night.

That the *Ati-ratra* is an ancient sacrifice is further proved by the occurrence of a similar ceremony in the Parsi scriptures. The word *Ati-ratra* does not occur in the Avesta, but in the Vendibad, XVIII, 18, (43)-22 (48), we are told that there are three parts of the night and that in the first of these parts (*trishvai*), Fire, the son of Ahura Mazda, calls upon the master of the house to arise and put on his girdle and to fetch clean wood in order that he may burn bright; for, says the Fire, "Here comes *Azi* (Sans. *Ahi*) made by the Daevas (Vedic *Asuras*), who is about to strive against me and wants to put out my life." And the asme request is made during the second and the third part of the night. The close resemblance between this and the three *paryayas* of the *Ati-ratra* sacrifice does not seem to have been yet noticed; but whether noticed or not it shows that the *Ati-ratra* is an ancient rite performed during the night for the purpose of helping Indra, or the deity that fought with the powers of darkness, and that such sacrificial acts as putting on the girdle (*kosti*) or squeezing the Soma, were performed during this period of darkness.

Now what applies to the sacrifice of a single night may well be extended to cases where sacrifices had to be performed for two, three or more continuous nights. I have already shown before that the ancient sacrificers completed their sacrificial sessions in ten months and a long night followed the completion of these sacrifices. What did the sacrificers do during this long night? They could not have slept all the time; and as a matter of fact we know that the people in the extreme north of Europe and Asia do not, even at present sleep during the whole of the long night which occurs in their, part of the globe. Paul Du Chaillu, who has recently (1900) published an account of his travels in *The Land of the Long Night*, informs us (p. 75) that although the sun went below the horizon for several days in the Arctic regions, yet during the period "the Lapps could tell from the stars whether it was night or day, for they were accustomed to gauge time by the stars according to their height above the horizon, just as we do at home with the sun"; and what the Lapps do now, must have been done by the oldest inhabitants of the circum-polar regions. It is, therefore, clear that the ancient sacrificers of the Aryan race could not have gone to sleep after sacrificing for ten months. Did they then sit idle with their hands folded when Indra was fighting for them with the powers of darkness?

They performed their sacrifices for ten months with a view to help Indra in his war with Vala; and just at the time when Indra most needed the help of invigorating songs and Soma libations, are we to suppose that these sacrificers sat idle, gave up the sacrifices and left Indra to fight with Vala alone and single-handed as best as be could? The whole theory of sacrifices negatives such a supposition. Therefore, if the Arctic theory is true, and if the ancestor of the Vedic Rishis ever lived in a region where the darkness of the night lasted for several days (a day being taken as a measure of time equal to 24 hours), we naturally expect to find a series of nightly Soma sacrifices performed during the period, to help the gods in their struggle with the demons of darkness; and as a matter of fact, there are in the Vedic sacrificial literature, a number of sacrifices which, if we include the *Ati-ratra* in it, extend from one to a hundred nights. The Mimamsakas and even the authors of the Brahmans, who knew little about the ancient Arctic home, have converted these night-sacrifices into day-sacrifices; but the explanation evidently appears to be in vented at a time when the true nature of the *Ratri-kratus* or *Ratri-sattras* was forgotten, and it does not, therefore, preclude us from interpreting these facts in a different way. I have already stated above that if we accept the explanation of the Mimamsakas, we cannot explain why the series of the night-sacrifices should abruptly end with the *Shata-ratra* or a hundred nights' sacrifice; but by the Arctic theory we can explain the fact satisfactorily by supposing that the duration of the long night in the ancient home varied from one night (of 24 hours) to a hundred continuous nights (of 2400 hours) according to latitude, and that the hundred nightly Soma sacrifices corresponded to the different durations of the night at different places in the ancient home.

Thus where the darkness lasted only for ten nights (240 hours) a *Dasharatra* sacrifice was performed, while where it lasted for 100 nights (2400 hours) a *Shata-ratra* sacrifice was necessary. There are no sacrifices after the *Shata-ratra* because a hundred continuous nights marked the maximum duration of darkness experienced by the ancient sacrificers of the race. We have seen that the legend of Aditi indicates a period of seven months' sunshine; join to it the Dawn and the Twilight of 30 days each, and there are left three months, (or if we take the year to consist of 365 days, then 95 days), for the duration of the long continuous night, — a result which remarkably corresponds to the longest duration of the night-sacrifices known in the Vedic literature.

The Dawn marked the end of the long night, and could not; therefore, be included in the latter at least for sacrificial purposes. In fact separate sacrifices are enjoined for the Dawn in sacrificial works; and we may, therefore, safely exclude the long Dawn from the province of the nightly sacrifices, and the same may be said of the period of the long evening twilight.

A hundred nights' sacrifice thus marked the maximum duration of darkness during which Indra fought with Vala and was strengthened by the Soma libations offered to him in this sacrifice. As there is no other theory to account for the existence of the night-sacrifices, and especially for their number, to wit, one hundred, these sacrifices may be safely taken to indicate the existence of an ancient year approximately divided into seven months' sunshine, one month's dawn, one month's evening twilight and three months' long continuous night.

There are other considerations which point out to the same conclusion. In the post-Vedic literature we have a persistent tradition that Indra alone of all gods is the master of a hundred sacrifices (*shata-kratu*), and that as this attribute formed, so to say, the very essence of Indraship, he always jealously watched all possible encroachments against it. But European scholars relying upon the fact that even Sayana prefers, except in a few places (III, 51, 2) to interpret *shata-kratu*, as applied to Indra in the Rig-Veda, as meaning, not "the master of a hundred sacrifices," but "the lord of a hundred mights or powers," have not only put aside the Puranic tradition, but declined to interpret the word *kratu* in the Rig-Veda except in the sense of "power, energy, skill, wisdom, or generally speaking, the power of body or mind." But if the above explanation of the origin of the night sacrifices is correct, we must retrace our steps and acknowledge that the Puranic tradition or legend is, after all, not built upon a pure misunderstanding of the original meaning of the epithet *shata-kratu* as applied to Indra in the Vedic-literature. I am aware of the fact that traditions in the post-Vedic literature are often found to have but a slender basis in the Vedas, but in the present case we have something more reliable and tangible to go upon. We have a group, an isolated group of a hundred nightly Soma sacrifices and as long as it stands unexplained in the Vedic sacrificial literature it would be unreasonable to decline to connect it with the Puranic tradition of Indra's sole mastership of hundred sacrifices, especially when in the light of the Arctic theory the two can be so well and intelligibly connected. The hundred sacrifices, which are regarded as constituting the essence of Indraship in the

Puranas, are there said to be the Ashvamedha sacrifices and it may, at the outset, be urged that the *shata-ratra* sacrifice mentioned in the sacrificial works is not an Ashvamedha sacrifice. But the distinction is neither important, nor material. The Ashvamedha sacrifice is a Soma sacrifice and is described in the sacrificial works along with the night-sacrifices.

In the Taittiriya Samhita (VII, 2, 11) a hundred offerings of food to be made in the Ashvamedha sacrifice are mentioned, and the Taittiriya Brahmana (III, 8, 15, 1) states that Prajapati obtained these offerings "during the night," and consequently they are called *Ratri-homas*. The duration of the Ashvamedha sacrifice is again not fixed, inasmuch as it depends upon the return of the horse and in the Rig-Veda (I, 163, 1) the sacrificial horse is identified with the sun moving in waters.

The return of the sacrificial horse may, therefore, be taken to symbolize the return of the sun after the long night and a close resemblance between the Ashvamedha and the night-sacrifices, which were performed to enable Indra to fight with Vala and rescue the dawn and the sun from his clutches, may thus be taken as established. At any rate, we need not be surprised if the *Shata-ratra* Soma sacrifice appears in the form of a hundred Ashvamedha sacrifices in the Puranas. The tradition is substantially the same in either case and when it can be so easily and naturally explained on the Arctic theory, it would not be reasonable to set it aside and hold that the writers of the Puranas created it by misinterpreting the word *Shata-kratu* occurring in the Vedas. We have seen that *shata-kratu* as applied to Indra is interpreted by Western scholars and in many places even by Sayana himself, as meaning the lord of a hundred powers.

Sayana now and then (III, 51, 2; X, 103, 7) suggests or gives an alternative explanation and makes Indra "the master of a hundred sacrifices"; but Western scholars have gone further and discarded all other explanations except the one noted above. It is, therefore, necessary to examine the meaning of this epithet, as used in the Rig-Veda, a little more closely in this place. If the word *kratu* in *shata-kratu* be interpreted to mean "might" or "power," the numeral*shata*, which strictly denotes "a hundred," will have to be taken as equivalent to "many" or "numerous" inasmuch as no definite set of a hundred powers can be pointed out as specially belonging to Indra. That the word *shata* may be so interpreted is evident from the fact that adjectives like *shata-nitha* (I, 100, 12) and shatam-uti (I, 102, 6; 130, 8), as applied to India in the Rig-Veda, are found in other places in the form of *sahasra-nitha* (III, 60, 7), and *sahasram-uti* (I, 52, 2). Again Indra's arrow is once called *shatabradhna* and also *sahasra-parna* in the same verse (VIII, 77, 7); while Soma is represented as going in a hundred ways (*shata-yaman*) in IX, 86, 16, and a few hymns after it is said to be *sahasra-yaman* or going in a thousand ways (IX, 106, 5). Even the adjective *shatamanyu* which Sayana interprets as meaning "the master of a hundred sacrifices" in X, 103, 7, has its counterpart, if not in the Rig-Veda at least in the Sama-Veda which reads *sahasra-manyu* for *sahasramushka* in Rig-Veda VI, 46, 3. This shows that the Vedic bards considered *shata* (a hundred) and *sahasra* (a thousand) as interchangeable numerals in some places and if the numeral *shata* in *shata-kratu* had been of the same character, we should naturally have met with a paraphrase of the epithet as *sahasra-kratu* somewhere in the Vedic literature. But although the epithet *shata-kratu*, as applied to Indra, occurs about sixty times in the Rig-Veda and several times in other Vedic works, nowhere do we find it paraphrased as *sahasra-kratu*, which shows that the Vedic bards did not feel themselves at liberty to alter or paraphrase it as they liked.,

The adjective *amita-kratu* is applied to Indra in I, 102, 6; but as *amita* does not necessarily mean more than "one hundred," it does not follow that on this account we should give up the ordinary meaning of *shata* in *shata-kratu*. If the word *kratu* had nowhere been used in the Rig-Veda to denote a sacrifice, we may have been justified in interpreting *shata-kratu* in the way suggested by Western scholars. But, as observed by Dr. Haug, when Vasishtha prayed to Indra (VII, 32, 26) "Carry, O Indra! our sacrificial performance (*kratum*) through, just as a father does to his sons (by assisting them). Teach us, O thou, who art invoked by many that we may, in this turn (of the night) reach alive the (sphere of) light (*jyotis*)," the prayer in all probability refers to the sacrificial performance (*kratu*) held for the purpose of enabling the sacrificers to safely reach the other end of the night. In fact, it refers to the *Ati-ratra* sacrifice and the Aitareya Brahmana (IV, 10) quotes and interprets it in the same way. Sayana in his commentary on the Aitareya Brahmana though not in the Rig-Veda Bhashya, also takes the same view; and as the *Ati-ratra* sacrifice is referred to expressly by its name in the Rig-Veda (VII, 103, 7) it is not at all unlikely that a verse referring to this Soma sacrifice should occur in other hymns. Hence if there are passages where *kratu* can be taken to mean "a sacrifice" there is no reason why the epithet *shata-kratu* be not understood ɔ mean "the master of a hundred sacrifices" as suggested by the Puranic tradition.

Another fact which favours this interpretation, is that in the Rig-Veda Indra is described as destroying 90, 99 or 100 fortresses or cities (*purah*) of his enemies (I, 130, 7; II, 19, 6; VI, 31, 4; II, 14, 6). Now *deva-purah*, which means "the fortresses of the gods," has been interpreted to mean "days" in the description of the *dash ratra* sacrifice in the Taittiriya Samhita VII, 2, 5, 3-4; and if *deva-purah* means "days," the *purah* (cities, fortresses) of Shambara may well be taken to mean "nights." This view is confirmed by the statement in the Aitareya Brahmana previously quoted, which says that the Asuras found shelter with the night, or in other words, the darkness of the night was, so to say, their fortress. Indra's destroying a hundred forts of Shambara is, therefore, equivalent to his fighting with the enemy for a hundred continuous nights, a period during which the ancient sacrificers offered him Sonia libations in order that he may be better prepared for the struggle with Vala.

The destruction of 99 or 100 forts of the enemy, a group of a hundred nightly sacrifices, the nine and ninety rivers (*sravantih*) which Indra is described as crossing during his fight with Ahi (I, 32, 14), and a hundred leather straps with which Kutsa is said to have bound down Indra to his sacrifice in the Tandya Brahmana IX, 2, 22, and from which he is invoked to free himself in Rig. X, 38, 5, are but so many different kaleidoscopic views of the same idea which makes Indra and Indra alone the lord of a hundred sacrifices; and if we take all these together they undoubtedly point out to the existence of a hundred continuous nights in the ancient home of the ancestors of the Vedic people. In V, 48, 3, "*a hundred,*" moving in the abode of Indra are said to turn *on* and turn *off* the course of ordinary days when Indra strikes Vritra with his bolt; and I think we have here a distinct allusion either to a hundred sacrifices performed or to a hundred continuous nights required for securing a complete victory over the powers of darkness in the nether world, and which nights (or rather one long night of hundred days) may well be described as *breaking off* and *bringing back* the succession of ordinary days and nights, inasmuch as the long night immediately follows and precedes the period of sunshine in the Arctic regions.

But a far more striking corroboration of the above view is furnished by certain passages in the Avesta which describe the fight of Tishtrya with the demon of draught called Apa osha or "the burner" in the Parsi scriptures. In the Rig-Veda the fight of Indra with Vritra (*Vritra-turya*) is often represented as "a struggle for waters" (*upturya*), or as "the striving for cows" (*go-ishti*), or "the striving for day" (*div-ishti*) and Indra is said to have released the cows or waters, and brought on the dawn or the sun by killing Vritra (I, 51, 4; II, 19, 3).

Now India, as *Vritra-han*, appears as *Verethraghna* in the Avesta; but the fight for waters is therein ascribed not to Verethraghna but to Tishtrya, the star of rain.

It is he, who knocks down Apaosha and liberates the waters for the benefit of man, "with the assistance of the winds, and the light that dwells in the waters." In short Tishtrya's conquest over Apaosha is an exact parallel of Indra's conquest over Vritra as described in the Rig-Veda; and as the legends are interpreted at present, they are said to refer to the breaking up of the clouds and the bringing on of the rains on the earth. Tishtrya being supposed to be the star of rain. But this theory fails to account for the fact how the recovery of the dawn and the rising of the sun, or the bringing on of light, were included amongst the effects of Indra's victory over Vritra. It will be shown in the next chapter that the struggle for waters has very little to do with rain, and that the fight for waters and the fight for light are really synchronous, being two different versions of the same story. In short, both of these legends really represent the victory of the powers of light over darkness.

Shushna or "the scorcher" is one of the names given to Indra's enemy in the Rig-Veda (I, 51, 11), and the result of the conflict between Indra and Shushna is the release of the waters, as well as the finding of the morning cows (VIII, 96, 17), and the winning of the sun (VI, 20, 5).

Apaosha is thus Shushna under a different garb, and the only difference between the two legends is that while Indra is the chief actor in the one, Tishtrya is the chief hero in the other. But this difference is immaterial inasmuch as the attributes of one deity are often transferred, even in Rig-Veda, to another.

The Avestic legend of Tishtrya is, therefore, rightly understood by Zend scholars to be a reproduction of the Vedic legend of Indra and Vritra. Now, in the Tir Yasht, Tishtrya is represented as eventually overcoming Apaosha with the help of the Haoma sacrifice offered to Tishtrya by Ahura Mazda (Yt. VIII, 15-25).

The fight is carried on in the region of the waters, the sea Vouru-Kasha, from which Tishtrya is described as rising up victorious after defeating Apaosha (Yt. VIII, 32). Daeva Apaosha is again said to have assumed the form of a dark horse, while Tishtrya is represented as opposing him in the form of a bright horse, hoof against hoof (Yt. VIII, 28), and eventually coming up victorious from out of the sea Vouru-Kasha, like the sacrificial horse rising from the waters in the Rig-Veda (I, 163, 1).

But the passage most important for our purpose is the one in which Tishtrya informs Ahura Mazda as to what should be done in order to enable Tishtrya to overcome his enemy and to appear before the faithful at the appointed time.

"If men would worship me," says Tishtrya to Ahura Mazda, "with a sacrifice in which I were invoked by my own name, as they worship the other Yazatas with sacrifices in which they are invoked by their own names, then I should have come to the faithful at the appointed time; I should have come in the appointed time of my beautiful immortal life, should it be one night, or two nights, or fifty, or a hundred nights," (Yt. VIII, 11).

As Tishtrya appears before man after his battle with Apaosha, the phrase "appointed time" signifies the time during which the battle is fought and at the termination of which Tishtrya comes to the faithful; and the passage, therefore, means (1) that the "appointed time," when Tishtrya was to appear before man after fighting with Apaosha, varied from one night to a hundred nights and (2) that Tishtrya required to be strengthened during the period by Haoma sacrifices in which he was to be invoked by his own name. We have seen above that a hundred nightly Soma sacrifices were offered to Indra by the ancient Vedic sacrificers to enable him to secure a victory over Vritra and that Indra was the only deity to whom the libations were offered in these sacrifices.

The legend of Tishtrya and Apaosha is, therefore, an exact reproduction of Indra's fight with Vritra or Vala; and with his correspondence before us, we should feel no hesitation in accepting the view stated above regarding the origin of the *Shata-ratra* sacrifice. Neither Darmesteter nor Spiegel explains why the appointed time for the appearance of Tishtrya is described as "one night, or two nights, or fifty or a hundred nights," though both translate the original in the same way. The legend also forms the subject of chapter VII of the Bundahish, but there, too, we find no explanation as to why the appointed time is described as varying from one to a hundred nights.

It is, however, suggested by some that the appointed time may refer to the season of rains. But rains cannot be said to come after "one night, two nights, or fifty, or a hundred nights," and the latter expression would therefore, be utterly inappropriate in their case; nor, as stated above, does Tishtrya's fight with Apaosha represent only a struggle for rain, since we know that it is a struggle for light as well.

We have also seen that the existence of night-sacrifices in the Vedic literature, extending over one, two, three, or ten, or a hundred nights, indicates the long darkness during which Indra fought with Vala; and the coincidence between this fact and the "appointed time," of Tishtrya cannot be regarded as accidental.

The legends are undoubted in identical character, and taking the one to illustrate the other, the only conclusion deducible from them is that, a hundred nights was regarded to be the maximum duration of the fight between Indra and Vala, or Tishtrya and Apaosha, so far as the ancestors of the Indo-Iranian people were concerned, and that the sea Vouru-Kasha, or the ocean "encompassed with darkness," as the Rig-Veda has it (II, 23, 18), was the scene of this battle between the powers of light and darkness. We also learn from them that the hero of the battle, whether he was Indra or Tishtrya, stood in need of help, derived from the performance of the sacrifices *specially offered* to him during the period; and that as a matter of fact such sacrifices were performed in ancient times.

The word *shata-kratu* does not occur in the Avesta, but in the Ashi Yasht (Yt. XVII, 56) "a ram of hundred-fold energy" (*maeshahe satokarahe*) is spoken of; and considering the fact that in the Bahram Yasht (Yt. XIV, 23) "a beautiful ram, with horns bent round" is said to be one of the incarnations of Verethraghna, and that Indra is also described as appearing in the form of a ram in the Rig-Veda (VIII, 2, 40), it is very probable that the phrase *sato-karahe maeshahe* refers to Vere-thraghna in the Ashi Yasht, and like the epithet *shata-kratu*, the adjective *sato-karahe* means not "possessed of hundred powers," but "the master of a hundred deeds or sacrifices."

There is thus a very close correspondence between the Vedic and the Avestic ideas on this subject, and this strengthens the conclusion that the night sacrifices in the Vedic literature had their origin in the existence of a long continuous night of varying durations in the original home of the Vedic people. We can now also satisfactorily explain why Tishtrya is described (Yt. VIII, 36, *vide* Spiegel's Trans.) as "bringing hither the circling years of men."

It is the Avestic parallel of the Vedic story of the Dawn setting in motion "the ages of men, or *manusha yuga*," discussed in the last chapter, and stews that when Tishtrya's fight with Apaosha, or India's war with Vala, was over, the new year commenced with the long dawn, followed by the months of sunshine varying from seven to eleven in number, according to the latitude of the place.

In the light of what has been stated above, we can now better understand the original nature and meaning of the *Ati-ratra* sacrifice. It is a nightly sacrifice, performed during the night, even at present, and the Mimamsakas have not succeeded in converting it into a daysacrifice.

So far it is all right; but the question is why should the sacrifice be called Ati-ratra? The prefix *ati* (corresponding with Latin *trans*) ordinarily denotes "something beyond" "something on the other side, or at the other end," and not "something pervading, extending, or spreading the whole extent of anything." Even Sayana in his commentary on VII, 103, 7, the only place where the word *Ati-ratra* occurs in the Rig-Veda, explains it to mean "that which is the past or beyond the night" (*ratrim atitya vartate iti ati-ratrah*), and Rudradatta in his commentary on the Apasthamba Shrauta Sutra (XIV, 1, 1), gives the same explanation.

The *Ati-ratra* therefore, denotes a *trans nocturnal* sacrifice that is, performed at either end of the night. Now according to the Aitareya Brahmana (IV, 5), The passage about Tishtrya's connection with the year is noticed by Mr. Meherjibhai Nosherwanji Kuka, M.A., in his essay "On the order of Parsi months," published in the *Cama Memorial Volume*, and of which he was kind enough to send me a separate copy. The passage is in the Tir Yasht, § 36: — "*Tishtrim starem raevantem* kharenanghuantem yazamaide, yim yare-charecho machyehe Ahuracha khratu-guto aurunacha gairichacho sizdaracha ravascharato uziyoirentem hisposentem huyairyaicha danghve uzjasentem duzyairyaicha, kata Airyao *danghavo huyairyao bavaonti*." Spiegel translates it thus, "We praise the star Tishtrya, the shining, the majestic, who brings here the circling years of men."

Darmesteter takes *yare-charecho* &c., with the words following, *viz.*, *uziyoirentem hisposentem*, and translates, "We praise Tishtrya &c., whose rising is watched by men, who live on the fruits of the year." According to Dastur Erachji Mleherjirana (see his *Yasht ba maeni*), the meaning of the whole paragraph, in which this passage occurs, is: — "We praise Tishtrya, &c, who maketh the year revolve in accordance with the notions of the mountaineers and the nomads. He riseth and is visible towards the regions where there is no correct calculation of the year."

But whatever the difficulties of interpretation may be, one thing the *Ati-ratra* sacrifice is performed for the purpose of driving out the Asuras from the darkness of night; and the Tandya Brahmana (IV, 1, 4-5) tells us that Prajapati, who first perceived the sacrifice, created from it the twin of day and night (*aho-ratre*). It follows from this that the *Ati-ratra* was performed at the close of such night as give rise-to the ordinary days and nights, or, in other words, the regular succession of days and nights followed its performance. This can only be the case if we suppose that the *Ati-ratra* was performed at the end of a long continuous night in regions where such night occurred.

With us in the temperate or the tropical zone, ordinary days and nights regularly succeed each other throughout the year without any break, and it is meaningless, if not absurd, to speak of the cycle of day and night as produced from a particular night in the year.

Again, on the theory of a daily struggle between light and darkness the Asuras must be turned out of darkness every night, and strictly speaking the performance of the *Ati-ratra* is necessary on every one of the 360 nights of the *Sattra*. But as a matter of fact the *Ati-ratra* is performed only at the beginning and the end of the *Sattra*; and even then the regular *Sattra* is said seems to be quite clear from this passage, *viz.*, that Tishtrya was the star by which the year was reckoned. In the Tir Yasht § 5, springs of water are said to flow at the rising of Tishtrya, who in § 16 is described as "mingling his shape with light," or "moving in light," § 46.

All these incidents can be satisfactorily explained if we suppose that, after Tishtrya's fight with Apaosha, lasting for 100 nights at the longest; the aerial waters, which communicated motion to the sun and other heavenly bodies (see Faravardin Yasht 53-58) and which lay still or stagnant during the time, were set free to move again along the path made by Mazda, bringing on with them the light of the sun and thus commencing the new year after the long winter night in the Arctic region.

The simultaneous character of the motion of waters, the commencement of the new year, and the winning of light after Tishtrya's fight with Apaosha, can be explained only in this way, and not by making the legend refer to the rainy season (see the discussion about "waters" in the book).

The Pairika *Duz-yairya*, or the Bad Year, which Tishtrya is said to break asunder, is on this theory, the wearisome dark Arctic night to commence on the Chaturvimsha and close on the Mahavrata day, and not on the concluding Atiratra day. It seems, therefore, that the performance of the *Ati-ratra* was not originally intended to drive away the Asuras from only the first of 360 nights over which the *Sattra* now extends. For in that case there is no reason why the Asuras were not required to be expelled from everyone of the 360 nights. It follows, therefore, that the Ati-ratra or the traps-nocturnal sacrifice refers to some night not included in the regular nights of the *Gavam-ayanam*.

It is true that the *Ati-ratra* is performed at the beginning and the end of every *Sattra* and in one sense it is therefore, a *trans-sattra* or *atisattra* sacrifice. But that does not account for the name *Ati-ratra* as the *Sattra* is not held during night. We must, therefore hold that the two *Ati-ratras* were originally performed not at the beginning and the end of a *Sattra* but at the beginning and the end of a night which occurred or intervened between the last and the first day of the *Sattra*. When this night ended with an *Ati-ratra* the usual *Sattra* began and as the sun was above the horizon during the period producing the regular succession of days and nights no *Ati-ratra* was needed during the *Sattra*, for as stated in the Tandya Brahmana the object of the *Ati-ratra* was gained.

But the *Sattra* closed with the long night and the *Ati-ratra* had therefore again to be performed at the end of the *Sattra* to drive the Asuras from this night. I have shown before that we have direct and reliable authority in the Taittiriya Samhita to hold that the *Gavam-ayanam* was once completed in ten months or 300 days and it was therefore appropriately closed with and introduced by an *Ati-ratra*.

The word *Ati-ratra* is thus rationally explained, for the sacrifice was performed at the beginning and the close of the long night and, was therefore, adequately called a trans-nocturnal sacrifice. Between these two *Ati-ratras* came all the night-sacrifices mentioned above, offered exclusively to Indra.

The old *Gavamayanam* of ten or less than ten months, the *Ati-ratra* or the transnocturnal, the *Ratri-kratus* and *Ratri-sattras*, or nightly Soma sacrifices of two, three, &c., up to a hundred continuous nights' duration, and lastly the *Ati-ratra*, to be again followed by the *Gavam-ayanam*, thus formed the complete yearly round of sacrifices performed by the primeval ancestors of the. Vedic people; and each of these sacrifices had originally the same place in the yearly round as is indicated by the root-meaning of its name.

But when the year of ten months was converted into one of twelve to suit the altered conditions of the new home, the *Gavam-ayanam* expanded into a performance of 360 days, and the elastic nature of the greater portion of the performance, as pointed out above, permitted the change to be easily carried out.

But though the annual *Sattra* expanded in this way, encroaching upon the night-sacrifices of the long night, which were no longer needed, the *Ati-ratra* was retained as an introductory sacrifice and was incorporated in the ceremonies of the *Sattra* itself.

Thus the two *Atiratra* sacrifices, which were originally performed, as shown by the etymology, at the two termini of the long night, came to be converted into the introductory and concluding sacrifices of the annual *Sattra*; and if the word *Ati-ratra* had not been retained, we could not have got any clue to reveal to us the-story of its changing fortune. But the night-sacrifices, the *Ratri-kratus* or *Ratri-sattras*, which were performed during the long night between the two *Ati-ratras*, were no longer needed and their nature came to be oon misunderstood, until at last the Mimamsakas finally made room for them in the class of daily Soma sacrifices, partly under *Ahinas* and partly under *Sattras*, by means of the equation that *ratri* (night) is equal to *aho-ratre* (day and night) in the sacrificial literature.

How this change was carried out is a question beyond the scope of this book; but I may-here state that, in my opinion, it was the authors of Brahmans, or the Brahmavadins who preceded them, that had to perform the difficult task of adapting the ancient sacrificial calendar to the changed conditions of their new home, somewhat after the manner of Numa's reform of the ancient Roman calendar.

The sacrifice was the main ritual of the Vedic religion, and naturally enough the priests must have tried to preserve as much of the old sacrificial system as they possibly could in adapting it to the new conditions. The task was by no means an easy one, and those that find fault with the Brahmans as full of fanciful speculations must bear in mind the fact that an ancient and sacred system of sacrifices had to be adapted to new conditions, by assigning plausible reasons for the same, at a time when the true origin of the system was almost forgotten.

The Brahmans could not have indulged in free speculations about the origin of the rites and ceremonies mentioned by them, had the latter originated in their own time, or in days so near to them that the real traditions about the origin of these ceremonies could be preserved intact.

But so long as these traditions were fresh, no explanation was probably needed; and when they became dim, their place had to be supplied by plausible reasons based on such traditions as were known at the time. This throws quite a new light on the nature and composition of the Brahmans: but as the discussion is not pertinent to the subject in hand, we cannot enter into it more fully in this place. We have now reviewed the leading features of the system of Soma sacrifices as described in the Vedic literature, so far as our purpose is concerned, and seen that by the aid of the Arctic theory, some hard facts therein, which have been hitherto incomprehensible, can be easily and naturally explained. A history of the whole sacrificial system from the point of view indicated above is a work quite outside the pale of this book; but so far as we have examined the subject and especially the question about the isolated group of a hundred nightly Soma sacrifices, I think, we have sufficient evidence therein to warrant us in holding that these sacrifices are a relic of the ancient times when the ancestors of the Vedic Rishis performed them with the object of helping Indra to fight with the powers of darkness.

It has been already shown in the first part of this chapter that the *Gavam-ayanam* or the "Cows' walk" like the Roman year, once lasted only for ten months; and a series of suitable nightsacrifices is a natural supplement to such sessions. Both are relics of ancient times, and taken along with the evidence regarding the existence of a long dawn of thirty days and of the long day and night discussed in previous chapters, they conclusively establish the existence of an ancient home of the ancestors of the Vedic people in the circum-polar region.

The sacrificial sessions of the Navagvas and the Dashagvas, the legend of Dirghatamas growing old in the tenth month, the tradition about the ancient year of five seasons, or the yoking of seven or ten horses to the chariot of the sun, all go to strengthen the same view; and the Avestic passages regarding the duration of Tishtrya's fight with Apaosha, the Puranic tradition about Indra's being the master of a hundred sacrifices or the destroyer of a hundred cities, the existence of a series of one hundred nightly Soma sacrifices, which, though obsolete long since, could not have found place in the sacrificial works as *Ratri-sattras*, unless they were ancient sacrifices performed, as their name indicates, during night, — these and many other minor facts noticed before, further corroborate, if corroboration be needed, our theory regarding the original home of the Aryans near the North Pole. It must, however, be stated here that I do not wish to imply in any way that the numerous sacrificial details found in the later Vedic literature were in vogue or were known in these ancient times. On the contrary I am prepared to believe that in all probability these ancient sacrifices were very simple in character. The ancient priests probably went on sacrificing from day today and afterwards from night to night, without any idea that the system was capable of giving rise to various rigid annual *Sattras*. The sacrifice was the only ritual of their religion; and howsoever simple such sacrifices might have been in ancient times, it was almost a matter of duty, at least with the priests, to perform them every day.

It was also a means, as remarked by me elsewhere, to keep up the calendar in ancient times, as the yearly round of sacrifices closely followed the course of the sun. It is from this latter point of view that the ancient sacrificial system is important for historical or antiquarian purposes, and I have examined it above in the same light. This examination, it will be seen, has resulted in the discovery of a number of facts which lead us directly to, and can be satisfactorily explained only by the theory of the original Arctic home; and when our conclusions are thus supported by the hymns of the Rig-Veda on the one hand, and the sacrificial literature on the other, I think, we need have no doubt about their correctness.

5

Educational Views of Tilak

NATURE AND OBJECTIVES OF EDUCATION

While taking decisions about the education to be given to the natives and its medium of instruction, there were lots of agreements, for and against, put forth by the British thinkers, missionaries, Company officials, and the members of the Board of Directors. Preservation of the oriental knowledge, encouragement to study and research moral and religious reformation of Indians, sifting the good in the native culture and coupling it with the good in the western culture, these were some of the points debated.

They also discussed whether education of the natives was the responsibility of the rulers for the atonement, for the acquisition of their land, and how to win the confidence of the upper strata of society which had lost its importance under the British rule.

Out of these the most powerful decisions which proved fruitful were:

1) The English rulers need a large number of class II officers to sustain their rule in the subcontinent. If these officers were to discharge their duties promptly and efficiently, they needed to be educated. In the new regime, the traditional knowledge acquired in old-fashioned schools was not going to help. So the rulers had to get a well-educated or atleast just educated class of servants. It was not only expensive and impracticable but literally impossible to bring such people from England.

   At the foundation ceremony of the Elphinstone Institute some of the Directors expressed hope that "a class of persons qualified by their intelligence and morality for high employment in the civil administration of India would be producted by the Institute".

   This makes clear with what purpose they were running the Institute.

2) A class of people would be produced, who took English education and therefore got to know the English culture and so would be in favour of the English regime "we must do our best to form a class who may be interpreters between us and the millions whom we govern, a class of persons Indian in blood and colour but English in taste, in opinion, words and intellect". Without education there was no other means of realising the dream of Macaulay.
3) The main objective of imparting education was spread of Christianity." Western light and knowledge should take the place of eastern culture and religion" was the expectation of Charles Grant.
4) The Anglicised class would also be helpful for trade and spread of Christianity. Though the policy of religious neutrality was adopted for the sake of political stability, it was but natural that the Christian rulers, would have, in their minds sympathy for the missionaries.
5) Since English was made the official language, the top British Officers would not need to learn the native languages in this country of many dialects, nor would they have to depend on their subordinates for the purpose of governance. On the contrary an English knowledge servant class was going to be easily available. "It is neither our aim nor desire to substitute the English language for the vernacular dialects of the country—.The vernacular languages must be employed to teach the far large classes-" Despatch of the honourable court of Directors no 49. 19 July 1854.

Although such assurance was given, it was obvious that whenever principles came in conflict with practical convenience, the rulers always gave priority to the latter.

Though the Government adopted the policy of giving western education in English medium, they had never intended to train the natives for highest posts like Generals, Diplomats or legal experts. By making education accessible to a small group of people, the Government thought its responsibility was over. They thought that education given at the top would automatically percolate to the lower strata of the society. There was no need of any special efforts; this was the Government's role in taking education to the masses. The Government which expressed a desire to reform the natives had no intention of making primary education free or compulsory for the poor people.

The British Government also did not bother to promote vocational education. In this context it must be noted that after taking the responsibility of the native education, only one engineering class was opened in Bombay over a period of twelve years, and that too was meant to meet the requirements of the Government.

The Government policy was to be frugal in expenses on education.

In the 1870-71 report of the Department of Education, the disparity between the salaries of employees in other departments and the Department of Education is highlighted. In the Department of education nobody's salaries were like Rs. 800, Rs. 700 or Rs. 600 per month. Monthly salary of Rs. 500 per month was given only to two native professors, whereas even a class III subordinate or Deputy Collector got the same salary.

Three Headmasters got Rs. 200/-per month, which is the salary of class V. Judge or a Deputy Collector.

A Deputy Inspector gets Rs. 100/-per month, which is also the salary a small size school headmaster. This is the minimum scale for mamlatdars.

The Director of Education complains that because of the lower grades of salary bright or really well-educated people do not like to work in this field, and even if a few come they take the first opportunity to move out for a better paid job.

On the whole, education that will help the British regime, its administration and stability, was the objective of education.

Consequences of this kind of Education

1) *Dominance of English:* As English was the medium of education, it also became the language of communication of the educated class. Book writing and even private correspondence was done in English. Vishnushastri Chiplunkar and Lokmanya Tilak also were no exceptions to this rule. The prefaces and covers of Marathi books were written in English. "From this, we can see how the influence of the foreign language of a foreign government spreads in all walks of life. Marathi is banished", says V. K. Rajwade.
2) The Government wanted the people who had acquired knowledge in English to take it to their countrymen through Marathi medium. But these people had no love for Marathi. Already a note of anger was being heard. In September 1860 issue of 'Marathi Jnanaprasarak' Vinayak Janardan Kirtane writies:

"Many of us have got to taste the sweet diet of modern European sciences and Literature, and some others have got the unparalleled juice of Sanskrit language to taste, so both classes of people are neglecting their own language. Those who have studied English say "sheer nonsense. What is there in Marathi? What we have to do with it"-and those who have studied Sanskrit say-"There is nothing interesting in Marathi. Why Should we bother to study it?"

In the end, Kirtane earnestly requests the English and Sanskrit scholars, "There are millions of your country men around you, who look up to you as their saviours from the whirlpool of ignorance. Take them out of it. Take them out of the darkness and show them a ray of light. This will give you the great satisfaction of fulfilment of your duties".

In the very first year of 'Vijvidh jnana Vistar' in the November 1867 issue, the same note is struck at a higher pitch. In an article entitled 'Marathi Bhasha' the writer says:

> *"In the first Convocation ceremony the chairman had said, `The purpose of these degrees and honours conferred on you is that you should make a good use of them. You must try hard to pass on the knowledge we have given you with so much effort, cost, to your countrymen who speak your language'. But has anyone followed this suggestion in practice? Some people make an excuse saying that there are no corresponding words in Marathi. This is only a hollow excuse. The Government has appointed teachers on big salaries for the education of their people. But if they cannot pass on what they have received from others, then what is so great about taking those degrees?"*

In the 1870-71 report of the Education Department, J. B. Paile has expressed the same kind of disapproval in the following words—"Even if it be granted that there neither is nor even will be an original vernacular literature worthy to take its place with the literature of the west,—but it is no reason why the educated Indian should not learn to use with force and correctness the language to which he was born, and in which alone the mass of his fellow-country men can be addressed".

3) *Stunted Growth of Regional Languages:* In the Bombay Province, Regional languages were used as mediums of instruction, for some years in the beginning. Some book writing-may be just translated text books of physical sciences was stimulated. As these branches of knowledge were new to Marathi, new terminology was created. If this policy had continued, after some time Marathi would have given up dependence on the walker of translations, and would have become not only the carrier of knowledge, but would have also undertaken original and varied book-writing. In time to come Marathi would have become a source of knowledge. Marathi, as well as other regional languages would have developed, but because of the universal dominance of English, the regional languages were suppressed and their growth was stunted.
4) *A New Awakening to History:* The history of India was included in the curriculum of those days. The early writers were English men. The history books studied in schools and colleges were written by foreigners,

especially foreign rulers. Prejudice, inadequacy, misinterpretation, one sidedness, and contempt for the natives appeared at many places.

"Shivaji was a Whimsical Person. Many of his deeds were evil conquering a fort or land by fighting Guerilla wars. He liked deceitful ways more than the straight forward ones. This was one of the defects of his character. He has proved his cruelty and harmfulness on many occasions".

This is a quotation from Capt. Dough. He says, "Shivaji's behaviour was just like what we find everywhere in Asia or backward countries. He showed his bad qualities on various occasions just like a king, a plunderer, or a head of dacoits tribe, in those countries. He dealt with situation as they arose. For success in his undertaking, he did not hesitate to do anything. It is difficult to call this man a man of principles. It was his principle to hate all those who opposed his religion and towards the end he, like Aurangzeb, had started persecuting people belonging to other religions".

Even Elphinstone wrote on the same lines. He writes, "Shivaji was a son of a great General. He started his career like an adventurous and treacherous dacoit, but in the end he became an independent, sagacious ruler".

This example is significant enough. Of course there were many reactions to it. In the April 1860 issue of 'Marathi Jnanaprasarak', there was a series of articles entitled 'Shivaji Maharajancha Vrittanta'. In the final article the writer says, "The foreign historians take Shivaji for a dacoit and plunderer, and many learned men amongst us have accepted this improper view. The historians who would clap for Wallace, Bruce or Tell, who worked for the betterment of their countries, would shamelessly use word of abuse for Shivaji. We wouldn't have thought it worthwhile to refute the opinions of these partial historians. But when so many Hindu Scholars do not hesitate to support this view, we feel it necessary to refute it" The articles end as follows.

"Shivaji did not have a desire to wipe out other kingdoms by fighting crooked and unfair battles. Shivaji rose against people who were making life difficult for his countrymen, and hurt the interest of those who did not belong to their religion. He rose to protect his country, his religion and his people against these onslaughts. Is it right to call him a dacoit, only because there were a few lapses on his part while achieving his goal. There is no doubt that if they bother to take notice of his praiseworthy cause, they will be convinced that Shivaji was one like Wallace, Bruce and Tell who loved their country".

In a paper read by Nilkantha Janardan Kirtane in 'Poona Young Men's Association' it is said, "Grantsahib has made one mistake. While writing of Shivaji's biography he did not trust the works of a Maratha. He himself has said that the parts which defile Shivaji were taken from the writings of the

Muslims". Around the same time, Mahadeo Govind Ranade, who was still a student, wrote harsh articles of the true Marathi nature of Nana Phadnavis. Vitthalrao Pathak told the essence of Maratha history in 'Jnaprasarak'. V. J. Kirtane read a play on the senior Mahadevrao Peshwe, in a meeting held by 'Marathi Janaprasarak'.

Thus there was at least a little, just a seed's, consciousness of self-respect and their ego began to wake up. Seeds of inclination for independent thinking were sown. That the need for putting forth such a view was felt, was itself great. Even the British would not have expected this to happen so soon.

The history of England was included in the curriculum. The concepts of control of the king's power by public opinion, participation of the people in governance, individual freedom, establishment of Democracy etc., became familiar to the newly educated natives, who in the beginning thought that the rulers who enforced the rules in their country would be true to their sense of fairness and enforce them in India too.

Although they showered praise on the British regime, the thought that the British would have to leave this country one day, kept on recurring to their minds.

"The British Government is making efforts to educate the natives through the local Government and the English people. If they educate the natives, the latter will acquire the capability for self-rule.

The historical annals show that no nation which can have self-rule has ever allowed others to rule them. So it should happen in this country, and it will be for the good of both the countries India and England". This was what Balashastri Jambhekar has written in the May 1840 issue of "Digdarshan".

Lokhitwadi too, who often praised the British rule, and mercilessly hammered the defects on the natives, is seen expressing the hope that "when people become enlightened they will gently tell the British, "We are educated just like you, why not have powers? "Then, probably, they will get the posts of Governors also. When they get powers, they will become independent like Americans, and ask the British to go back to their country. "Now we can govern our country very well. We don't want your advice and we don't want your domination". This will be the condition of our country".

This awakening is a consequence of English education.

5) *Loyal Government Servants:* The British changed the traditional subjects and the mediums of education, but the change was not limited to these factors. With education the mode of thinking also changed. After some time this educated class adopted even the clothing of the British. A new

class of loyal government servants came into existence. This class was self-satisfied and totally cut off from the society.

6) *Lack of Religious Education:* In the government run or government aided schools, there was no place either for Christianity or for any of the native religions. The moral education was given through translated books like 'Balmitra', or 'Isapneeti'. Students were not introduced to the religious and cultural traditions of this country. Getting it impressed on the mind or taking pride in it was far away dream.

7) *Inferiority Complex:* The English medium, the western content of education, teachers indebted to the fixed British curriculum and text-books. There were few teachers who would go beyond this and enkindle a flame of nationalism, mothertongue, own religion and culture in the minds of students. Most of the student's aim was to get a government job. Very few took education for the sake of knowledge. In this condition everything English-Their language their material progress, their achievements, their ettiquettes and thoughts, their culture, in short, everything of theirs was superior, great, for most of the students. As a result, we natives are backward and can never be their equals',-such inferiority complex took hold of their minds.

In short the class of people who had the capacity for independent thinking and forms the very backbone of a nation, was a slave of the British. This was most unfortunate for this Country.

If the Hindu subjects would be allowed to use native languages for practical purposes, they would not follow the English, and would desire to re-establish their rule of their own religion. So Lord Bentinck insisted on English medium and his expectations were fulfilled, because, in fact, most of the people were Pro-English. Those who aimed only at a government job, were influenced by the British rule, Still, the Indian patriots should be grateful to the British diplomats who though for selfish reasons, imparted education to the natives and allowed their gradual participation in politics"

The above remark by Acharya Javdekar is quite apt. Because of the English education, intelligent students who were not contented just with the curriculum and text-books, had a new vista of knowledge opened to them.

They became conscious of their identify. They started comparative studies of occidental and oriental cultures. They began to think it necessary to preserve the immortal in our culture and couple it with the useful in the western culture.

In order to fulfil this purpose, though in government services, without crossing its limits, and avoiding sychophancy, Balshastri Jambhekar, Lokhitwadi, Krishnashastri Chiplunkar, Kerunana Chhachtre, Mahadev

Moreshwar Kunte, Justice Ranade and some others preserved their self-respect and began their movement of mass-education through meeting, institutions, newspapers, writings etc.

Their objectives were progress and prosperity of their own nation, language, people and religion. They did imply total Independence in the time to come on the scene.

Soon after this Vishnushastri Chiplunkar spurned the bondage of the government services and founded the "New English School" on 1st Jan., 1880. After him Tilak and Agarkar took a vow of patriotism and service to the country, without even thinking of joining government service.

EDUCATION THROUGH NATIONAL FESTIVALS

Tilak wanted to extend his sphere of education through other methods. He had read the History of Greece in which there was a description of different cultural festivals. The Greek, enthusiastically participated in them and were thus involved in the affairs of the state. Tilak wanted to involve the generality of the people in social and political activities in a similar manner. He therefore thought of starting public festivals which would become instruments of public education. He then started the Ganapati festival as a social event and got a very enthusiastic response from the people in Pune and also in some other places.

Traditionally, the worship of the idol of Ganapati was a domestic celebration. Tilak gave a new orientation to this practice and widened its significance to educate the people. He advocated that the Ganapati festival be celebrated publicly and besides the ritual of worship and Aarati, it should include lectures by eminent persons on different subjects, group singing and other cultural programmes by groups of youths. Tilak thus created a new public platform for educating the people. Tilak also launched the Shivaji Festival. He was quite explicit about its object which was the celebration of the glory and achievements of Chhatrapati Shivaji Maharaj. Tilak told the people that Shivaji was a National Hero, and a perennial source of inspiration for patriotism. Tilak observed that in times when national qualities such as patriotism, sense of solidarity and brotherhood, and hatred of tyranny were absent, it was necessary to celebrate the achievements of the National Hero, Shivaji who was a symbol of all these noble national virtues.

Tilak in his speech at Amravati said," On one day at least in a year, every person should think about his village or town, about his country. He should ask himself the question whether the condition of the country was in a flourishing state or had decayed. If it had decayed, he must try to find out the means for its improvement. It is with this end in view that the Shivaji festival is being celebrated." Tilak wrote that no other hero in Maratha History was so respected by all sections of the public as Shivaji Maharaj. Tilak drew the attention of the people to the fact that the forts standing in different parts of Sahyadri ranges in Maharashtra were a living testimony to Shivaji's prowess and a number of places were remembered for their association with the exploits of Shivaji Maharaj.

In an article in 'Mahratta' Tilak wrote, "Hero-worship is a feeling deeply implanted in human nature and our political aspirations need all the strength which the worship of a swadeshi hero is likely to inspire into our minds. For this purpose Shivaji is the only hero to be found in Indian history. He was born at a time when the whole nation required relief from mis-rule and by his self-sacrifice and courage, he proved to the world that India was not a country forsaken by providence".

While launching the Shivaji festival and Ganapati festival Tilak was using the revivalist method in order to awaken the sense of hope and self-confidence among the people. He regarded these festivals as a means to national awakening and also as a means to giving an ethical basis to the political aspirations. Tilak wanted to revive the creative spirit of the old times and not the form of the old institutions or religion. He regarded the traditional way of life like a tree and wanted to graft on it, the new ideas such as nationalism. Tilak's criticism of liberal leaders like Ranade was, that they were trying to implant alien ideas in Indian soil. Tilak said that it was necessary to utilise the vitality of the indigenous way of life and give it a new orientation. He once said, "Love for one's country is a natural instinct. We have to give a new orientation to it and make people accept the ideology of nationalism". Thus, through the Shivaji Festival and Ganapati Festival, Tilak was playing a significant role as a teacher who wanted to mould public opinion and inculcate in people the spirit of patriotism.

In spite of his editorial responsibilities and in spite of his continuous efforts to give a momentum to the Shivaji Festival and Ganpati Festival, Tilak still found time to pursue his research on the chronology of Vedas with the help of astronomy. Tilak submitted a Paper to the Ninth Oriental Congress held in London in 1882. The Paper which was based on his research on the "antiquity of the Vedas" by giving astronomical evidence with the help of Vedanga Jyotisha put forth the theory that the Vedas were written during the period 4000-2500 B.C. Though there were different opinions about the proposition put forth by Tilak, it was accepted as a serious effort by Oriental scholars.

During this period, Tilak also wrote in Kesari detailed reviews of the new editions of the Mahabharata and Ramayana and stated his own theories about their dates, origin and several important and textual interpretative problems connected with them. Apart from these, Tilak wrote extensive reviews of two important books of a political nature Dadabhai Naoroji's "Poverty and Un-British rule in India" and Digby's "Prosperous British India." Tilak wrote the reviews under the caption 'Two Good Books'. As a conscientious teacher of his readers, he first gave a detailed summary of these books, and after stating clearly the main proposition in these two serious works, analysed their contents and made his own detailed comments on them. Dadabhai Naoroji, the great sage "Maharshi" of Indian politics, showed in a convincing manner that the British Empire had carried on a relentless economic exploitation of India, destroyed its agro-industrial pattern of life and reduced India to beggary. Both Dadabhai Naoroji and Digby had thrown light on the growing poverty in India caused by the British rule. Tilak's reviews were models of educative journalism. Tilak's obituary articles on some of his great contemporaries like Justice Ranade, Prin. Agarkar, Vivekanand, Max Mueller and Herbert Spencer, were also written with the same educative approach. In these articles he did not just pay tributes to these great men. He evaluated the significant contribution of these eminent persons, in the context of the social and political situation prevailing in India. In his article on "Vishnu Shastri Chiplunkar", Tilak expressed his criticism of English education. He wrote: "English education was responsible for destroying that essential bond of relationship between learning, ethics, religious faith and family life."

Tilak participated in the work of the Indian National Congress from its very inception and made a fervent plea that instead of following the moderate method of petition and prayer, the Congress should create a political sanction to support their demand for political rights. At the same time, Tilak always sought an opportunity to draw the attention of the people to the problems of education. In the seventeenth session of the Indian National Congress at Calucutta, Tilak seconded the resolution on the appointment of an Education Commission.

In his speech Tilak made a comparison between the Japanese and Indian systems of education and said, "It was because of the independent system of education, with facilities for technical training that Japan had forged ahead. On the contrary, education in India had dwarfed the intellect of young men. You might point out a Jagadeesh Chandra Bose here or a Dr. R. P. Paranjpye there, but let me remind you that they are exceptions which prove the rule. Our ancient system of education cultivated a love for learning and produced men, whose intellectual attainments are still the wonder of the world. Education in India had been reduced to the position of a subordinate handmaid of administration and unless it is raised to a real position of the Goddess of learning, India could not be raised to the status of the civilised nations of the West."

TILAK AND MANAGEMENT OF EDUCATIONAL INSTITUTIONS

Training has been one little part of Lokmanya Tilak's commitment to Indian Social Life. There are distinctive sides to Tilak's life of which the most unmistakable is his political commitment. Be that as it may, he was a political pioneer as well as an incredible researcher and a writer. He lit up each subject he took up. In spite of the fact that Education involved just a couple of years of his open and social life, his commitment in this field is interesting as in amid the whole 20 century the nation took after the example of training he chose and imitated the administration style he claimed.

Four critical occasions of. Tilak's instructive commitment which have been considered in this paper are (i) The establishment of the New English School at Pune, (ii) The development of the Deccan Education Society, (iii) The foundation of the Fergusson College, and (iv) His acquiescence of Life Membership of the Deccan Education Society. Tilak voiced his thoughts and conclusions fundamentally through articles in Kesari and through letters composed by him to his associates in the Deccan Education Society. Give us a chance to take up these occasions one by one.

Foundation of New English School, Pune

The closing of the East India Company's regime in India was the beginning of a new era in our country. The failure of the uprising of 1857 had signified that the emancipation of our land and people was to be achieved through peaceful and constitutional means. Raja Ram Mohan Roy in Bengal and Mahadeo Govind Ranade in Maharashtra were the heralds of this new orientation. A very important aspect of this Indian Renaissance was the recognition of the vital part that education had to play in the creation of modern India. The historic debate on the type of education to be imparted to our people had already been settled in favour of the modern West rather than of the ancient East.

The verdict in favour of western rather than oriental education had not only meant the virtual suppression of the old by foreigners and christian missionaries. Such a transfer of educational power, though natural and inevitable under the circumstances, was neither necessary for all the time nor wholesome. Nation building education, national education, was what we wanted, and this could not be at the hands of foreigners and missionaries, for obvious reasons. National education, education of the entire nation to achieve national ends, education of the people, for the people and by the people, was the need of the hour.

The famous Wood's Education Despatch was released in 1854. It provided for establishing administrative machinery and colleges for training teachers. The despatch, no doubt, provided the essential framework for our educational system. It was highly appreciative of western education but it introduced a very tight bureaucratic control over the educational system in the country. The despatch appreciated the value of liberal education and education for women. Though the provisions in the despatch were good in character, in effect they proved useful to the Government and to missionaries than to the people. Govt. got an assured supply of servants. In addition as the despatch had provided for grants-in-aid to institutions the missionaries were mainly benefited because of this provision. They got grants without sacrificing their religious activities.

The good intentions expressed in the despatch regarding popular education and encouragement to Indian vernaculars remained unrealised. The despatch did not refer to universal literacy although it expected education to spread over a wider field, through the grant-in-aid system. It did not recognize the obligation of the State to educate every child under a certain age; it did not declare that poverty shall be no bar to education of the deserving. The despatch did not visualise education for leadership, or for industrial regeneration nor for the defence of the motherland. As private enterprise was often discouraged, christian missionaries were the only private agency in the field of education.

Under the above mentioned circumstances a band of patriotic and enterprising young men in Pune launched the New English School on 1 January, 1880. These young men were Chiplunkar, Tilak, Namjoshi, Apte and Agarkar. Opening of the New English School proved a new era in the educational and public life of Maharashtra.

Bal Gangadhar Tilak and Gopal Ganesh Agarkar later played a vital role in their chosen fields of Politics and Social Reforms. New English School, Pune was singular in having such eminent personalities as its founders. They looked upon education as the surest way to the regeneration of our mother land. In their view, Education was to be the means of rousing the intellect, the drooping will and the slumbering conscious of their countrymen. They kept before the people a very moderate objective of cheapening and facilitating education by starting schools and colleges. This venture was very bold and ambitious particularly in 1880, though it was considered 'mad', 'hopeless', 'criminal' and 'utopian' by Tilak's contemporaries.

The founders were too determined and too full of faith to be depressed by apathy or opposition shown by the contemporaries. Through their writings about education they created among youngsters the ideas of patriotism and national self-respect. Tilak and his colleagues achieved the success to the school project through self-sacrifice. All these men had the idealism and enterprise of the pioneers in them. At the time there was a Govt. School and a few private coaching classes in Pune. While the Govt. school was fully supported by the Govt. financing, the private classes conducted by Mahagaonkar, Bhave and others were purely conducted for financial benefits. New English School was different than these. Chiplunkar, Tilak, Agarkar and Apte were so gifted that in their own way they had other things to do than teaching. New English School was extremely fortunate in having them as founders.

A few things are worth noting here at this stage. May be due to the fact that Tilak, Agarkar and their colleagues were educated in the Deccan College where western education was imported, they never thought of going back to oriental education. They accepted what Macauley and the Wood's Despatch had professed. But the starting of New English School in Pune heralded a new movement in Maharashtra. Tilak's influence over the people was so strong that people opened schools in their towns and named them 'New English School'. People were convinced that Education was a tool towards achieving freedom of the country.

Formation of Deccan Education Society

It was essential for the success of the scheme of popular education sponsored by the founders of the New English School that they should form themselves into a corporate body to ensure continuity of effort in that cause and to win public confidence as to the stability and permanence of institutions they might establish. If the public was to be invited to contribute to funds on a scale adequate to the undertaking, the administration of such funds would have to vest in the hands of the organised body, including men interested in education and possessing influence in the Society. From the very outset the founders regarded themselves not as proprietors but as temporary trustees, who on their own personal responsibility and by their own personal sacrifices, would place the school on a firm footing, and then convert it into a public institution, accepting for themselves the status of its life-long servants. When the opening of a college was in sight the formation of a corporate body became a matter of urgency.

The earliest mention of the idea of forming a Society occurred in a report of the Superintendent of the New English School for the year 1883. He mentioned in that report that in order to establish a college and to open schools all over Maharashtra it was desirable to constitute a "Board of Trustees with a Managing Committee attached to it". These words gave some idea of the constitution of the proposed Society. When this preliminary work was over, an application for the Registration of the Society was made on 5 August, and the Society was registered on 13 August, 1885 under Act XXI of 1860 (Societies Registration Act) of the Legislative Council of India. The Memorandum of Association stated the object of the Society to be "to facilitate and cheapen education by starting, affiliating or incorporating at different places as circumstances might permit, schools and colleges under native management, or by any other ways best adopted to the wants of the people". The constitution of the Society as originally framed in 1884 provided for setting up three bodies to carry on the business of the Society: (1) Local Managing Boards, one for each Centre, consisting of Life-Members working at that Centre, and entrusted with the internal management of the Societies Institutions situated therein; (2) The Council of the Society for general supervision and control made up of all Life-Members in active service, and an equal number of representatives of the Patrons and Fellows of the Society; and (3) Trustees to take charge of the permanent funds and property of the Society. This constitution provided for day-to-day management of the Society's Institutions, and initiative as regards the development and extension of the Society's activities for the collection of funds for the purposes of the Society lay with the Life-Members. The Council on which Fellows and Patrons of the Society *i.e.* those contributing Rs. 200 or more, and those contributing Rs. 1000 or more respectively to the funds were represented and through which they could exert influence on the management of the Society's affairs, had powers of control rather than on initiation. The Council held the purse—strings on behalf of the Society and could use that power to exert its influence. Life-Members individually and collectively supplied the driving force to the activities of the Society.

The constitution and the working of the Board was thoroughly democratic. Every Life-Member, senior or junior, stood absolutely on the same footing as regards the right of voting and eligibility to office. On their capacity to visualise educational needs and formulate well-considered plans, as also their readiness to carry out these plans depended the progress and prosperity of Society's institutions. The founders of the New English School, Pune succeeded in setting up an altogether new standard of public duty, and made the name of a Life-Member of the Society synonymous with service, sacrifice and integrity. The non-members on the Council had to give a word of counsel now and again, and blessings with their good wishes to any project the Life-Members had put before them. If we look at the private institutions run in Maharashtra at that time, they lacked corporate organisation and consequent lack of guarantees of permanence. They were at a disadvantage as compared to government and missionary institutions. The constitution evolved by the founders of the New English School and Deccan Education Society overcame this difficulty.

We must look at the Constitution of the D.E. Society very carefully. As Tilak, Agarkar, Gokhale and others were involved in framing it, it served as a model to institutions existing at that time as also to those which were started even at later dates. A major weakness of this Constitution, absence of the Governing Council which had a majority of Non-Life Members was pointed out by the then Government and was ultimately accepted by D.E. Society in 1898. Excepting this modification the Constitution of the D.E. Society as framed by the founders continued to function well for over 100 years.

It may be said that the founders of the New English School were influenced by a two-tier management system that prevailed in England for more than two centuries. They had the House of Lords and House of Commons. The administrators came from the House of Commons while the House of Lords had a control over the working of the Govt. Similarly the Board of Life-Members was similar to House of Commons as all the Heads of Institutions were Life-Members. The Managing Council was similar to House of Lords as they had control over the working of the Board of Life-Members. Later on the concept of General Body was also introduced. The General Body had no powers whatsoever but could express their opinion on the Balance Sheet and Income and Expenditure Statement of the Society. In addition they had the power to elect non-life-members to the General Body of the Society.

Life-Membership was a new concept introduced in the constitution of the D.E. Society. Life-Membership stood for service, sacrifice and integrity. Eventually Life-Members became centres of power in the Society. Life-Members were selected by Life-Members and they continued to be Life-Members till they retired. They had the initiative in every matter concerned with the Society and its institutions. This concept attracted the attention of all the prominent educational institutions in Pune and eventually the Shikshan Prasarak Mandali, Maharashtra Education Society, Progressive Education Society, Modern Education Society adopted the institution of Life-Members. Rayat Shikshan Sanstha, Satara and Vivekanand Shikshan Sanstha, Kolhapur which have schools and colleges all over Western Maharashtra introduced this system in their constitutions.

The system has been adopted by many more Societies all over the country. However, like the degradation of political and social systems in the country, the institution of Life-Members also deteriorated. There evolved groupis and nepotism. Life-Members started taking undue advantages and less work. That led to laziness among them. On the one hand life-members became a matter of envy while on the other hand a matter of ridicule. Concentration of power and initiative among the Life-Members was not liked by many non-life-members. Thinkers like Prof. A.B. Shah and Prof. G.P. Pradhan opposed the system on matters of principle saying that selecting Head-Masters or Principals only from among the Life-Members was undemocratic and it was perpetuating power in the hands of a chosen few who may not be men of efficiency and character.

By 1980 some political parties took interest in the affairs of educational institutions in Pune and Maharashtra and amended constitutions of some educational societies in such a way that the Governing Councils were now prominent in the affairs of Societies though the institution of Life-Members remained alive on paper. No doubt Life-Members are the only link between Schools and Colleges and the Management that conducts these institutions. No initiative is now left with Life-Members. However, it must be admitted that the Institution of Life-Members was a prominent administrative system in educational institutions for over a century.

The Fergusson College

When Lokmanya Tilak passed his LLB examination, he had decided to launch educational activity in Pune. He wanted to start a College but could muster enough friends to start a school only when the school started. Because of their social-political activities both Agarkar and Tilak got popularity among the people, got new acquaintances and got donations from princely states. The atmosphere was ripe to start a College. A band of workers like Tilak, Agarkar, Apte, Gole, Kelkar and Dharap were already available for the school. Student strength also grew. Matriculation results of the School were also good. The Deccan Education Society was formed in 1884 and Life-Members were available to it as devoted workers. The time was ripe to open a college.

Teachers who had joined the New English School were efficient teachers in their own subjects; Tilak taught Mathematics and Sanskrit, Agarkar History and Economics, Chiplunkar English and Sanskrit, Apte English and Gole Physics. They were eligible to teach in Colleges also as per the prevailing rules. This impressed the teachers in Mumbai University who included Prin. Wordsworth, Oxenham, Dr. McKikan and Dr. Bhandarkar, Ranade and Telang. They were in favour of allowing the D.E. Society to open a College in Pune.

Shri. Vaman Shivram Apte represented the New English School before the Hunter Commission. He stressed the need of (i) Expanding facilities of Education, (ii) Education to be made cheaper, (iii) Improving quality of education imparted in Govt. Institutions, (iv) Independence to private institutions, (v) Freedom to institutions taking grant-in-aid, (vi) Improving education in Indian Languages, (vii) Developing Indian models of education, (viii) Developing Text-Books in India, (ix) Delegating the management of higher education to Indians. The Commission was quite impressed with this deposition. Tilak and his colleagues thought Education, if controlled and imparted by Indians would produce men of quality who would also improve the social and political life of the country. Ultimately that would lead to freedom of the country. They believed that Education was the only force that could bring about material, moral and religious regeneration of fallen countries and could raise them to the level of most advanced nations by slow and peaceful revolutions.

On 24 October, 1884 a meeting of prominent citizens of Pune was held in which the Deccan Education Society was formed. Shri. Apte suggested that opening of a College could be undertaken only when sufficient donations were received from the people. Money thus collected must be vested in the hands of those who were known to be socially and morally of a high standard. In this meeting Tilak proposed a Committee to be formed for that purpose consisting of Mandlik, Telang, Wordsworth, Waderburn, V. M. Kelkar and others. Dr. Bhandarkar in his resolution praised the work of Tilak and six other colleagues.

In December, 1884 the Syndicate of the Mumbai University recommended to the Senate that the D. E. Society be allowed to start a College in Pune and if the College worked well for a period of three years the University should grant it affiliation. Fergusson College was opened on 2 January, 1885 in Gadrewada near Holkarwada. The D. E. Society had requested the Govt. to allow it to use Shaniwarwada, but the Govt. declined. For some time it was decided to house the College in Budhwarwada. On that occasion Sir James Fergusson made a speech and praised Tilak and his colleagues for their efforts. However, this function proved to be futile as the foundation stone had to be shifted from Budhwarwada to the present site owned by Shirole. From 1892 the College became full-fledged as it was allowed to conduct final year B.A. class. For some time Govt. was inclined to hand-over the Deccan College to D. E. Society but these negotiations fizzled out.

Opening of the Fergusson College was no doubt a triumph for Tilak and his colleagues. The reputation of the College spread all over the country in later years. Many eminent personalities have recorded their appreciation of the work done by Tilak and others. Lala Lajpat Rai, Shriniwas Shastri and Pandit Madan Mohan Malviya have been some of them.

Tilak's Resignation of Life-Membership of D.E. Society

The Fergusson College was started in 1885. While the School and the College were making rapid progress, the internal differences among life-members began to increase. Life-members on whose hearty team-work depended the continued success and progress of the Society's institutions were divided in two opposite camps around Tilak and Agarkar. The difference that now divided them arose partly from differing views about the management of institutions and irreconcilable outlooks upon the social and political questions of the day, and partly from incompatibility of temperament, together working to produce extreme bitterness of feeling. Tilak resigned his Life-membership in October 1890. It was a fateful decision. He cut himself off from the proud handiwork of his own and his comrades' youthful idealism and set out on the rough sea of public life. It was in the circumstances a wise decision, too, because the gulf between others and himself was too wide. It was no use wasting the energies of all in endless friction and opposition. It was the question of child-marriage that first brought the elements of discord to the surface. Not only on the question of child-marriage and enforced widowhood but on others too relating to social reform. Agarkar was a radical, advocating drastic action on the part of the individuals and the Government to root out the cankerous diseases of Hindu Society.

In the view of his colleagues, education and the consciousness of social evils it was bound to produce were the most potent instruments of social reform. They were opposed to State-action to accelerate the pace of social reform too much in advance of public opinion. Tilak's opposition to social reform legislation was particularly outspoken and continuous and this circumstance must have tended to produce estrangement between these two persons. This line of cleavage was intensified by other differences regarding the management of the school and the college. In these matters Apte, and later on, Gokhale were one with Agarkar, while Namjoshi and Dharap sided with Tilak. Whatever the grouping of other individuals, Tilak and Agarkar were always to be found on opposite sides on all important issues, and an impassable barrier of thought and feeling gradually raised itself between them.

As regards pay and earnings to Life-Members, Tilak's contention was that the principle of self-sacrifice demanded that the life-members should content themselves with the pay and family provision secured by the Society, and that extra earning should go to the Society. In case of necessity, gratuities might be given to individual life-members, but no regular outside work ought to be undertaken with a view to supplementing the ordinary salary. It were best to put a stop to outside work altogether, because it created divergent interests and imported inconvenient questions into the working of the Society. If outside work was to be allowed, however, it was necessary to rule that profits thereof shall go to the common fund of the Society.

Such a rule would secure that outside work shall be undertaken out of disinterested motives purely as a labour of love. Agarkar's views on these matters stood in sharp contrast to Tilak's. He says, "I seriously differ from him on the question of private work. He suggests that no life-member should be allowed to undertake any extensive private work without the consent of the Board. He thinks that such a restriction is necessary in the interests of the Body. Now I am not quite sure that the interests of the Body would be promoted by such a restriction. In proposing the restriction he is solely influenced by the desire that every life-member should expend the whole of his energy on the work of the institutions and that nothing should distract his mind from it. This is extremely desirable; but the restriction proposed will launch us into almost inseperable difficulties... Further, the strict rules about pay and gratuities may induce some to secretly set aside this restriction to make up their pressing wants, and some may do it for the sake of helping their friends with interested motives or without them.

Thus the Board will soon have to convert itself into a most frightful Court of Inquisition producing disgust about it in the mind of every life-member, and thus this restriction will ultimately defeat its own end .... No Body can imitate the discipline of the order of Jesuits without making important modifications in it. No Jesuit is a married man; no Jesuit has private property, nor is he allowed to make any; the Jesuits have a common mess and they lodge in a common house." Life-members were pretty equally divided on the question at issue. It must be clearly borne in mind that the outside work that Agarkar and those of his thinking had in mind was of the literary, journalistic, political or public character. They were not pleading for liberty to engage without let or hindrance in any sort of money-making activities or business, but only in such categories of activities as are indicated above. Traditions have always been held to preclude life-members from the pursuit of business as ordinarily understood. Even private tuition for gain is considered as tabooed to life-members, and regular paid service is ruled out by the pledge of life-membership itself.

It must be remembered that three of the most conscientious and devoted men in the Society—Agarkar, Apte and Gokhale—were ranged against Tilak in the fight over principles. It is not to be imagined for a moment that they wanted to dilute the principle of self-sacrifice, or lower the standard of devotion to Society. Their own sacrifice left no room for any such misgiving. The Secretaryship of the Sarvajanik Sabha was an honorary unpaid post, and the only gain that Gokhale could have looked for in accepting it was the opportunity of serving a period of political apprenticeship under the guidance of Ranade.

For conscientious and unflagging work in the interest of Society's institutions, a greater figure than Apte could not have been found among life-members. If such men differed from Tilak it must have been from disinterested motives, and for worthy objects. They must have considered the vow of Jesuitical poverty impracticable for married men belonging to Hindu Society, with their undefined family obligations to relatives far and near, and in claiming for life-members the freedom to supplement their salaries by extra earnings they were facing the facts of the situation in a spirit of realism.

It would have been intolerable to have to place one's domestic difficulties before others and appeal to them for monetary help. A regular system of gratuities would have been most difficult to work equitably. It would have been a source of personal misunderstandings and heart-burnings. It was best to allow a fixed salary and leave to each life-member the freedom to supplement it if he liked and if he could. The Society's work must always be understood to have the supreme claim on the time and energy of everyone; but after that was satisfied, according to such energy of everyone, according to such a standard as his colleagues might apply, there was wisdom in leaving a life-member free to engage in outside work according to his lights.

To cut him off from outside work was not the most effective way of making a life-member devote himself absorbingly to the Society's interests. Devotion to academic and administrative work in connection with the Society must come from the urge of his own heart and conscience, and the compelling force of tradition and example. In opposing Tilak on the ground of principle, therefore, Agarkar and Gokhale were striving for the establishment of what was practicable and attainable. The principles they proposed for the working of the Society have stood the test of time, and that their faith in them was deep and disinterested was proved by the events of 1898. The spirit of self-sacrifice did not dry up after Tilak's leaving the Body; it flowed steady and strong and asserted itself again and again in defence of the cherished principles.

TILAK'S VIEWS ON WOMEN'S EDUCATION

As we enter the new century, it is an appropriate time to look back and take a review of the historical changes that this country has brought in the field of education and especially women's education. Women's education cannot be thought of without its relationship with the other social aspects of women's life such as child marriage, widow remarriage, women's position in the society. In Tilak's time his contemporaries like Gopal Ganesh Agarkar, Mahatma Phule, Vitthal Ramji Shinde, Maharshi Dhondo Keshav Karve, held a different view. It will be interesting to study the reasons for such a different view.

Tilak has written editorials in his newspapers Kesari and Mahratta. Firstly he objected to the curriculum of the girls school because it was just like that of British schools. The cultural and social background of Indian girls is totally different from that of British girls, and so should be the curricula. Secondly he objected the full day school timing *i.e.* six hours a day for the girls. If necessary they should attend the half-day school, after finishing their duties in the house which according to him was their first moral obligation. His third objection for women's education was that the education given to them would help them become clerks in the British offices. If they start working in these offices they will neglect their first duty which is household work. This is most disgusting and hence should be abandoned. His fourth objection was against hasty reforms. Educating few women would not help the society, but educating the common masses would only help. Spending money hastily on women's education would be a waste if very few women get education.

All these views of Tilak about women's education came as a reaction to the extreme views of the reformists of his time.

TILAK THE PIONEER OF NATIONAL EDUCATION

Lokmanya Bal Gangadhar Tilak was one of the architects of our freedom. He taught people that Swarajya was their birth-right. His teachings had a great impact on the minds of the people because he practised what he preached. Like many of our political leaders Tilak started his public life as a teacher because he regarded education as a powerful instrument of moulding the impressionable minds of students and of bringing about a change in our society's outlook on life.

An Idealist

It is necessary to study how Tilak's mind was moulded and how and why later on he took this decision to become a teacher. During his childhood his father Gangadhar Shastri, made him recite Sanskrit and Marathi verses, which sharpened his memory. During his school days, he developed a special liking for Mathematics. His sharp intellect prompted him to study the basic principles of different subjects, instead of just preparing for examinations. After passing the Matriculation examination, Bal Gangadhar Tilak joined Deccan Collage in Pune. As he was staying in the college-hostel, he could take the advantage of the college library and read books by eminent writers and thinkers on different subjects. He was also greatly influenced by the teaching of Prof. Chhatre, who inspired him to study the fundamentals of Mathematics. He offered Mathematics as his principal subject for the B.A. examination. Tilak formed a close friendship with his classmate Gopal Ganesh Agarkar who was a student of philosophy.

Tilak and Agarkar were idealist youths who were restless owing to the degenerate condition of their country. They were greatly impressed by the efforts made by Justice Mahadev Govind Ranade for enlightening the society through institutions like Vasant Vyakhyana Mala, and Sarvajanik Sabha. Tilak and Agarkar were also impressed by the writings of a young, powerful writer, Vishnu Shastri Chiplunkar, who appealed to people to develop a sense of self-respect, instead of imitating the British rulers. Tilak and Agarkar had heated discussions about the future course of action in life. Unlike most of their contemporaries, these two young idealists decided not to join Government service and instead work for the uplift of their country. Tilak argued that it was necessary to start political work first, while Agarkar argued that they should first strive to bring about reforms in society, and then start political work. After long and heated discussions, these two young idealists took the decision to work on the common platform of education.

Both of them realized that it was necessary to educate the people in general and the youths in particular before working for either social reforms or the political movement. After taking this bold decision, Tilak and Agarkar along with Vishnu Shastri Chiplunkar decided to start a High School. Shri. Vaman Shivram Apte, an eminent Sanskrit Scholar, and V.B.Namjoshi-a young idealist who was also a realist, also joined the trio. Starting of the New English School was an event which shook the student world of Pune, and as the young teachers proved their ability, the response both of the students and their guardians became more and more enthusiastic.

The trio, Chiplunkar, Agarkar and Tilak were not content with just their work as teachers. They were searching fresh fields and new pastures. They decided to undertake the work of educating the people and launched two news-papers-'Kesari' in Marathi and 'Mahratta' in English in January 1881. The editorials in Kesari were written in a direct and simple style and the editor never lost sight of the main purpose of educating public opinion. The profession of journalism has its trials. Tilak and Agarkar as editors championed the cause of the ruler of Kolhapur. They however wrote something which was challenged in the court and as the young editors could not produce evidence supporting their statements, they were sentenced to three months' imprisonment.

Tilak and Agarkar boldly accepted the punishment and their prestige as editors rose, in society, During this period of imprisonment, Tilak and Agarkar picked up the thread of their discussions in college and realized that the gap between their views was widening. Tilak made a fervent plea for political activity while Agarkar was equally emphatic about the need for social reforms. After their release from prison, Tilak and Agarkar once again devoted themselves to educational work, while carrying out their responsibility as editors. The next step in the field of education was the founding of the Deccan Education Society in 1884. This gave an institutional base to the educational effort, the next step of which was the starting of Fergusson College in January, 1885. The statement made on the occasion of the establishment of the Deccan Education Society, throws light on the ideological position of Tilak, Agarkar, Apte and their colleagues. It reads as follows:

> *"We have undertaken this work of popular education, with the firmest conviction and belief that of all agents of human civilization, Education is the only one that brings about material, moral and religious regeneration of fallen countries, and raises them up to the level of the most advanced nations by slow and peaceful revolutions."*

Prin. Apte gave evidence before the Education Commission presided over by William Wilson Hunter on 9th September 1882. His views were representative of the point of view of his colleagues in the Deccan Education Society. There was a strong plea for an indigenous agency for educational effort.

It was also stated that greater opportunities for collegiate and university education should be given to the students coming from those sections of society which had a tradition of learning. The ground for this demand was that through this enlightened class education would percolate to other strata of society. This view was in sharp contrast with the view expressed by Jyotirao Phule, the great social reformer, that it was the primary responsibility of the Government to give education for seven years to students from all sections of society. He argued that the more intelligent students would then take advantage of the facilities for higher education. Phule made a fervent plea for equal opportunities for learning to all and said that the level of enlightenment of the entire society must be raised and education should not become the monopoly of the chosen few. Phule showed a progressive vision but his plea was not accepted by the Government.

It was evident that Apte and Tilak, who came from families with a tradition of learning, did not understand the aspirations of the masses and putforth the elitist point of view which perpetuated social inequality and gave special advantages to the so-called higher communities.

Due to differences among the Life-Members of DE Society Tilak resigned from the Deccan Education Society and Fergusson College, but he continued his vocation as a teacher. He started conducting Law Classes for the High Court Pleader's examination. Tilak had passed the LL.B. exam. with merit and owing to his analytical mind, he developed a rare insight in different branches of Law and particularly in Hindu Law. He elucidated the different topics in such a manner that the students, besides getting the necessary guidance for the examination, were stimulated to think in a novel and original manner.

Editor as Educator

After the parting of ways in the Deccan Education Society, Tilak took over the 'Kesari' and the 'Mahratta'. Tilak regarded the work of an Editor as a sacred vocation where it was his responsibility to educate the people and enlighten them. He felt that his sphere of activity as a teacher had widened. Tilak never lost sight of the principle that a Teacher has to remain a student for life time and that a person gets the moral right to educate others only when he has studied the subject which he is teaching or on which he is writing. He read extensively and carefully and only when he was convinced that he had fully grasped all the implications of the topic which he wanted to elucidate, that he expressed his point of view through the editorial. He first gave the information about the concerned subject, then analysed it and out of such delineation of facts, emerged his editorial comment.

It was no wonder, therefore, that the readers, on most occasions, were persuaded to accept his point of view. Tilak, who was a keen student of mathematics, was always logical in his argument and was very disciplined in his exposition of ideas. Tilak did not like stylistic flourishes and always avoided rhetoric. His style of writing was simple and direct. He explained the subject but avoided superfluous expression. His style of writing was compressed and had a masculine dignity.

He mainly appealed to the intellect of his readers rather than striving to arouse their emotions. In 1886, there was a famine in Maharashtra. Tilak first carefully studied The Famine Relief Code, published by the Government after the famine in 1872. He immediately understood the significance and the implications of the Government's Resolution. In the Famine Relief code, the Government had committed itself to certain relief measures such as distributing food grains at a cheap rate, a concession in land-revenue etc. Tilak first published in Kesari, the summary of the Famine Relief Code in Marathi. He then explained to the readers that it was the moral responsibility of the Government to implement their own decision and it was the moral right of the people to demand the relief measures, incorporated by the Government in their own Famine Relief Code. Tilak then printed a small booklet which contained the important provision of the code and, with the help of the volunteers, of the Sarvajanik Sabha, distributed the copies of the booklet in the famine affected parts of Bombay Presidency.

In the then Colaba district, when the Government prosecuted the volunteers, Tilak rushed to the Tehsil town Pen and in a hugely attended meeting of peasants, condemned the prosecution. He challenged the Government to prosecute him, because he had printed the booklet which contained a part of the G. R.-The Famine Relief Code-and that as the Secretary of the Sarvajanik Sabha, he had asked the volunteers to distribute it. The collector of Colaba district was present and he then withdrew the prosecution. Tilak thus repudiated the saying that 'he who can does, he who cannot, teaches'. Tilak taught the people to become conscious of their rights; he also acted boldly and challenged the Government. He succeeded because his action was based on the knowledge of the contents and also the implications of the Famine Relief Code.

When Tilak was teaching in the New English School and later on in Pune, his students were not adults and the classrooms were enclosed with walls. When Tilak started his work as Editor and social-worker, he had undertaken the job of educating adult people. This was a public-school for grown up persons and this school had no walls. Through his writings he reached a wide section of society. Although Tilak did not appoint any deputies, many enthusiastic young people in different towns and villages in Maharashtra read out before a group of adult audience the Kesari and particularly the editorials of Tilak. Thus communication was established between Tilak and the people. The editor became educator.

EDUCATION-AN INSTRUMENT OF NATIONAL AWAKENING

It is argued by some people that politics and education go ill together. This observation can be valid only if politics is regard as a game for grabbing power and money. If on the other hand, politics means an effort of the people to fight against injustice and to end tyranny, education forms a major part of political action. Tilak as the leader of the movement launched against the partition of Bengal by Lord Curzon, made national education a major part of the four point progamme which developed in to a nationwide movement. Tilak always regarded education as a powerful instrument of social transformation and used it as a weapon not only in the movement against Bengal Partition but in the struggle for Swaraj. I think it is necessary to describe in some details the political situation in which national education emerged as an important programme.

In 1905 Lord Curzon, the Viceroy of India, announced his decision of the 'partition' of the province of Bengal. The autocratic decision was an attack on the growing spirit of nationalism and the sense of solidarity among the people of Bengal. The sinister motives of Lord Curzon had become clear from his speeches in East Bengal wherein he made an effort to create enmity between the Hindus and the Muslims in pursuance of the imperialist policy of "Divide and Rule". However, Curzon's attempt to divide Bengal, made Bengal united. All sections in Bengal, rich and poor, landlords and tenants, young and old, moderates and extremists saw in the partition an insult to their honour and a threat to their solidarity. The Partition of Bengal and people's protest against it might have become only a local affair confined only to the people of Bengal. But the trio of India's political leaders-Lala Lajpat Rai, Bal Gangadhar Tilak and Bipin Chandra Pal-Lal, Bal and Pal-showed great political foresight and lifted the struggle of the people of Bengal to the national plane. These three leaders converted Curzon's onslaught into an opportunity for creating national solidarity. Protests against Bengal's partition were held all over India and the people of India demonstrated their solidarity against the tyranny of the British Empire. It is, however necessary to know the difference in the attitude of the leaders who represented three different trends of thought, three different currents in Indian politics, not merely at that juncture but through out India's freedom struggle. The first trend was that of moderate leaders like Gopal Krishna Gokhale and Pherozshah Mehta, who followed only constitutional methods. These liberal leaders rendered yeoman's service to the nation during the first phase by laying the foundation of our future political movement. But theirs was the politics of the elite, only of eminent personalities with a rare ability to represent the cause of India before the British Parliament.

At the other end, there were the revolutionaries, who believed that freedom could be won only through armed struggle. Some of them had become martyrs and their supreme sacrifice had kindled the flame of patriotism in the hearts of many Indian youths. However only extraordinarily brave persons who were prepared to lay down their lives at the altar of liberty could follow this path. The moderates and the revolutionaries were poles apart from each other in their methods, However, the common people could not follow either of these groups. There was the third group of leaders-the trio of Tilak, Lala Lajpat Rai, and Bipin Chandra Pal, who had realized that it was necessary to bring the common people of India in the freedom struggle.

They therefore placed before the nation a constructive and combative programme which would develop into a mass movement. When Bengal was partitioned, moderate leaders like Gokhale expressed their protest only through circulars, memoranda, and speeches. Aurobindo Ghosh wanted to follow the path of armed revolution. But Tilak and his colleagues, Lajpat Rai and Pal, put forth the four point programme of Swadeshi, Boycott, National Education and Swaraj. This programme enabled these leaders to involve thousands of people in this apparently modest political action. Tilak firmly believed that such a constructive and combative programme alone would arouse the uncommon strength of the common man. It must be noted that national education formed an important part of the nation-wide agitation. Tilak expressed his views on National Education, through the editorials in Kesari and through many of his speeches. Tilak never did anything in a half-hearted manner. In the editorial on the programme of boycott of foreign goods Tilak described Boycott as "Yoga". He also regarded "National Education" as "Yoga" which implied highest level of concentration, resulting in rare skills- "योग: कर्मसु कौशलम्". He expected teachers to work with a missionary zeal. In one of his speeches Tilak said that he wanted "Graduate Ramdasis" (The followers of Saint Ramdas who aroused the sense of self-respect and patriotism in people) to carry on the movement for Swaraj. Tilak expected that teachers must have love for knowledge, love for students and the ability to develop the personalities of youth is by inculcating in them the spirit of patriotism. He expected the guardians to co-operate with this effort of moulding and sharpening the new generation by making their wards accept the discipline of the novel experiment in the field of education.

Tilak expected the students to instil in themselves the virtues of courage, truthfulness, sacrifice and above all an attitude of self-reliance. He expected educationists like Prof. Vijapurkar to make bold experiments and evolve the pattern of National Education. Tilak, in one of his speeches said that learning and character must be blended so that instead of producing clerks required for the administration of British rule, National Education would train students in such a manner that in future life they would build India as a Nation.

Tilak wrote a number of editorials in Kesari on the subject of National Education and elucidated his ideas. Tilak made a fervent plea for making Marathi the medium of instruction in Maharashtra. He observed that education imparted through the mother-tongue stimulated the thought process of students.

On the other hand, while learning through English, the students faltered because they were not familiar with that language and found it difficult to express whatever they know. As a result, many students were obsessed with the notion of fluency in English and their thinking process was dwarfed. In one of his editorials Tilak wrote, "If I had learnt through Marathi, the knowledge that I have accumulated at the age of fifty-two, would have easily been gained by me at the age of thirty."

In one of the editorials he developed the idea that knowledge was power, while in one of his speeches he developed the idea 'सा विद्या या विमुक्तये'. That is knowledge which liberates the mind. Tilak said that because of the rule of the British many educated people had developed a sense of inferiority. If the right type of education *i.e.* national education was imparted to students, they would be mentally liberated and would boldly think in an independent manner. Tilak while elucidating his concept of National Education, always emphasised the need for removing the bifurcation of the life of the people and the education imparted to them. He said, "education must make people fearless, truthful and enable them to earn their livelihood with self-respect; but the purpose of the British rulers was to create a class which would help them carry on their administration by acting as a link between the rulers and the ruled.

They expected from this class not just obedience but a servility of what was taught in schools and colleges was a means of conditioning the mind of students for promoting in them a slavish outlook. The purpose of national education is just the opposite. We want a new generation of youths who would respect our nation. our religion and language."

Communicating the Message of Bhagwad-Gita

At Mandalay, Tilak used his imprisonment for the pursuit of knowledge in right earnest. He learnt two foreign languages, *viz.* French and German, in order to read the works of philosophers like Comte in the original French language. One is amazed at the long list of books read by Tilak during his incarceration in the Mandalay prison. Tilak once again felt that he would be able to play the role of a teacher of the people only if he would explain to them the message of the 'Bhagwad Gita'. To Tilak, the Gita was a perennial source of inspiration. While passing through the trials and ordeals of his life, it intensified his faith. 'Gita-Rahasya' was the quintessence of this life's message.

Tilak had not just read about Karma-Yoga in Bhagwad-Gita, he had lived as a Karma Yogi through out his life. He felt that the message of Bhagwad-Gita would inspire the people to lead a life of action in order to realize their dream of swarajya. Tilak, who because of his sacrifice and suffering, had become Lokmanya was confident that if he would communicate to them the message of the Bhagwad-Gita, they would try to follow it and strive for Swaraj. Tilak was conscious of the fact that his efforts would not bear fruit in his life-time; but the ideal of 'निष्काम कर्मयोग' "action without any expectation" as stated in Bhagwad Gita enabled him to carry on his effort vigorously, throughout his life. Lokmanya Tilak wrote 'Gita Rahasya' and in doing this he was carrying on the tradition sages-Rishis-in ancient India, whose teachings transcended the limitations of time and distance. Through 'Gita Rahasya', Tilak emerged as a teacher of teachers, and also as a guide and philosopher to many of his countrymen.

After his release from Mandalay jail in 1914, Lokmanya Tilak, who was the accredited leader of the whole India, directed his energies to the task of consolidating the political forces. His efforts were successful in the Lucknow Session of the Indian National Congress held in 1916. The last five years of his life were full of hectic political activities and he hardly had any time to give impetus to the effort of national education. He taught people the lesson that Swarajya was their birth-right and that they should strive to get it. In his speeches on the political ideal of Swarajya, he time and again referred to education as a powerful means of instilling the spirit of patriotism in youth. On 17th April 1917, Lokmanya Tilak delivered a speech at Chikodi, near Belgaum and the subject of his speech was 'My ideal of Education'. In that speech he made a fervent plea for free and compulsory primary education. He told the people that through national education, they would become conscious of their right to get Swarajya and would also realize that it was their responsibility to strive for it.

Tilak made a fervent plea for the spread of education. However, owing to his traditional mental make-up, he did not advocate the cause of women's education. He was brought up in the society dominated by men and he, therefore, felt that the primary duty of women was to look after the family and bring up children. When a female High School was started in Pune, Tilak wrote against it. He was of the opinion that if at all education is to be given to girls in schools, it must be such as would make them good mothers and efficient house-wives. His views were diametrically opposite to those of Prin. Gopal Ganesh Agarkar who wrote in his journal 'Sudharak' that there should be co-education and that education imparted to girls should not be different from the education given to boys. When there was a growing demand for women's education, Tilak said that time was not ripe for such a reform. He did not want to oppose the prevalent conservatism in Hindu society so far as women's education was concerned.

When Prof. Dhondo Keshav Karve started a residential school where widows were given admission, Tilak did not write anything in support of that effort. In 1916, owing to the efforts of Prof. Karve, the first women's University was started in Pune, Tilak did not welcome that event, which had a great social significance.

When Lokmanya Tilak went to England in 1917, with the help of Barrister Baptista, he brought out an excellent pamphlet 'Self Determination' which made a fervent plea for Home Rule in India. Tilak sent copies of this pamphlet to all the editors of newspapers in England and also to the members of British Parliament. When one of his followers asked him about this, Tilak said, "We have to educate the British people about the conditions in India and I am confident that owing to our pamphlet on self-determination, I would ensure the support of the Labour Party to our cause."

A Pioneer of National Education

Tilak had sown the seeds of the ideal of national education. After Tilak's demise when Gandhiji emerged as the leader of the freedom struggle, he gave great emphasis on national education. After the non-co-operation movement of 1920, Gandhiji asked many of his followers to dedicate themselves to the work of national education. The Gujrat Vidyapeeth at Ahmedabad, The Tilak Maharashtra Vidyapeeth in Pune and many Rashtriya Shalas were started in different parts of the India. In Tilak Maharashtra Vidyapeeth at Pune, teachers like Acharya Bhagwat, Acharya Jawadekar and others, while delivering inspiring lectures on politics, history and literature, inculcated in students a national outlook. Almost all these students participated in the Satyagraha movement in 1930. Thus the seed sown by Tilak had grown into a huge banyan tree. Tilak titled as 'Lokmanya' by the people of India, is regarded by all as one of the main architects of our freedom struggle. However, it is equally necessary for us to understand the significance of his efforts for giving a new orientation to education and developing it as an instrument of guarding our freedom.

ELPHINSTONE'S EDUCATIONAL POLICY

Elphinstone was the Resident in the court of Peshwas from 1811 to 1818. In 1819 he was appointed the Governor of Bombay, and retired from the same post in 1827. He had keen interest in the education of the natives. He was of the opinion that teaching and learning in the mother tongue saved time and toil, and so if the mother-tongue was used as the medium of instruction, education could reach the power centres at different levels. He firmly believed that the vicious customs in this country would be uprooted only through education. He also maintained that the education of the poor and the funds required for it was the Government's responsibility.

In the licence issued in 1813, though the general objectives of Indian education were mentioned, the details had yet to be worked out. Elphinstone recommended new western education through regional languages-Marathi or Gujrathi.

In 1815 the "Bombay Education Society" was established for the education of the English and the Anglo-Indian children. In August 1820, a meeting of the Society was held under the chairmanship of Elphinstone. Jagannath Shankarseth, Jamshethji Jijibhai, Framji Kawasji, Mohammed Ibrahim Makwa and some respectable businessmen of Bombay were present at this meeting. Resolutions were passed regarding writing of text-books in English, Marathi and Gujrathi, giving grants to the native schools working at that time, and establishment of new schools. Another very important resolution was passed by which the medium of instruction in those schools would be regional languages.

For the execution of this new policy 'The Native School and School Book Committee' was constituted. But the scope of this committee was more extensive than the original policy of the society, so the Bombay Education Society restricted its own activities to European and Anglo-Indian students. As the Bombay Education Society thus changed its policy, in 1822 a new society called 'The Bombay Native School Book and School Society' was formed.

This Society started new type of schools in native languages on the Island of Bombay. In 1824, an English school was also opened. Many parents hesitated to send their children to English medium schools for the fear of conversion.

"In order to remove their misconceptions and make modern education acceptable to them, along with Capt. Jervis, Kashinath alias Bapu Chhatre was appointed Native Secretary on Rs. 100/-per month". In 1830 Balshastri Jambhekar was appointed as Deputy Native Secretary, and in 1832, he who was in his twenties (born in 1812) was promoted to the post of Deputy Secretary. This was really a great honour to the achievement of a native scholar.

The secretary of the 'Bombay Native—' used to be a government servant and the members used to be private citizens. This institution used to get a government grant to the tune of Pounds 5000 per annum. They also collected donations from private sources. From that fund they used to run schools in Bombay and else where. There were thirteen Europeans and eleven Indians on the Managing Committee. The European persons were names like Candy, Jervis etc. Elphinstone was the first chairman followed by Malcom.

The job of spreading education in the Bombay Province was entrusted to this society. Elphinstone has many times expressed his views on education for the natives. While recommending the Institutions for financial aid, he made the following suggestions.

"(i)to improve the mode of teaching at the native schools and to increase the member of schools, (ii) to supply them with books, (iii) to hold out some encouragement to the lower orders of natives to avail themselves of the means of instructions thus offered to them, (iv) to establish schools for teaching the European Sciences and improvements in the higher branches of Education, (v) to provide for the preparation and publication of books and moral and physical science in native languages, (vi) to establish schools for the purpose of teaching

English to those disposed to pursue it as a classical language and as a means of acquiring knowledge of the European discoveries, and (vii) to hold forth encouragement to the natives in the pursuit of those lost branches of knowledge".

If the medium of instruction was to be a vernacular, it was necessary to write books in that language. Elphinstone appointed a committee for this purpose. That committee produced some really good text books.

During the years 1818 to 1827 three books were published in Marathi and all the three books were translations of English books on mathematics. During the period 1827 to 1838, ten books were published-two on medical science, two of Jambhekar's on Mathematics and Geometry, two Readers by Major Candy, Dadoba Pandurang's Grammar, and Hari Keshavji Pathare's book on Physics. From 1837 to 1847, thirty books were published, and from 1847-1857 the number rose to hundred and two. During the course of eight years from 1857 to 1864, five hundred and fifty books were published.

Till the year 1850, a Marathi dictionary with grants from the Government, Moulsworth's Marathi-English dictionary, Major Candy's dictionary, Shrikrishna Shastri's concise dictionary were published. A dictionary and Grammar were new to Marathi and was encouraging for the language.

Among the books written during this period, text-books written for schools had a large share. But it was a welcome trend that books in Astronomy, Geography, Physics, Chemistry, Mechanics etc., albeit through translations, were brought in to Marathi. On the whole the number of books translated from Sanskrit and English was very large. But as time passed the number of original works increased. In the beginning the authors were mostly from Bombay and so their diction had an influence of Konkani, but later, authors who had studied in grammar schools in Pune, had their prose style influenced by Sanskrit.

Bombay was a business centre, bustling with followers of different religions. It had been under the British rule since 1665, So the Bombayites were conversant with the English culture. No wonder their mode of thinking was influenced by it. Puneites hated the English whom they considered responsible for the loss of their Kingdom.

"Robertson was appointed the Collector of Pune. One day his Secretary received an application saying, "Let us know in your reply when the British rule will come to an end". However the applicant had concealed his identity. The collector said, "Write at the bottom of the application that our Kingdom will fall only when either we get divided, or the natives get united. Not till then". Writing their remarks on the application, he gave orders to stick it like a decree near the gate of Tulsibag if the applicant did not come forth; accordingly, it was stuck there". The city of Pune was orthodox and conservative. "A man by name Gangadhar Dikshit Phadke was a teacher in Bombay from 1820 to 1825, where he taught the English people. When he later came to Pune, he was ostracized because the Puneites thought that he could not have escaped eating or doing things not permitted in the Hindu community. In the end he had to leave Pune and lead a life of renunciation".

At the same time there was a large number of Brahmins who had once enjoyed power, but now had no patronage. "A few days back, the Brahmins were most honoured, they were the religious and political leaders. But all of a sudden they lost their prosperity and progress. Their `mantra' became powerless and they themselves helpless".

The sting of fall was still fresh in their minds. "This class of Brahmins was not only strong in numbers, but had in them the seeds of systematic governance, a good social order and ancient culture. It was on the strength of these qualities the Hindu Society stayed stable and integrated for centuries. In this class of Brahmins there was no dearth of scholars, soldiers, learned people or civilized householders. Who else was required for administration?"

Elphinstone knew that the British rulers could not afford to keep this class discontented or neglected. It was absolutely necessary to pacify their anger and win their sympathy, if the British rule was to stabilize. That was why, Elphinstone who advocated modern education through regional languages, opened a college for Sanskrit studies in Pune, on the auspicious day of Dasshera.

Shastris and Vedics were appointed as teachers in this College. Subjects like the Vedas, Grammar, medicine, figures of speech, were taught there. "At Diwali time, besides a good bath in the early morning, students were served special Diwali sweets like Ladu, Karanjya, Anarase and so on. It was all Peshwa style in that College. The British Principal was not allowed to enter the College building. It is said that on one occasion when he did, `Udakshanti' was performed". The Managing Committee was opposed to spending money on this Sanskrit College. But Elphinstone convinced them that the expenditure was permissible because the money was spent from the amount which had already been sanctioned for Shravanmas charity. The establishment of the Sanskrit College was a part of Elphinstone's policy of the appeasement of the people and the Brahmins. It was mainly for the sake of stability for the English rule.

Later on, the nature of this Pathashala underwent a lot of change. English classes were incorporated, and ultimately it got transformed, first as the Poona College, and later as the Deccan College.

Lokmanya Tilak says, "The task of destroying self rule and establishing foreign rule is an extremely difficult task because the natives keep smarting under the insult. In such circumstances the ruler needs great tact", and Elphinstone did possess it.

The fact that he adopted two different policies for Bombay and Pune proves his cleverness.

1827 to 1840: The Bombay Native Education Society

In 1827, 'The Bombay Native School Book and School Society' was renamed as the 'Bombay Native Education Society', in keeping with the changed objectives. This Society enjoyed Elphinstone's support and guidance. He invited some highly respectable contemporary Indian personalities, and introduced them to the working of the Society.

In 1827, Elphinstone retired. In commemoration of his excellent services the Bombay Native Education Society decided to collect Rs. 1,20,500 for creation of a professorship in his name. In this context the following resolution was passed.

To enable the Society to erect an educational memorial to Elphinstone, people voluntarily collected a fund of Rupees 2,00,000/-. The Board of Directors contributed sumptuously. In 1834 the Elphinstone Institute was founded, which started the Elphinstone College. The English medium school in Bombay was renamed as the Elphinstone School. Upto 1840, the Bombay Native Education Society did substantial work in the field of education in the Bombay Province. The Society used to run schools in Bombay, Thane, Panvel, and Pune. The principals of these schools used be Europeans. Though these schools were called primary schools, their nature was just like that of our middle schools. Subjects like Reading, Writing, Arithmetic, Euclidean Geometry, History of England, History of India, Astronomy, Philosophy, Algebra etc. were taught there.

Due to this attitude, the Society gave priority to opening more and more primary schools of the above type. In 1840 the society ran as many as 115 schools. Inadequate funds and scarcity of trained teachers, were the two factors which brought the Society's standard down.

During 1825 to 1832, the society spent more than Rs. 2,00,000/-on book-writing, publications and encouragement awards. In the history of a native language this was the first event when rulers and thinkers made such a concerned effort.

However, later on, when the supporters of English as the medium of instruction became more powerful, the Regulatory Body of the Company

Government sent a letter in 1832 expressing displeasure at the way the Bombay Province was squandering money on the native languages.Gradually the pace of the Society's work slowed down.

In those days the Bombay Government used to manage the colleges in Bombay and Pune, and also the 63 primary schools in the Purandar Taluka in Pune District. These Purandar primary schools were unique in the sense they were different from the primary schools mentioned above. Their curriculum was similar to that of 'Tatya Pantoji Schools', but the teachers were government employees. These schools were established in 1837 on the suggestion of the Assistant Collector of that region Capt. Shortrede. They were under the control of the Revenue Department till 1840. These schools were used for promotion of education of the masses.

1840 to 1854 : The Board of Education

In 1840, the Bombay Government constituted the 'Board of Education' to look after the management of all the institutions. That was the end of the Bombay Native Education Society. There were seven members on the Board, out of which three were recommended by the Bombay Native Education Society. All the three were natives. All the schools managed by the Society and the Government as well as the colleges in Bombay and Pune, were handed over to the Board for management. In 1842 the Bombay Province was divided into three sectors for administrative convenience, each of which was supervised by a European inspector. The Board opened primary schools in the villages having a population of two thousand and above, if the villagers gave land for the school and were ready to pay one anna as the monthly fee. Generally speaking, the Board continued the policies of the Bombay Native Society. In 1845 a training class for primary teachers was started in Elphinstone Institute in Bombay. In 1854 the report on the Board's performance, the following statement is found, "Considerable attention has also been paid in Bombay to education through the medium of vernacular languages It appears that 215 vernacular schools are under management of the Board of Education—the schools are reported to be improving and masters trained in the Government College have been recently appointed—. These results are very creditable to the residency of Bombay".

The question of the medium of instruction was controversial and especially in Bengal, Raja Ram Mohan Roy also insisted on English. There it was Arabi, Sanskrit or English. In 1934 Macaulay came to India. He was the Chairman of the 'General Committee of Public Instruction' and the law Member of the Executive Committee of the Governor General. In his opinion "A single shelf of a good European library was worth the whole native literatures of India and Arabia".

Such was his ignorance of the oriental culture. He did not know Sanskrit or Arabic languages and had no interest in them either. His opinion of the native languages was that they were backward. He propagated English emphatically. The Governor General Bentinck was also of the same opinion. In 1835 he gave orders. "The great object of the British Government ought to be the promotion of European literature and science among the natives of India and that all the funds appropriated for the purpose of education would be best employed on English education alone".

In the Bombay Province the choice was not between English and Sanskrit, it was between a regional language and English. This policy of the Governor General had its impact in Bombay too.

In 1843, Eraskin Perry became the chairman of the Board of Education. He was a supporter of English as the medium of instruction. He did not agree with the policy of the Bombay National Education Society, of using an Indian language to impart higher education as far as possible. He put forth a proposal that like Bengal, Bombay also should adopt English as the medium of instruction. But Jagannath Shankarseth, Framji Kawasji and Mohammed Ibrahim Makwas opposed it vehemently. They supported the use of Indian languages. In the end the question was referred to the Government and in 1848 the Government took the decision, "When examinations in Marathi, Gujrathi and English were conducted, it was doubtlessly proved that those who study in the mother tongue learn quickly. So, the Government's opinion is that learning should be in one's own language".

Taking into consideration the differences between the situations in Bengal and Bombay, it was decided that the vernacular would be used in primary schools, where-as in colleges English would be the medium of instruction.

By that time English was granted the status of the official language. Knowledge of English was obligatory for the Government service. The demand for English went up because of the financial benefits of knowing it. The inevitable consequence was that, schools using Indian languages began to be considered inferior, and even in the Bombay Province English got an entry everywhere except the lowest standards.

Bibliography

Alva, Joachim: *Leaders of India,* Bombay, Thacker & Co., Ltd., 1943

Anthony, J. Parel : *Hind Swaraj or Indian Home Rule,* Cambridge University Press, 1925.

Arabinda Poddar : *Tagore : The Political Personality*, Kolkata, Indiana, 2004.

Athlye, D.V.: *Lokmanya Tilak,* Annasaheb Chiploonkar, 1921.

Atri, Ajit : *Gandhi's View of Legal Justice,* New Delhi, Deep and Deep Pub., 2007.

Bapat, S. V.: *Tilak Sukti Sangraha,* A Kesari Prakashan, Pune, 1926.

Barua, B. P.: *Raja Rammohun Roy and the New Learning*. Hyderabad, 1988.

Bhat, V. C.: *Lokmanya Tilak,* Prakash Publications, Pune, 1956.

Bhattacharya, Sabyasachi : *Vande Mataram : The Biography of a Song,* New Delhi, Penguin, 2003.

Bourai, Himanshu : *Gandhi and Modern Indian Liberals,* Delhi, Abhijeet Pub., 2004.

Butalia, Urvashi: *The Other Side of Silence: Voices from the Partition of India,* New Delhi, Penguin, 1998.

Campbell-Johnson, Alan: *Mission with Mountbatten,* London: Hale, 1982.

Chatterji, Joya: *Bengal Divided: Hindu Communalism and Partition, 1932-1947,* Cambridge, Cambridge UP, 1994.

Collier, Richard: *The Great Indian Mutiny*. New York, 1963.

Dabholkar, Kunda: *Bharatiya Stree Shikshan,* Joshi Lokanade Prakashan, Pune, 1973.

Dasgupta, Subrata : *The Bengal Renaissance : Identity and Creativity from Rammohun Roy to Rabindranath Tagore*, Delhi, Permanent Black, 2007.

Guha, Ramachandra : *India After Gandhi : The History of the World's Largest Democracy,* New Delhi, Picador, 2007.

Hasan, Mushirul: *India's Partition: Process, Strategy and Mobilization,* New Delhi, Oxford UP, 1993.

Heisner and Goldberg: *Tilak and the Struggle of Freedom,* Peoples Publishing House, New Delhi, 1956.

Joshi, V.C.: *Rammohun Roy and the Process of Modernization in India,* Delhi, 1975.

Keer Dhananjay: *Lokmanya Tilak,* Pub. S. B. Kangutkar, Mumbai, 1959.

Kelkar, B. K.: *Tilak Vichar,* Shri Vidya Prakashan, Pune, 1981.

Kesari-Maratha: *Tilak Birth Centenary Number,* Pune, 1956.

Lohia, Ram Manohar: *Guilty Men of India's Partition,* Allahabad, Navahind, 1960.

Manto, Saadat Hasan: *Kingdom's End and Other Stories,* Delhi, Penguin, 1987.

Mathur, Y. B.: *Women's Education in India 1813-1966*, Asia Publishing House, 1973.

Nagendranath Chattopadhyaya: *Mahatma Raja Rammohan Rayer Jiban Charit*,Calcutta, 1881.

Naik, J. P.: *Political Content of Education*, Socio Research Publications Centre, Calcutta, 1917.

Pandey, B. N.: *The Break-up of British India*, London, Macmillan, 1969.

Parvate, T. V.: *Bal Gangadhar Tilak*, Navjeevan Publishing House, Ahmedabad, 1958.

Phadke, Y. D.: *Shodh Bal-Gopalancha*, Shri Vidya Prakashan, Pune 1977.

Richard I. Cashman: *The Myth of the Lokamanya: Tilak and Mass Politics in Maharashtra*, Berkeley, 1975.

Samaddar, Ranabir: *Reflections on Partition in the East*, New Delhi, Vikas Publishing House, 1997.

Tinker, Hugh: *Experiment with Freedom, India and Pakistan 1947*, London, Oxford UP, 1967.

Index

A

Agreement, 76.
Alipore Bomb Case, 21.

B

Bombay Province, 35, 188, 215, 218, 219, 220.
British Colonial Period, 18.
British Rule, 20, 21, 22, 25, 27, 30, 43, 44, 45, 46, 185, 210, 211, 213, 220.

C

Civil Disobedience, 31.
Colonial Rule, 18, 45, 47.
Comparative Mythology, 3, 58, 64.

D

Democracy, 25, 190.
Development Projects, 25.
Dharma, 40, 73, 76, 84, 93.

E

Educational Institutions, 43, 199, 200.
Educational Policy, 214.

F

Formation of Indian National Congress, 19.
Formation of Muslim League, 21.
Freedom Struggle, 31, 36, 38, 39, 210, 214, 215.

G

Gandhi, 20, 22, 28, 29, 31, 33, 39, 47, 48, 74, 76, 78, 80, 81, 82, 85, 88.
Governor General, 219, 220.

H

Hardinge Bomb Case, 22.
Hindu Dharma, 84.
Hindu Mahasabha, 81, 82, 83, 84.
Hindu Nationalism, 27, 28, 82.
Home Rule Movement, 36, 48.

I

Indian Independence Movement, 1, 40.
Indian National Congress, 2, 3, 19, 20, 22, 25, 32, 35, 36, 43, 44, 50, 51, 87, 107, 220.

L

Liberation, 45, 47, 79.

M

Muslim League, 21, 22, 27, 46, 49, 91.

N

National Awakening, 32, 34, 193.
National Education, 30, 35, 195, 196, 209, 211, 212, 213, 214.
Nationalism, 23, 24, 25, 27, 28, 31, 47, 74, 79, 82, 87, 191, 193, 209.

Non-cooperation Movement, 33.

P

Partition of Bengal, 3, 19, 20, 21, 28, 32, 36, 47, 209, 210.
Political Apprenticeship, 203.
Political Power, 25, 45, 85.
Political Strategy, 39.
Projects, 25, 86.
Promotion of Hindu Nationalism, 74.

R

Revolutionary Movement, 21, 28.

S

Slaves, 33.
Social Reformer, 1, 38, 207.
Superiority of Hinduism, 73.

T

Tolerant Religion, 74.

U

Untouchability, 33, 34, 44, 82.

V

Vedas, 5, 51, 52, 69, 70, 71, 72, 73, 75, 79, 94, 129, 161, 183, 184, 203, 217, 220.

❑❑❑